C++ Reactive Programming

Design concurrent and asynchronous applications using the
RxCpp library and Modern C++17

Praseed Pai
Peter Abraham

BIRMINGHAM - MUMBAI

C++ Reactive Programming

Commissioning Editor: Richa Tripathi
Acquisition Editor: Sandeep Mishra
Content Development Editor: Rohit Singh
Technical Editor: Ketan Kamble
Copy Editor: Safis Editing
Project Coordinator: Vaidehi Sawant
Proofreader: Safis Editing
Indexer: Aishwarya Gangawane
Graphics: Jason Monteiro
Production Coordinator: Shraddha Falebhai

First published: October 2018

Production reference: 2110119

Published by Packt Publishing Ltd.
Livery Place
35 Livery Street
Birmingham
B3 2PB, UK.

ISBN 978-1-78862-977-5

www.packtpub.com

`mapt.io`

Mapt is an online digital library that gives you full access to over 5,000 books and videos, as well as industry leading tools to help you plan your personal development and advance your career. For more information, please visit our website.

Why subscribe?

- Spend less time learning and more time coding with practical eBooks and Videos from over 4,000 industry professionals

- Improve your learning with Skill Plans built especially for you

- Get a free eBook or video every month

- Mapt is fully searchable

- Copy and paste, print, and bookmark content

PacktPub.com

Did you know that Packt offers eBook versions of every book published, with PDF and ePub files available? You can upgrade to the eBook version at `www.PacktPub.com` and as a print book customer, you are entitled to a discount on the eBook copy. Get in touch with us at `service@packtpub.com` for more details.

At `www.PacktPub.com`, you can also read a collection of free technical articles, sign up for a range of free newsletters, and receive exclusive discounts and offers on Packt books and eBooks.

Contributors

About the authors

Praseed Pai has been working with Software Industry for the last 25 years, starting his career as a MS-DOS systems programmer using ANSI C. He has been actively involved in developing large scale cross-platform system using C++ on Windows, GNU Linux, and macOS. His areas of interest include Engineering Software Development, Enterprise Software Development, and Native Code Programming. He is the co-author of a book .*NET Design Patterns*, by Packt Publishing.

I would like to acknowledge the contributions of Peter Abraham, Sarath Soman, Vaisakh Babu, Shine Xavier, Aneesh Revi, Benoy Vijayan, Joseph Abraham, and so on, while working on the content of the book.

I would like to thank my parents, Mrs. Mohana and Late K.J. Thrivikrama Pai, who taught me the value of continuous learning. I whole heartedly thank my wife Sandhya L, for giving encouragement, while I was writing this book. Last, but not the least, Sidharth and Karthik Pai, my two sons, for co-operating with me, while writing this book.

Finally, I thank Sandeep Mishra and Rohit Kumar Singh from Packt Publishing. I also thank Sumant Tambe, who reviewed the content of this book.

Peter Abraham has been a performance fanatic and a C/C++ programming language enthusiast right from his college days, where he excelled in Microsoft Windows programming and GNU Linux programming. He garnered experience in working with CUDA, image processing, and computer graphics programs by virtue of working with companies such as Quest Global, Siemens, and Tektronix.

Peter has been eagerly following the C++ standard and RxCpp libraries as part of his profession. He has worked with C++ based GUI toolkits such as Qt and MFC.

I would like to start off thanking Praseed Pai for choosing me to co-author this book. In addition, I would like to thank: friends and members of computers science fraternity (Joseph Abraham, Benoy Vijayan, Sarath Soman, Vaishak Babu, Soma Jose, Pranav P.S, Stanly Soby, Gururaj Badiger) for their contributions. My parents (Abraham and Susamma) without whom I would cease to exist. My brothers (Joseph and Sebastian) for their whole-hearted support throughout my life. My patrons (Rev. Fr. Varghese Kalarickal, Reena Peter) for believing in me.

Finally, I thank the members of Packt Publishing. I also thank Sumant Tambe, who reviewed the content of this book.

About the reviewer

Sumant Tambe is a software engineer, researcher, open source contributor, blogger, speaker, author, and gamer. He is experienced in using Modern C++, Kafka, data distribution service, reactive programming, and stream processing to solve new problems in big data and industrial IoT.

He has authored *C++ Truths* blog and the *More C++ Idioms* wikibook. He shares his learnings on his blog, and at local code camps, meetups, and conferences. He has been a recipient of the Microsoft MVP Award in development technologies for 5 years. He has a PhD in computer science from Vanderbilt University.

Packt is searching for authors like you

If you're interested in becoming an author for Packt, please visit `authors.packtpub.com` and apply today. We have worked with thousands of developers and tech professionals, just like you, to help them share their insight with the global tech community. You can make a general application, apply for a specific hot topic that we are recruiting an author for, or submit your own idea.

Table of Contents

Preface   1

Chapter 1: Reactive Programming Model – Overview and History   7
Event-driven programming model   8
Event-driven programming on X Windows   8
Event-driven programming on Microsoft Windows   10
Event-driven programming under Qt   12
Event-driven programming under MFC   13
Other event-driven programming models   14
Limitations of classical event processing models   14
Reactive programming model   15
Functional reactive programming   15
The key interfaces of a reactive program   16
Pull-versus push-based reactive programming   18
The IEnumerable/IObservable duality   18
Converting events to IObservable<T>   22
The philosophy of our book   26
Summary   28

Chapter 2: A Tour of Modern C++ and its Key Idioms   29
The key concerns of the C++ programming language   30
Zero cost abstraction   30
Expressivity   30
Substitutability   33
Enhancements to C++ for writing better code   34
Type deduction and inference   34
Uniform initialization of variables   36
Variadic templates   37
Rvalue references   39
Move semantics   40
Smart pointers   42
Lambda functions   44
Functors and Lambdas   45
Composition, currying, and partial function application   48
Function wrappers   50
Composing functions together with the pipe operator   51
Miscellaneous features   53
Fold expressions   53
Variant type   54
Other important topics   55

Range-based for loops and observables 55
Summary 59

Chapter 3: Language-Level Concurrency and Parallelism in C++ 61
What is concurrency? 62
Hello World of concurrency (using std::thread) 63
Managing threads 64
  Thread launch 65
  Thread join 66
  Passing arguments into a thread 67
Using Lambdas 70
  Ownership management 71
Sharing data between threads 73
  Mutexes 75
  Avoiding deadlock 77
  Locking with std::unique_lock 80
  Condition variables 82
A thread-safe stack data structure 84
Summary 87

Chapter 4: Asynchronous and Lock-Free Programming in C++ 89
Task-based parallelism in C++ 90
  Future and promise 90
  std::packaged_task 93
  std::async 94
C++ memory model 96
Memory access and concurrency 97
The modification contract 98
Atomic operations and types in C++ 98
Atomic types 99
  std::atomic_flag 101
  std::atomic<bool> 103
    Standard atomic integral types 105
  std::atomic<T*> – pointer arithmetic 106
  std::atomic<> primary class template 107
Memory ordering 108
  Sequential consistency 108
  Acquire-release ordering 110
  Relaxed ordering 112
A lock-free data structure queue 113
Summary 116

Chapter 5: Introduction to Observables 117
The GoF Observer pattern 118
The limitations of the GoF Observer pattern 121

A holistic look at GoF patterns	122
The OOP programming model and hierarchies	123
A Composite/Visitor pattern for expression processing	125
Flattening the composite for iterative processing	129
Map and filter operations on the list	132
Reversing the gaze for Observables!	133
Summary	137
Chapter 6: Introduction to Event Stream Programming Using C++	**139**
What is Stream programming model?	140
Advantages of the Stream programming model	140
Applied Stream programming using the Streams library	141
Lazy evaluation	142
A simple Stream program	142
Aggregating values using the Stream paradigm	143
The STL and the Stream paradigm	144
A word about the Streams library	144
Event Stream programming	145
Advantages of Event Stream programming	145
The Streamulus library and its programming model	146
The Streamulus library – a peek into its internals	149
The Streamulus Library – a look into expression processing	150
The spreadsheet Library — a change-propagation engine	151
RaftLib – another Stream-processing library	153
What do these things have to do with Rx programming?	154
Summary	155
Chapter 7: Introduction to Data Flow Computation and the RxCpp Library	**157**
The data flow computation paradigm	158
An introduction to the RxCpp library	159
The RxCpp library and its programming model	160
A simple Observable/Observer interaction	160
Filters and Transformations with Observables	161
Streaming values from C++ containers	161
Creating Observables from the scratch	162
Concatenating Observable Streams	162
Unsubscribing from Observable Streams	163
An introduction to marble diagrams for visual representation	164
RxCpp (Stream) Operators	164
The average Operator	165
The Scan Operator	165
Composing Operators through the pipe Operator	166
Working with Schedulers	167
A tale of two Operators – flatmap versus concatmap	169

Other Important Operators 174
A peek into the things we haven't covered yet 176
Summary 177
Chapter 8: RxCpp – the Key Elements 179
Observables 179
What's a Producer? 180
Hot versus Cold Observables 180
Hot Observables 181
Hot Observables and the replay mechanism 183
Observers and their variants (Subscribers) 184
Subjects 185
Schedulers 188
ObserveOn versus SubscribeOn 191
The RunLoop Scheduler 193
Operators 194
Creational Operators 195
Transformation Operators 196
Filtering Operators 196
Combining Operators 197
Error-handling Operators 197
Observable utility Operators 198
Conditional and Boolean Operators 198
Mathematical and Aggregate operators 199
Connectable Observable Operators 200
Summary 200
Chapter 9: Reactive GUI Programming Using Qt/C++ 201
A quick introduction to Qt GUI programming 202
Qt object model 203
Signals and slots 204
Event system 206
Event handlers 206
Sending events 207
Meta-object system 207
Hello World – Qt program 208
Qt event model with signals/slots/MOC – an example 210
Creating a custom widget 210
Creating the application dialog 212
Executing the application 216
Integrating the RxCpp library with the Qt event model 217
Qt event filter – a reactive approach 218
Creating the window – setting layouts and alignments 220
Event type specific observables 221
An introduction to RxQt 223

Summary   226

Chapter 10: Creating Custom Operators in RxCpp   229
  Philosophy of Rx operators   229
  Chaining stock operators   230
  Writing basic RxCpp custom operators   232
    Writing an RxCpp operator as a function   232
    Writing an RxCpp operator as a Lambda   234
    Composing custom RxCpp operators   234
  Different genres of custom operators   235
    Writing a custom creational operator   236
    Writing a custom transformation operator   238
    Writing a custom operator that involves Schedulers   239
  Writing custom operators that can be chained   240
    Using the lift<t> operator to write a custom operator   240
    Converting an arbitrary Lambda to a custom Rx operator   242
    Creating a custom RxCpp operator in the library   245
  Summary   248

Chapter 11: Design Patterns and Idioms for C++ Rx Programming   249
  The OOP and Design patterns movement   249
  Key Pattern catalogs   250
    The GOF catalog   251
    The POSA catalog   251
  The Design pattern redux   253
  From Design patterns to Reactive programming   254
    Flattening the hierarchy to navigate through it   259
    From Iterators to Observables   261
  The Cell pattern   262
  The Active object pattern   265
  The Resource Loan pattern   266
  The Event bus pattern   268
  Summary   272

Chapter 12: Reactive Microservices Using C++   273
  The C++ language and web programming   274
    The REST programming model   274
  The C++ REST SDK   274
    HTTP client programming using the C++ REST SDK   275
    HTTP server programming using the C++ REST SDK   277
  Testing the HTTP server using CURL and POSTMAN   280
    The libcurl and the HTTP client programming   281
    Kirk Shoop's libCURL Wrapper library   282
  The JSON and HTTP protocol   284
  The C++ REST SDK-based REST server   288

Invoking REST services using the RxCurl library   296
A word about the Reactive micro-services architecture   299
  Fine-grained services   300
  Polyglot persistence   301
  Independent deployment   301
  Service orchestration and choreography   301
  Reactive web service call   302
Summary   302

Chapter 13: Advanced Streams and Handling Errors   303
A short recap of the characteristics of a reactive system   304
RxCpp error and exception handling Operators   305
  Executing an action on an error   306
  Resuming when an error occurs   308
  Retry when an error occurs   310
  Cleanup with the finally() Operator   313
Schedulers and error handling   314
Event-based Stream handling – some examples   319
  Aggregation based on Stream data   319
  Application event handling example   322
Summary   325

Other Books You May Enjoy   327

Index   331

Preface

This book will help you learn how to implement the reactive programming paradigm with C++ for building asynchronous and concurrent applications. The reactive programming model requires tremendous amount of pre-requisites in terms of proficiency in programming models (OOP/FP), event-driven GUI programming, language-level concurrency, lock free programming , design Patterns, and event stream programming. The first six chapters cover the these topics in a detailed manner. For the remaining chapters, we have based our discussions on industrial-strength RxCpp library. The topics covered include introduction to the RxCpp programming model, five key elements of the RxCpp programming model, GUI programming using Qt, writing custom operators, Rx design patterns, reactive microservices, and advanced exceptions/operators. By the end of the book, you will be able to confidently embed Rx constructs in your programs to write better concurrent and parallel applications using C++.

Who this book is for

If you're a C++ developer interested in using reactive programming to build asynchronous and concurrent applications, you'll find this book extremely useful. This book doesn't assume any previous knowledge of reactive programming. We cover the modern C++ constructs necessary to write reactive programs in Chapter 2, *A Tour of Modern C++ and its Key Idioms*, Chapter 3, *Language-Level Concurrency and Parallelism in C++*, and Chapter 4, *Asynchronous and Lock-Free Programming in C++*. Any C++ programmer with reasonable familiarity with Classic C++ can easily follow the book without any difficulty.

What this book covers

Chapter 1, *Reactive Programming Model – Overview and History*, takes a look at the various event handling techniques implemented by GUI toolkits such as Windows API, XLib API, Qt, and MFC. This chapter also introduces some key data structures of the Rx programming model in the context of writing cross platform Console applications and GUI applications using the MFC library.

Chapter 2, *A Tour of Modern C++ and its Key Idioms*, covers the Modern C++ constructs necessary for writing reactive programs. The chapter focuses on new C++ features, type inference, variadic templates, rvalue references, move semantics, lambda functions, elementary functional programming, pipeable operators, implementation of iterators, and observers.

Chapter 3, *Language-Level Concurrency and Parallelism in C++*, discusses the threading library available with the C++ standard. You will learn how to launch and manage a thread. We will discuss different aspects of the threading library. This chapter lays a good foundation for concurrency support introduced in Modern C++.

Chapter 4, *Asynchronous and Lock-Free Programming in C++*, discusses the facilities provided by the standard library for implementing task-based parallelism. It also discusses the new multithreading-aware memory model that is available with the modern C++ language.

Chapter 5, *Introduction to Observables*, talks about the GoF Observer pattern and explains its shortcomings. You will learn how to transform a program which implements the GoF Composite/Visitor pattern to Observable streams, using a technique devised by us, in the context of modelling an expression tree.

Chapter 6, *Introduction to Event Stream Programming Using C++*, focuses on the topic of Event Stream programming. We will also look at the Streamulus library, which provides a **Domain Specific Embedded Language** (**DSEL**) approach to the manipulation of event Streams.

Chapter 7, *Introduction to Data Flow Computation and the RxCpp Library*, starts with a conceptual overview of the data flow computing paradigm and moves quickly to writing some basic RxCpp-based programs. You will learn about the set of operators supported by the RxCpp library.

Chapter 8, *RxCpp – the Key Elements*, gives you an understanding of how pieces of the Rx programming fit together in the context of Rx programming model in general and RxCpp library in particular. The topics covered in detail are Observables, Observer, Operators, Subscribers, Schedulers (five key elements of the Rx programming model).

Chapter 9, *Reactive GUI Programming Using Qt/C++*, deals with the topic of reactive GUI programming using the Qt framework. You will learn about concepts in the Qt framework, such as Qt object hierarchy, meta-object system, signals, and slots. Finally, you will write an application to handle mouse events and filter them in a reactive way using the RxCpp library.

Chapter 10, *Creating Custom Operators in RxCpp*, covers the advanced topic of how we can create custom reactive operators in RxCpp, should an existing set of Operators not suffice for the purpose. We cover how to leverage Lift Meta Operator and adding Operators to the RxCpp library. This topic also helps you create Composite Operators by composing existing Operators.

Chapter 11, *Design Patterns and Idioms for C++ Rx Programming*, delves into the wonderful world of design patterns and idioms. Starting with GOF design patterns, we will move on to reactive programming patterns. We will cover Composite/Visitor/Iterator (from GoF catalogue), Active Object, Cell, Resource Loan, and the Event Bus Pattern.

Chapter 12, *Reactive Microservices Using C++*, covers how the Rx programming model can be used to write reactive microservices using C++. It introduces you to the Microsoft C++ REST SDK and its programming model. You will learn how to leverage the RxCpp library to write aggregate services and access HTTP based services in a reactive manner.

Chapter 13, *Advanced Streams and Handling Errors*, discusses error handling in RxCpp, along with some of the advanced constructs and Operators that handle Streams in the RxCpp library. We will discuss how to continue Streams when an error comes, how to wait for the producer of the Stream to correct the error and continue the sequence, and how to perform common operations that are applicable to both success and error paths.

To get the most out of this book

In order to follow the topics in this book, you need to have knowledge of C++ programming. All other topics have been covered in this self-contained book. Of course, one need to search the web or read additional material to have an expert level understanding on some of the topics (which is true for any subject).

Download the example code files

You can download the example code files for this book from your account at www.packtpub.com. If you purchased this book elsewhere, you can visit www.packtpub.com/support and register to have the files emailed directly to you.

You can download the code files by following these steps:

1. Log in or register at www.packtpub.com.
2. Select the **SUPPORT** tab.
3. Click on **Code Downloads & Errata**.
4. Enter the name of the book in the **Search** box and follow the onscreen instructions.

Once the file is downloaded, please make sure that you unzip or extract the folder using the latest version of:

- WinRAR/7-Zip for Windows
- Zipeg/iZip/UnRarX for Mac
- 7-Zip/PeaZip for Linux

The code bundle for the book is also hosted on GitHub at `https://github.com/ PacktPublishing/CPP-Reactive-Programming`. In case there's an update to the code, it will be updated on the existing GitHub repository.

We also have other code bundles from our rich catalog of books and videos available at `https://github.com/PacktPublishing/`. Check them out!

Download the color images

We also provide a PDF file that has color images of the screenshots/diagrams used in this book. You can download it here: `https://www.packtpub.com/sites/default/files/ downloads/CPPReactiveProgramming_ColorImages.pdf`.

Conventions used

There are a number of text conventions used throughout this book.

`CodeInText`: Indicates code words in text, database table names, folder names, filenames, file extensions, pathnames, dummy URLs, user input, and Twitter handles. Here is an example: "The preceding code snippet initializes a structure by the name of `WNDCLASS` (or `WNDCLASSEX` for modern systems) with a necessary template for a window."

A block of code is set as follows:

```
/* close connection to server */
XCloseDisplay(display);

return 0;
}
```

When we wish to draw your attention to a particular part of a code block, the relevant lines or items are set in bold:

```
/* close connection to server */
XCloseDisplay(display);
```

```
    return 0;
  }
```

Any command-line input or output is written as follows:

```
$ mkdir css
$ cd css
```

Bold: Indicates a new term, an important word, or words that you see onscreen. For example, words in menus or dialog boxes appear in the text like this. Here is an example: "In Windowing parlance, it is called a **message** loop."

Warnings or important notes appear like this.

Tips and tricks appear like this.

Get in touch

Feedback from our readers is always welcome.

General feedback: Email feedback@packtpub.com and mention the book title in the subject of your message. If you have questions about any aspect of this book, please email us at questions@packtpub.com.

Errata: Although we have taken every care to ensure the accuracy of our content, mistakes do happen. If you have found a mistake in this book, we would be grateful if you would report this to us. Please visit www.packtpub.com/submit-errata, selecting your book, clicking on the Errata Submission Form link, and entering the details.

Piracy: If you come across any illegal copies of our works in any form on the Internet, we would be grateful if you would provide us with the location address or website name. Please contact us at copyright@packtpub.com with a link to the material.

If you are interested in becoming an author: If there is a topic that you have expertise in and you are interested in either writing or contributing to a book, please visit authors.packtpub.com.

Reviews

Please leave a review. Once you have read and used this book, why not leave a review on the site that you purchased it from? Potential readers can then see and use your unbiased opinion to make purchase decisions, we at Packt can understand what you think about our products, and our authors can see your feedback on their book. Thank you!

For more information about Packt, please visit packtpub.com.

Reactive Programming Model – Overview and History

The X Windows system, Microsoft Windows, and IBM OS/2 Presentation Manager made GUI programming popular on the PC platform. This was a major shift from the character mode user interface and batch process style programming models that existed before them. Responding to events became a major concern for software developers worldwide and platform vendors resorted to the creation of low-level C-based APIs that relied on function pointers and callbacks to enable programmers to handle the events. The programming models were mostly based on the co-operative multithreaded model, and with the advent of better microprocessors, most platforms began to support pre-emptive multithreading. Handling events (and other asynchronous tasks) became more complex and responding to events in the traditional way became less scalable. Even though excellent C++-based GUI toolkits made their appearance, event handling was done mostly using message IDs, function pointer based dispatches, and other low-level techniques. A prominent compiler vendor even tried adding language extensions to the C++ language to enable better Windows programming. Handling events, asynchrony, and associated issues require a fresh look at the problem. Luckily, the Modern C++ standard has support for Functional Programming, language-level concurrency (with a memory model), and better memory management techniques to enable programmers to work with asynchronous data streams (by treating events as streams). This is achieved using a programming model called reactive programming. To put things in perspective, this chapter will outline the following topics:

- Event-driven programming model and how it has been implemented in various platforms.
- What is reactive programming?
- Different models of reactive programming.
- Some simple programs to make conceptual understanding better.
- The philosophy of our book.

Event-driven programming model

Event-driven programming is a programming model where flow control is determined by events. Examples of events are mouse clicks, key presses, gestures, sensor data, messages from other programs, and so on. An event-driven application has the mechanism to detect events on a near real-time basis, and respond or react to them by invoking the appropriate event handling procedure. Since the bulk of the earlier event processing programs were written using C/C++, they resorted to low-level techniques such as callbacks (using function pointers) to write those event handlers. Later systems such as Visual Basic, Delphi, and other rapid application development tools did add native support for event-driven programming. To make matters more clear, we will take a tour of the event handling mechanism of the various platforms. This will help readers appreciate the issues that reactive programming models are solving (from a GUI programming context).

Reactive programming treats data as streams and events in windowing systems can be treated as streams to be processed in a uniform manner. The Reactive programming model provides support for gathering events from different sources as streams, filtering streams, the transformation of streams, performing actions on streams, and so on. The programming model handles asynchrony, scheduling details as part of the framework. This chapter is mostly based on the key data structures of the Reactive programming model and how we can implement basic Reactive programs. In an industrial-strength reactive program, the code written will be asynchronous and the examples from this chapter are synchronous. We give the necessary background information and language constructs in the following chapters before out of order execution and schedules are discussed. These implementations are here for elucidation and can be treated as learning examples.

Event-driven programming on X Windows

The X Windows programming model is a cross-platform API, is mostly supported on POSIX systems, and has even been ported to Microsoft Windows. In fact, X is a network windowing protocol, which required a Window manager to manage the Windows stack. The screen contents are managed by the X server and the client library will pull the contents and display them on the local machine. In desktop environments, the server runs locally on the same machine. The following program will help the reader understand the gist of the XLib programming model and how events are handled in the platform:

```
#include <X11/Xlib.h>
#include <stdio.h>
```

```
#include <stdlib.h>
#include <string.h>

int main(void)
{
    Display *display;
    Window window;
    XEvent event;
    char *msg = "Hello, World!";
    int s;
```

The preceding code snippet includes the proper header files that a programmer is supposed to include to get the function prototypes provided by the XLib C library. There are some data structures that a programmer should be aware of while writing XLib programs from scratch. Nowadays, people use libraries such as Qt, WxWidgets, Gtk+, Fox toolkit, and so on to write commercial-quality X Programs.

```
    /* open connection with the server */
    display = XOpenDisplay(NULL);
    if (display == NULL){
        fprintf(stderr, "Cannot open display\n");
        exit(1);
    }
    s = DefaultScreen(display);
    /* create window */
    window = XCreateSimpleWindow(display,
            RootWindow(display, s), 10, 10, 200, 200, 1,
            BlackPixel(display, s), WhitePixel(display, s));

    /* select kind of events we are interested in */
    XSelectInput(display, window, ExposureMask | KeyPressMask);

    /* map (show) the window */
    XMapWindow(display, window);
```

The preceding code snippet initializes the server and creates a window to certain specifications. Traditionally, most X Windows programs run under a window manager that manages the cascading windows. We selected the messages that are of interest to us by invoking the XSelectInput API call before displaying the window:

```
    /* event loop */
    for (;;)
    {
        XNextEvent(display, &event);

        /* draw or redraw the window */
        if (event.type == Expose)
```

```
    {
        XFillRectangle(display, window,
            DefaultGC(display, s), 20, 20, 10, 10);
        XDrawString(display, window,
            DefaultGC(display, s), 50, 50, msg, strlen(msg));
    }
    /* exit on key press */
    if (event.type == KeyPress)
    break;
}
```

Then, the program goes to an infinite loop while polling for any events, and the appropriate Xlib API will be used to draw a string on the Window. In Windowing parlance, it is called a **message** loop. The retrieval of events will be done by the XNextEvent API call:

```
/* close connection to server */
XCloseDisplay(display);

return 0;
}
```

Once we are out of the infinite message loop, the connection to the server will be closed.

Event-driven programming on Microsoft Windows

Microsoft Corporation created a GUI programming model, which can be considered as the most successful windowing system in the world. The third edition of the Windows software was a runaway success (in 1990) and Microsoft followed this with the Windows NT and Windows 95/98/ME series. Let us look at the event-driven programming model of Microsoft Windows (consult Microsoft documentation for a detailed look at how this programming model works). The following program will help us understand the gist of what is involved in writing Windows Programming using C/C++:

```
#include <windows.h>
//----- Prtotype for the Event Handler Function
LRESULT CALLBACK WndProc(HWND hWnd, UINT message,
                    WPARAM wParam, LPARAM lParam);
//-------------- Entry point for a Idiomatic Windows API function
int WINAPI WinMain(HINSTANCE hInstance,
        HINSTANCE hPrevInstance, LPSTR lpCmdLine, int nCmdShow)
{

MSG msg = {0};
```

```
WNDCLASS wc = {0};
wc.lpfnWndProc = WndProc;
wc.hInstance = hInstance;
wc.hbrBackground = (HBRUSH)(COLOR_BACKGROUND);
wc.lpszClassName = "minwindowsapp";
if( !RegisterClass(&wc) )
  return 1;
```

The preceding code snippet initializes a structure by the name of WNDCLASS (or WNDCLASSEX for modern systems) with a necessary template for a Window. The most important field in the structure is lpfnWndProc, which is the address of the function that responds to the event inside an instance of this Window:

```
if( !CreateWindow(wc.lpszClassName,
                "Minimal Windows Application",
                WS_OVERLAPPEDWINDOW|WS_VISIBLE,
                0,0,640,480,0,0,hInstance,NULL))
    return 2;
```

We will invoke the CreateWindow (or CreateWindowEx on modern systems) API call to create a window based on the class name provided in the WNDCLASS.lpszClassname parameter:

```
    while( GetMessage( &msg, NULL, 0, 0 ) > 0 )
        DispatchMessage( &msg );
    return 0;
}
```

The preceding code snippet gets into an infinite loop where messages will be retrieved from the message queue until we get a WM_QUIT message. The WM_QUIT message takes us out of the infinite loop. The Messages will sometimes be translated before calling the DispatchMessage API call. DispatchMessage invokes the Window callback procedure (lpfnWndProc):

```
LRESULT CALLBACK WndProc(HWND hWnd, UINT message,
                        WPARAM wParam, LPARAM lParam) {
switch(message){
  case WM_CLOSE:
    PostQuitMessage(0);break;
  default:
    return DefWindowProc(hWnd, message, wParam, lParam);
}
return 0;
}
```

The preceding code snippet is a minimalist `callback` function. You can consult Microsoft documentation to learn about Windows API programming and how events are handled in those programs

Event-driven programming under Qt

The Qt Framework is an industrial-strength, cross-platform, and multi-platform GUI toolkit that runs on Windows, GNU Linux, macOS X, and other Mac systems. The toolkit has been compiled into embedded systems and mobile devices. The C++ Programming model has leveraged something called **Meta Object Compiler** (**MOC**), which will peruse the source code for directives (a bunch of macros and language extensions embedded in the source code) and generate appropriate additional source code to generate event handlers. So, before the C++ compiler gets the source code, the MOC pass has to run to generate legal ANSI C++ by removing those extra linguistic constructs specific to the Qt system. Consult the Qt documentation to learn more about this. The following simple Qt program will demonstrate the key aspects of Qt programming and its event processing system:

```cpp
#include <qapplication.h>
#include <qdialog.h>
#include <qmessagebox.h>
#include <qobject.h>
#include <qpushbutton.h>

class MyApp : public QDialog {
  Q_OBJECT
public:
    MyApp(QObject* /*parent*/ = 0):
    button(this)
    {
      button.setText("Hello world!"); button.resize(100, 30);

      // When the button is clicked, run button_clicked
      connect(&button,
              &QPushButton::clicked, this, &MyApp::button_clicked);
    }
```

The macro `Q_OBJECT` is a directive to the MOC to generate an `Event Dispatch` table. When we connect the event source to an event sink, an entry will be given to the `Event Dispatch` table. The generated code will be compiled along with the C++ code to produce an executable:

```cpp
public slots:
    void button_clicked() {
      QMessageBox box;
```

```
      box.setWindowTitle("Howdy");
      box.setText("You clicked the button");
      box.show();
      box.exec();
    }

protected:
  QPushButton button;
};
```

The language extension *public slots* will be stripped away by the MOC (after doing the job of source code generation) to a form compatible with the ANSI C/C++ compiler:

```
int main(int argc, char** argv) {
  QApplication app(argc, argv);
  MyApp myapp;
  myapp.show();
  return app.exec();
}
```

The preceding code snippet initializes the Qt application object and displays the main window. For all practical purposes, Qt is the most prominent application development framework for the C++ language and it also has got a good binding to the Python Programming language.

Event-driven programming under MFC

The Microsoft Foundation class library is still a popular library with which to write Microsoft Windows-based desktop programs. It does have some support for web programming if we mix **ActiveX Template Library** (**ATL**) along with it. Being a C++ library, MFC uses a mechanism called Message Mapping to handle events. A sample event handling table given as macros is part of every MFC program:

```
BEGIN_MESSAGE_MAP(CClockFrame,CFrameWnd)
    ON_WM_CREATE()
    ON_WM_PAINT()
    ON_WM_TIMER()
END_MESSAGE_MAP()
```

The preceding message map will respond to `OnCreate`, `OnPaint`, and `Ontimer` standard Windows API messages. Deep down these message maps are arrays on to which we will use `message id` as an index for dispatching the events. On closer examination, it is not much different from the standard Windows API messaging model.

The code listing is not given here because we have globally a GUI implementation of one of the key interfaces for the Reactive Programming model using MFC. The implementation is based on the MFC library and the reader can go through the annotated listing to gain an understanding of non-trivial event processing in MFC.

Other event-driven programming models

Distributed object processing frameworks such as COM+ and CORBA do have their own event processing framework. The COM+ event model is based on the notion of Connection Points (modeled by `IConnectionPointContainer`/`IConnectionPoint` interfaces) and CORBA does have its own event service model. The CORBA standard provides both pull-based and push-based event notifications. COM+ and CORBA are beyond the scope of this book and the reader is expected to consult the respective documentation.

Limitations of classical event processing models

The whole purpose of making a tour of the event processing supported by various platforms was to put things into the proper perspective. The event response logic in these platforms is mostly coupled with the platform where the code is written. With the advent of multi-core programming, writing low-level multi-threaded code is difficult and declarative task-based programming models are available with the C++ programming language. But the event sources are mostly outside the C++ standard! The C++ language does not have a standard GUI programming library, an interface standard to access external devices, and so on. What is the way out? Luckily, events and data from external sources can be aggregated into streams (or sequences) and by using functional programming constructs such as Lambda functions can be processed very efficiently. The added bonus is that if we resort to some kind of restrictions regarding the mutability of variables and streams, concurrency, and parallelism are built into the stream processing model.

Reactive programming model

Simply put, reactive programming is nothing but programming with asynchronous data streams. By applying various operations on stream, we can achieve different computational goals. The primary task in a reactive program is to convert data into streams, regardless of what the source of the data is. While writing modern graphical user interface applications, we process mouse move-and-click events. Currently, most systems get a callback and process these events as and when they happen. Most of the time, the handler does a series of filtering operations before it invokes the action methods associated with the event calls. In this particular context, reactive programming helps us in aggregating the mouse move-and-click events into a collection and sets a filter on them before notifying the handler logic. In this way, the application/handler logic does not get executed unnecessarily.

The stream-processing model is well known, and it is very easy to encode by application developers. Pretty much anything can be converted into a stream. Such candidates include messages, logs, properties, Twitter feeds, blog posts, RSS feeds, and so on. Functional programming techniques are really good at processing streams. A language such as Modern C++, with excellent support for Object/Functional programming, is a natural choice for writing reactive programs. The basic idea behind reactive programming is that there are certain datatypes that represent a value over time. These datatypes (or rather data sequences) are represented as Observable sequences in this programming paradigm. Computations that involve these changing (time-dependent) values will, in turn, themselves have values that change over time, and will need to asynchronously receive notifications (as and when the dependent data changes).

Functional reactive programming

Almost all modern programming languages support functional programming constructs. Functional programming constructs such as Transform, Apply, Filter, Fold, and so on are good for processing streams. Programming asynchronous data streams using functional programming constructs are generally called functional reactive programming (for all practical purposes). The definition given here is an operational one. Consult the work done by Conal Elliott and Paul Hudak as part of the Haskell community to understand the strict definition. Mixing Reactive Programming with FP is gaining traction among developers these days. The Emergence of libraries such as Rx.Net, RxJava, RxJs, and RxCpp and so on is a testimony to this.

Even though reactive programming is the core subject of this book, in this chapter we will be sticking to an OOP approach. This is necessitated because of the fact that we need to introduce some standard interfaces (emulated in C++ using virtual functions) necessary for doing Reactive programming. Later on, after learning about FP constructs supported by C++, readers can do some mental model mapping from OOP to FP constructs. We will also keep away from concurrency stuff to focus on software interfaces in this chapter. Chapters 2, *A Tour of the Modern C++ and Its Key Idioms*, Chapter 3, *Language-Level Concurrency and Parallelism in C++*, and Chapter 4, *Asynchronous and Lock-Free Programming in C++*, will give the necessary background to understand reactive programming using FP constructs.

The key interfaces of a reactive program

To help you understand what is really happening inside a reactive program, we will write some toy programs to put things in proper context. From a software design point of view, if you keep concurrency/parallelism aside to focus on software interfaces, a reactive Program should have:

- An event source that implements `IObservable<T>`
- An event sink that implements `IObserver<T>`
- A mechanism to add subscribers to an event source
- When data appears at the source, subscribers will be notified

In this particular chapter, we have written code using classic C++ constructs. This is because we have not yet introduced Modern C++ constructs. We have also used raw pointers, something which we can mostly avoid while writing Modern C++ code. The code in this chapter is written to conform to the ReactiveX documentation in general. In C++, we do not use inheritance-based techniques like we do in Java or C#.

To kickstart, let us define Observer, Observable, and a `CustomException` class:

```
#pragma once
//Common2.h

struct CustomException /*:*public std::exception */ {
```

```
        const char * what() const throw () {
            return "C++ Exception";
        }
};
```

The `CustomException` class is just a placeholder to make the interface complete. Since we have decided that we will only use classic C++ in this chapter, we are not deviating from the `std::exception` class:

```
template<class T> class IEnumerator {
public:
        virtual bool HasMore() = 0;
        virtual T next() = 0;
        //--------- Omitted Virtual destructor for brevity
};
template <class T> class IEnumerable{
public:
        virtual IEnumerator<T> *GetEnumerator() = 0;
        //---------- Omitted Virtual destructor for brevity
};
```

The `Enumerable` interface is used by the data source from which we can enumerate data and `IEnuerator<T>` will be used for iteration by the client.

 The purpose of defining interfaces for Iterator (`IEnuerable<T>`/`IEnumerator<T>`) is to make the reader understand that they are very closely related to the `Observer<T>`/`Observable<T>` pattern. We will define `Observer<T>`/`Observable<T>` as follows:

```
template<class T> class IObserver
{
public:
        virtual void OnCompleted() = 0;
        virtual void OnError(CustomException *exception) = 0;
        virtual void OnNext(T value) = 0;
};
template<typename T>
class IObservable
{
public:
        virtual bool Subscribe(IObserver<T>& observer) = 0;
};
```

`IObserver<T>` is the interface that the data sink will use to receive notifications from the data source. The data source will implement the `IObservable<T>` interface.

We have defined the IObserver<T> interface and it has got three methods. They are OnNext (when the item is notified to the Observer), OnCompleted (when there is no more data), and OnError (when an exception is encountered). Observable<T> is implemented by the event source and event sinks can insert objects that implement IObserver<T> to receive notifications.

Pull-versus push-based reactive programming

Reactive programs can be classified as **push-based** and **pull-based**. The pull-based system waits for a demand to push the data streams to the requestor (or subscriber in our case). This is the classic case where the data source is actively polled for more information. This employs the iterator pattern, and IEnumerable <T>/IEnumerator <T> interfaces are specifically designed for such scenarios that are synchronous in nature (the application can block while pulling data). On the other hand, a push-based system aggregates events and pushes through a signal network to achieve the computation. In this case, unlike the pull-based system, data and related updates are handed to the subscriber from the source (Observable sequences in this case). This asynchronous nature is achieved by not blocking the subscriber, but rather making it react to the changes. As you can see, employing this push pattern is more beneficial in rich UI environments where you wouldn't want to block the main UI thread while waiting for some events. This becomes ideal, thus making reactive programs responsive.

The IEnumerable/IObservable duality

If you take a closer look, there is only a subtle difference between these two patterns. IEnumerable<T> can be considered the pull-based equivalent of the push-based IObservable<T>. In fact, they are duals. When two entities exchange information, one entity's pull corresponds to another entity pushing the information. This duality is illustrated in the following diagram:

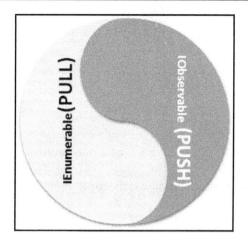

Let's understand this duality by looking at this sample code, a number sequence generator:

We have striven to use classic C++ constructs to write programs for this particular chapter as there are chapters on Modern C++ language features, language level concurrency, lock-free programming, and related topics for implementing Reactive constructs in Modern C++.

```cpp
#include <iostream>
#include <vector>
#include <iterator>
#include <memory>
#include "../Common2.h"
using namespace std;

class ConcreteEnumberable : public IEnumerable<int>
{
      int *numberlist,_count;
public:
      ConcreteEnumberable(int numbers[], int count):
            numberlist(numbers),_count(count){}
      ~ConcreteEnumberable() {}

      class Enumerator : public IEnumerator<int>
      {
      int *inumbers, icount, index;
      public:
      Enumerator(int *numbers,
            int count):inumbers(numbers),icount(count),index(0) {}
      bool HasMore() { return index < icount; }
      //---------- ideally speaking, the next function should throw
      //---------- an exception...instead it just returns -1 when the
```

```
        //---------- bound has reached
        int next() { return (index < icount) ?
                    inumbers[index++] : -1; }
        ~Enumerator() {}
        };
        IEnumerator<int> *GetEnumerator()
            { return new Enumerator(numberlist, _count); }
    };
```

The preceding class takes an array of integers as a parameter and we can enumerate over the elements as we have implemented the IEnumerable<T> interface. The Enumeration logic is implemented by the nested class, which implements the IEnumerator<T> interface:

```
int main()
{
        int x[] = { 1,2,3,4,5 };
        //-------- Has used Raw pointers on purpose here as we have
        //------- not introduced unique_ptr,shared_ptr,weak_ptr yet
        //-------- using auto_ptr will be confusting...otherwise
        //-------- need to use boost library here... ( an overkill)
        ConcreteEnumberable *t = new ConcreteEnumberable(x, 5);
        IEnumerator<int> * numbers = t->GetEnumerator();
        while (numbers->HasMore())
            cout << numbers->next() << endl;
        delete numbers;delete t;
        return 0;
}
```

The main program instantiates an implementation of the ConcreteEnuerable class and walks through each element.

We will write an even number sequence generator to demonstrate how these data types work together in converting a pull-based program to a push program. The robustness aspect is given low priority to keep the listing terse:

```
#include "stdafx.h"
#include <iostream>
#include <vector>
#include <iterator>
#include <memory>
#include "../Common2.h"
using namespace std;

class EvenNumberObservable : IObservable<int>{
        int *_numbers,_count;
public:
```

```
EvenNumberObservable(int numbers[],
        int count):_numbers(numbers),_count(count){}
    bool Subscribe(IObserver<int>& observer){
        for (int i = 0; i < _count; ++i)
            if (_numbers[i] % 2 == 0)
                observer.OnNext(_numbers[i]);
        observer.OnCompleted();
        return true;

    }
};
```

The preceding program takes an array of integers, filters out of the odd numbers, and notifies Observer<T> if an even integer is encountered. In this particular case, the data source is pushing data to observer. The implementation of Observer<T> is given as follows:

```
class SimpleObserver : public IObserver<int>{
public:
    void OnNext(int value) { cout << value << endl; }
    void OnCompleted() { cout << _T("hello completed") << endl; }
    void OnError( CustomException * ex) {}
};
```

The SimpleObserver class implements the IObserver<T> interface and it has the capability to receive notifications and react to them:

```
int main()
{
    int x[] = { 1,2,3,4,5 };
    EvenNumberObservable *t = new EvenNumberObservable(x, 5);
    IObserver<int>> *xy = new SimpleObserver();
    t->Subscribe(*xy);
    delete xy; delete t;
    return 0;
}
```

From the preceding example, you see how one can naturally subscribe for even numbers from an Observable sequence of natural numbers. The system will automatically push (publish) the values to the observer (subscriber) when an even number is detected. The code gives explicit implementations for key interfaces so that one can understand, or speculate what really happens under the hood.

Converting events to IObservable<T>

We have now understood how one can convert an `IEnumerable<T>`-based pull program to an `IObservable<T>/IObserver<T>`-based push program. In real life, the event source is not as simple as we found in the number stream example given earlier. Let us see how we can convert a `MouseMove` event into a stream with a small MFC program:

We have chosen MFC for this particular implementation because we have a chapter dedicated to Qt-based reactive programming. In that chapter, we will be implementing Reactive programs in idiomatic asynchronous push-based streams. In this MFC program, we simply do a filtering operation to see whether the mouse is moving in a bounding rectangle and, if so, notify the `observer`. We are using synchronous dispatch here. This example is synchronous too:

```
#include "stdafx.h"
#include <afxwin.h>
#include <afxext.h>
#include <math.h>
#include <vector>
#include "../Common2.h"

using namespace std;
class CMouseFrame :public CFrameWnd, IObservable<CPoint>
{
private:
     RECT _rect;
     POINT _curr_pos;
     vector<IObserver<CPoint> *> _event_src;
public:
     CMouseFrame(){
          HBRUSH brush =
               (HBRUSH)::CreateSolidBrush(RGB(175, 238, 238));
          CString mywindow = AfxRegisterWndClass(
               CS_HREDRAW | CS_VREDRAW | CS_DBLCLKS,
               0, brush, 0);
          Create(mywindow, _T("MFC Clock By Praseed Pai"));
     }
```

The preceding part of the code defines a `Frame` class that derives from the MFC library the `CFrameWnd` class and also implements the `IObservable<T>` interface to force the programmer to implement the `Subscribe` method. A vector of `IObserver<T>` will store the list of `observers` or `Subscribers`. For this example, we will have only one `observer`. There is no restriction on the number of `observer` in the code:

```
virtual bool Subscribe(IObserver<CPoint>& observer) {
    _event_src.push_back(&observer);
    return true;
}
```

The `Subscribe` method just stores the reference to the `observer` onto a vector and returns `true`: when the mouse is moved, we get notification from the MFC library and if it is in a rectangular area, `observer` will be notified (the notification code is as follows):

```
bool FireEvent(const CPoint& pt) {
    vector<IObserver<CPoint> *>::iterator it =
        _event_src.begin();
    while (it != _event_src.end()){
        IObserver<CPoint> *observer = *it;
        observer->OnNext(pt);
        //---------- In a Real world Rx programs there is a
        //--------- sequence stipulated to call methods...
        //--------- OnCompleted will be called only when
        //--------- all the data is processed...this code
        //--------- is written to demonstrate the call schema
        observer->OnCompleted();
        it++;
    }
    return true;
}
```

The `FireEvent` method walks through the `observer`'s and calls the `OnNext` method of the `observer`. It also calls the `OnCompleted` method of each instance of Observer's: The Rx dispatching mechanism follows certain rules while calling the `observer` methods. If `OnComplete` method is called, no more `OnNext` will be called on the same `observer`. Similarly, if `OnError` is called, no further messages will be dispatched to the `observer`. If we need to follow the conventions stipulated by the Rx model here, the listing will get complicated. The purpose of the code given here is to show how the Rx programming model works in a schematic manner.

```
int OnCreate(LPCREATESTRUCT l){
    return CFrameWnd::OnCreate(l);
}
void SetCurrentPoint(CPoint pt) {
```

```
    this->_curr_pos = pt;
    Invalidate(0);
}
```

The `SetCurrentPoint` method is invoked by `observer` to set the current point where the text has to be drawn. The `Invalidate` method is invoked to trigger a WM_PAINT message and the `MFC` subsystem will route it to `OnPaint` (as it is wired in the `Message` maps):

```
void OnPaint()
{
    CPaintDC d(this);
    CBrush b(RGB(100, 149, 237));
    int x1 = -200, y1 = -220, x2 = 210, y2 = 200;
    Transform(&x1, &y1); Transform(&x2, &y2);
    CRect rect(x1, y1, x2, y2);
    d.FillRect(&rect, &b);
    CPen p2(PS_SOLID, 2, RGB(153, 0, 0));
    d.SelectObject(&p2);

    char *str = "Hello Reactive C++";
    CFont f;
    f.CreatePointFont(240, _T("Times New Roman"));
    d.SelectObject(&f);
    d.SetTextColor(RGB(204, 0, 0));
    d.SetBkMode(TRANSPARENT);
    CRgn crgn;
    crgn.CreateRectRgn(rect.left, rect.top,
    rect.right , rect.bottom);
    d.SelectClipRgn(&crgn);
    d.TextOut(_curr_pos.x, _curr_pos.y,
    CString(str), strlen(str));
}
```

The `OnPaint` method is invoked by the MFC framework when the `Invalidate` call is made. The method draws the `literal` string, `Hello Reactive C++`, on the screen:

```
void Transform(int *px, int *py) {
    ::GetClientRect(m_hWnd, &_rect);
    int width = (_rect.right - _rect.left) / 2,
    height = (_rect.bottom - _rect.top) / 2;
    *px = *px + width; *py = height - *py;
}
```

The `Transform` method computes the bound of the client area of the `Frame` and converts `Cartesian` coordinates to devise coordinates. This computation can be better done through world coordinate transformations:

```
void OnMouseMove(UINT nFlags, CPoint point)
{
        int x1 = -200,y1= -220, x2 = 210,y2 = 200;
        Transform(&x1, &y1);Transform(&x2, &y2);
        CRect rect(x1, y1, x2, y2);
        POINT pts;
        pts.x = point.x; pts.y = point.y;
        rect.NormalizeRect();
        //--- In a real program, the points will be aggregated
        //---- into a list (stream)
        if (rect.PtInRect(point)) {
                //--- Ideally speaking this notification has to go
                //--- through a non blocking call
                FireEvent(point);
        }
}
```

The `OnMouseMove` method checks whether the mouse position is within a rectangle centered inside the screen and fires the notification to the `observer`:

```
        DECLARE_MESSAGE_MAP();
};

BEGIN_MESSAGE_MAP(CMouseFrame, CFrameWnd)
        ON_WM_CREATE()
        ON_WM_PAINT()
        ON_WM_MOUSEMOVE()
END_MESSAGE_MAP()
class WindowHandler : public IObserver<CPoint>
{
private:
        CMouseFrame *window;
public:
        WindowHandler(CMouseFrame *win) : window(win) { }
        virtual ~WindowHandler() { window = 0; }
        virtual void OnCompleted() {}
        virtual void OnError(CustomException *exception) {}
        virtual void OnNext(CPoint value) {
                if (window) window->SetCurrentPoint(value);
        }
};
```

The preceding class `WindowHandler` implements the `IObserver<T>` interface and handles the event notified by `CMouseFrame`, which implements the `IObservable<CPoint>` interface. In this canned example, we set the current point by invoking the `SetCurrentPoint` method to draw the string at the mouse position:

```
class CMouseApp :public CWinApp
{
      WindowHandler *reactive_handler;
public:
      int InitInstance(){
            CMouseFrame *p = new CMouseFrame();
            p->ShowWindow(1);
            reactive_handler = new WindowHandler(p);
            //--- Wire the observer to the Event Source
            //--- which implements IObservable<T>
            p->Subscribe(*reactive_handler);
            m_pMainWnd = p;
            return 1;
      }
      virtual ~CMouseApp() {
            if (reactive_handler) {
                  delete reactive_handler;
                  reactive_handler = 0;
            }
      }
};

CMouseApp a;
```

The philosophy of our book

The purpose of this chapter is to introduce readers to the key interfaces of the reactive programming mode they are—`IObservable<T>` and `IObserver<T>`. They are in fact the duals of the `IEnumerable<T>` and `IEnumerator<T>` interface. We learned how to model those interfaces in classic C++ (well, mostly) and had toy implementations of all of them. Finally, we implemented a GUI program that captures mouse movements and notifies a list of Observers. These toy implementations are to get our feet wet with the ideas and ideals of the Reactive programming model. Our implementations can be considered as implementing of OOP-based reactive programming.

To be proficient in C++ reactive programming, a programmer has to be comfortable with the following topics:

- Advanced linguistic constructs provided by Modern C++
- Functional programming constructs provided by Modern C++
- Asynchronous programming (RxCpp handles it for you!) model
- Event stream processing
- Knowledge of industrial-strength libraries such as RxCpp
- Applications of RxCpp in GUI and web programming
- Advanced reactive programming constructs
- Handling errors and exceptions

This chapter was mostly about key idioms and why we require a robust model for handling asynchronous data. The next three chapters will cover language features of Modern C++, handling concurrency/parallelism with C++ standard constructs, and lock-free programming (made possible by memory model guarantees). The preceding topics will give the user a firm foundation from which to master functional reactive programming.

In Chapter 5, *Introduction to Observables*, we will once again return to the topic of Observables and implement interfaces in a functional manner to reiterate some of the concepts. In Chapter 6, *Introduction to Event Stream Programming Using C++*, we will move towards the advanced event stream processing topics with the help of two industrial-strength libraries that use the **Domain Specific Embedded Language** (**DSEL**) approach towards event stream processing.

By now, the stage will be set for the user to be exposed to the industrial-strength RxCpp library and its nuances to write professional-quality Modern C++ programs. In Chapter 7, *Introduction to Data Flow Computation and the RxCpp Library* and Chapter 8, *RxCpp – the Key Elements*, we will cover this wonderful library. The following chapters will cover Reactive GUI programming using the Qt library and advanced operators in RxCpp.

The last three chapters cover advanced topics of Reactive design patterns, micro-services in C++, and handling errors/exceptions. By the end of the book, the reader who started with classic C++ will have covered a lot of ground, not only in writing Reactive programs but in the C++ language itself. Because of the nature of the topic, we will cover most of the features of C++ 17 (at the time of writing).

Summary

In this chapter, we learned about some key data structures of the Rx programming model. We implemented toy versions of them to familiarize us with the conceptual nuances underpinning them. We started with how GUI events were handled by Windows API, XLib API, MFC, and Qt. We briefly touched upon how events are handled in COM+/CORBA as well. Then, a quick overview of Reactive programming was given. After introducing some interfaces, we implemented them from scratch. Finally, a GUI version of these interfaces on top of MFC was implemented for the sake of completeness. We also dealt with the key philosophical aspects of the book.

In the next chapter, we will make a whirlwind tour of the key features of Modern C++ (C++ Versions 11/14/17) by emphasizing on move semantics, Lambdas, type inference, range-based loops, pipe-able operators, smart pointers, and so on. This is essential for writing even basic code for Reactive Programming.

2

A Tour of Modern C++ and its Key Idioms

The classic C++ programming language was standardized in 1998 and it was followed by a small revision (mostly corrections) in 2003. To support advanced abstractions, developers relied on the Boost (http://www.boost.org) library and other public domain libraries. Thanks to the next wave of standardization, the language (from C++ 11 onward) was enhanced, and now developers can encode most widely used abstractions (supported by other languages) without relying on external libraries. Even threads and file-system interfaces, which came squarely under the aegis of libraries, are now part of the standard language. Modern C++ (which stands for C++ versions 11/14/17) contains superb additions to the language and its libraries, that make C++ the de-facto choice for writing industrial strength production software. The features covered in this chapter are the minimum set of features that a programmer has to understand to work with Reactive Programming constructs in general and RxCpp in particular. The primary objective of this chapter is to cover the most important additions to the language which makes implementing Reactive Programming constructs easier without resorting to esoteric language techniques. Constructs such as Lambda functions, automatic type inference, rvalue references, move semantics, and language level concurrency are some of the constructs which the authors of this book feel that every C++ programmer should know. In this chapter, we will cover the following topics:

- Key concerns for C++ programming language design
- Some enhancements to C++ for writing better code
- Better memory management through rvalue references and move semantics
- Better object lifetime management using an enhanced set of smart pointers
- Behavioral parameterization using Lambda functions and expressions
- Function Wrappers (the `std::function` type)
- Miscellaneous features
- Writing Iterators and Observers (to put everything together)

The key concerns of the C++ programming language

As far as developers are concerned, the three key concerns that C++ programming language designers keep in mind were (and still are) as follows:

- Zero Cost Abstraction - No performance penalty for higher level abstraction
- Expressivity - A **user defined type** (**UDT**) or class should be as expressive as built-in types
- Substitutability - A UDT can be substituted wherever built-in-types are expected (as in generic data structures and algorithms)

We will discuss these briefly.

Zero cost abstraction

The C++ programming language has always helped developers to write code that exploits the microprocessor (on which generated code runs) and also raise the level of abstraction when it matters. While raising the abstraction, the designers of the language have always tried to minimize (almost eliminate) their performance overhead. This is called Zero Cost Abstraction or Zero Overhead Cost Abstraction. The only notable penalty you pay is the cost of indirect calls (through function pointers) while dispatching virtual functions. Despite adding tons of features to the language, the designers have maintained the "Zero Cost Abstraction" guarantee implied by the language from its inception.

Expressivity

C++ helps a developer to write user defined types or classes that can be as expressive as the built-in types of the programming languages. This enables one to write a arbitrary-precision arithmetic class (monikered as `BigInteger`/`BigFloat` in some languages), which contains all the features of a double or float. For the sake of explanation, we have defined a `SmartFloat` class that wraps IEEE double precision floating point numbers and most of the operators available to the double data type is overloaded. The following code snippets show that one can write types that mimic the semantics of built-in types such as int, float, or double:

```
//---- SmartFloat.cpp
#include <iostream>
#include <vector>
```

```
#include <algorithm>
using namespace std;
class SmartFloat {
    double _value; // underlying store
  public:
    SmartFloat(double value) : _value(value) {}
    SmartFloat() : _value(0) {}
    SmartFloat( const SmartFloat& other ) { _value = other._value; }
    SmartFloat& operator = ( const SmartFloat& other ) {
        if ( this != &other ) { _value = other._value; }
        return *this;
    }
    SmartFloat& operator = (double value )
     { _value = value; return *this; }
    ~SmartFloat(){ }
```

The `SmartFloat` class wraps a double value and has defined some constructors and assignment operators to initialize instances properly. In the following snippet, we will define some operators that help to increment the value. Both the prefix and postfix variants of operators are defined:

```
    SmartFloat& operator ++ () { _value++; return *this; }
    SmartFloat operator ++ (int) { // postfix operator
         SmartFloat nu(*this); ++_value; return nu;
    }
    SmartFloat& operator -- () { _value--; return *this; }
    SmartFloat operator -- (int) {
         SmartFloat nu(*this); --_value; return nu;
    }
```

The preceding code snippets implement increment operators (both prefix and postfix) and are meant for demonstration purposes only. In a real-world class, we will check for floating point overflow and underflow to make the code more robust. The whole purpose of wrapping a type is to write robust code!

```
    SmartFloat& operator += ( double x ) { _value += x; return *this; }
    SmartFloat& operator -= ( double x ) { _value -= x; return *this; }
    SmartFloat& operator *= ( double x ) { _value *= x; return *this; }
    SmartFloat& operator /= ( double x ) { _value /= x; return *this; }
```

The preceding code snippets implement C++ style assignment operators and once again, to make the listing short, we have not checked whether any floating point overflow or underflow is there. We do not handle exceptions as well here to keep the listing brief.

```
    bool operator > ( const SmartFloat& other )
      { return _value > other._value; }
    bool operator < ( const SmartFloat& other )
```

```
        {return _value < other._value;}
    bool operator == ( const SmartFloat& other )
        { return _value == other._value;}
    bool operator != ( const SmartFloat& other )
        { return _value != other._value;}
    bool operator >= ( const SmartFloat& other )
        { return _value >= other._value;}
    bool operator <= ( const SmartFloat& other )
        { return _value <= other._value;}
```

The preceding code implements relational operators and most of the semantics associated with double precision floating points have been implemented as shown:

```
    operator int () { return _value; }
    operator double () { return _value;}
};
```

For the sake of completeness, we have implemented conversion operators to `int` and `double`. We will write two functions to aggregate values stored in an array. The first function expects an array of `double` as parameter and the second one expects a `SmartFloat` array as parameter. The code is identical in both routines and only the type changes. Both will produce the same result:

```
double Accumulate( double a[] , int count ){
    double value = 0;
    for( int i=0; i<count; ++i) { value += a[i]; }
    return value;
}
double Accumulate( SmartFloat a[] , int count ){
    SmartFloat value = 0;
    for( int i=0; i<count; ++i) { value += a[i]; }
    return value;
}
int main() {
    // using C++ 1z's initializer list
    double x[] = { 10.0,20.0,30,40 };
    SmartFloat y[] = { 10,20.0,30,40 };
    double res = Accumulate(x,4); // will call the double version
    cout << res << endl;
    res = Accumulate(y,4); // will call the SmartFloat version
    cout << res << endl;
}
```

The C++ language helps us write expressive types that augment the semantics of basic types. The expressiveness of the language also helps one to write good value types and reference types using a myriad of techniques supported by the language. With support for operator overloading, conversion operators, placement new, and other related techniques, the language has taken the class design to a higher level compared to other languages of its time. But, with power comes responsibility and the language sometimes gives you enough rope to shoot yourself in the foot.

Substitutability

In the previous example, we saw how a user-defined type can be used to express all the operations done on a built-in type. Another goal of C++ is to write code in a generic manner where we can substitute a user-defined class that mimics the semantics of one of the built-in types such as float, double, int, and so on:

```
//------------- from SmartValue.cpp
template <class T>
T Accumulate( T a[] , int count ) {
    T value = 0;
    for( int i=0; i<count; ++i) { value += a[i]; }
    return value;
}
int main(){
    //----- Templated version of SmartFloat
    SmartValue<double> y[] = { 10,20.0,30,40 };
    double res = Accumulate(y,4);
    cout << res << endl;
}
```

The C++ programming language supports different programming paradigms and the three principles outlined previously are just some of them. The language gives support for constructs that can help create robust types (domain-specific) for writing better code. These three principles gave us a powerful and fast programming language for sure. Modern C++did add a lot of new abstractions to make the life of a programmer easier. But the three design principles outlined previously have not been sacrificed in any way to achieve those objectives. This was partly possible because of the meta programming support the language had due to the inadvertent Turing completeness of the template mechanism. Read about **template meta programming (TMP)** and Turing Completeness with the help of your favorite search engine.

Enhancements to C++ for writing better code

The programming language universe has changed a lot in the last decade and those changes should reflect in the C++ programming language in its new avatar. Most of the innovations in Modern C++ involve handling advanced abstractions and the introduction of functional programming constructs to support language level concurrency. Most modern languages have got a garbage collector and a run-time manages these complexities. The C++ programming language does not have automatic garbage collection as part of the language standard. The C++ programming languages with its implicit guarantee of Zero cost abstraction (you do not pay for what you do not use) and maximum run-time performance, has to resort to a lot of compile-time tricks and meta programming techniques to achieve the abstraction level supported by a language such as C#, Java, or Scala. Some of them are outlined in the following sections and you can delve into these topics yourself. The website http://en.cppreference.com is a good site for advancing your knowledge of the C++ programming language.

Type deduction and inference

The Modern C++ language compiler does a wonderful job of deducing types from the expressions and statements specified by the programmers. Most modern programming languages do have support for type inference and so does Modern C++. This is an idiom borrowed from Functional Programming languages such as Haskell and ML. Type inferences are already available with the C# and Scala programming languages. We will write a small program to kick-start us with type inference:

```
//----- AutoFirst.cpp
#include <iostream>
#include <vector>
using namespace std;
int main(){
    vector<string> vt = {"first", "second", "third", "fourth"};
    //--- Explicitly specify the Type ( makes it verbose)
    for (vector<string>::iterator it = vt.begin();
        it != vt.end(); ++it)
    cout << *it << " ";
    //--- Let the compiler infer the type for us
    for (auto it2 = vt.begin(); it2 != vt.end(); ++it2)
        cout << *it2 << " ";
    return 0;
}
```

The `auto` keyword specifies that the type of the variable will be deduced by the compiler based on initialization and the return values of functions specified in the expression. In this particular example, we do not gain much. As our declarations get more complicated, it is better to let the compiler do the type inference. Our code listings will use auto to simplify the code throughout the book. Now, let us write a simple program to make the idea even more clear:

```cpp
//----- AutoSecond.cpp
#include <iostream>
#include <vector>
#include <initializer_list>
using namespace std;
int main() {
    vector<double> vtdbl = {0, 3.14, 2.718, 10.00};
    auto vt_dbl2 = vtdbl; // type will be deduced
    auto size = vt_dbl2.size(); // size_t
    auto &rvec = vtdbl; // specify a auto reference
    cout << size << endl;
    // Iterate - Compiler infers the type
    for ( auto it = vtdbl.begin(); it != vtdbl.end(); ++it)
        cout << *it << " ";
    // 'it2' evaluates to iterator to vector of double
    for (auto it2 = vt_dbl2.begin(); it2 != vt_dbl2.end(); ++it2)
        cout << *it2 << " ";
    // This will change the first element of vtdbl vector
    rvec[0] = 100;
    // Now Iterate to reflect the type
    for ( auto it3 = vtdbl.begin(); it3 != vtdbl.end(); ++it3)
        cout << *it3 << " ";
    return 0;
}
```

The preceding code demonstrates the use of type inference while writing Modern C++ code. The C++ programming language also has a new keyword that helps to query the type of expression given as arguments. The general form of the keyword is `decltype(<expr>)`. The following program helps to demonstrate the use of this particular keyword:

```cpp
//---- Decltype.cpp
#include <iostream>
using namespace std;
int foo() { return 10; }
char bar() { return 'g'; }
auto fancy() -> decltype(1.0f) { return 1;} //return type is float
int main() {
    // Data type of x is same as return type of foo()
    // and type of y is same as return type of bar()
    decltype(foo()) x;
```

```
        decltype(bar()) y;
        //--- in g++, Should print i => int
        cout << typeid(x).name() << endl;
        //--- in g++, Should print c => char
        cout << typeid(y).name() << endl;
        struct A { double x; };
        const A* a = new A();
        decltype(a->x) z; // type is double
        decltype((a->x)) t= z; // type is const double&
        //--- in g++, Should print  d => double
        cout << typeid(z).name() << endl;
        cout << typeid(t).name() << endl;
        //--- in g++, Should print  f => float
        cout << typeid(decltype(fancy())).name() << endl;
        return 0;
    }
```

The `decltype` is a compile-time construct and it helps to specify the type of a variable (the compiler will do the hard work to figure it out) and also helps us to force a type on a variable (see the preceding `fancy()` function).

Uniform initialization of variables

Classic C++ had some kind of ad-hoc syntax for the initialization of variables. Modern C++ supports uniform initialization (we have already seen examples in the type inference section). The language provides helper classes to developers to support uniform initialization for their custom types:

```
//-----------------Initialization.cpp
#include <iostream>
#include <vector>
#include <initializer_list>
using namespace std;
template <class T>
struct Vector_Wrapper {
    std::vector<T> vctr;
    Vector_Wrapper(std::initializer_list<T> l) : vctr(l) {}
    void Append(std::initializer_list<T> l)
    { vctr.insert(vctr.end(), l.begin(), l.end());}
};
int main() {
    Vector_Wrapper<int> vcw = {1, 2, 3, 4, 5}; // list-initialization
    vcw.Append({6, 7, 8}); // list-initialization in function call
```

```
    for (auto n : vcw.vctr) { std::cout << n << ' '; }
    std::cout << '\n';
}
```

The preceding listing shows how one can enable initialization lists for a custom class created by a programmer.

Variadic templates

In C++ 11 and above, there is support for variadic templates as part of the standard language. A variadic template is a template class or template function that takes a variable number in a template argument. In classic C++, template instantiation happens with a fixed number of parameters. Variadic templates are supported both at class level and function level. In this section, we will deal with variadic functions as they are used extensively in writing functional-style programs, compile-time programming (meta programming), and pipeable functions:

```
//Variadic.cpp
#include <iostream>
#include <iterator>
#include <vector>
#include <algorithm>
using namespace std;
//--- add given below is a base case for ending compile time
//--- recursion
int add() { return 0; } // end condition
//---- Declare a Variadic function Template
//---- ... is called parameter pack. The compiler
//--- synthesize a function based on the number of arguments
//------ given by the programmer.
//------ decltype(auto) => Compiler will do Type Inference
template<class T0, class ... Ts>
decltype(auto) add(T0 first, Ts ... rest) {
    return first + add(rest ...);
}
int main() { int n = add(0,2,3,4); cout << n << endl; }
```

In the preceding code, the compiler synthesizes a function based on the number of arguments passed. The compiler understands that `add` is a variadic function and generates the code by recursively unpacking the parameters during compile time. Compile time recursion will stop when the compiler has processed all the parameters. The base case version is a hint to the compiler to stop recursion. The next program shows how variadic templates and perfect forwarding can be used to write a function that takes an arbitrary number of parameters:

```cpp
//Variadic2.cpp
#include <iostream>
#include <iterator>
#include <vector>
#include <algorithm>
using namespace std;
//--------- Print values to the console for basic types
//-------- These are base case versions
void EmitConsole(int value) { cout << "Integer: " << value << endl; }
void EmitConsole(double value) { cout << "Double: " << value << endl; }
void EmitConsole(const string& value){cout << "String: "<<value<< endl; }
```

The three variants of `EmitConsole` print the argument to the console. We have functions for printing `int`, `double`, and `string`. Using these functions as a base case, we will write a function that uses universal references and perfect forwarding to write functions that take arbitrary values:

```cpp
template<typename T>
void EmitValues(T&& arg) { EmitConsole(std::forward<T>(arg)); }

template<typename T1, typename... Tn>
void EmitValues(T1&& arg1, Tn&&... args){
    EmitConsole(std::forward<T1>(arg1));
    EmitValues(std::forward<Tn>(args)...);
}

int main() { EmitValues(0,2.0,"Hello World",4); }
```

Rvalue references

If you have been programming in C++ for a long time, you might be familiar with the fact that C++ references help you to alias a variable and you can do assignment to the references to reflect the mutation in the variable aliased. The kinds of reference supported by C++ were called lvalue references (as they were references to variables that can come in the left side of the assignment). The following code snippets show the use of lvalue references:

```
//---- Lvalue.cpp
#include <iostream>
using namespace std;
int main() {
  int i=0;
  cout << i << endl; //prints 0
  int& ri = i;
  ri = 20;
  cout << i << endl; // prints 20
}
```

`int&` is an instance of lvalue references. In Modern C++, there is the notion of rvalue references. rvalue is defined as anything that is not an lvalue, the kind of stuff that can appear on the right side of the assignment. In classic C++, there was no notion of an rvalue references. Modern C++ introduced it:

```
///---- Rvaluref.cpp
#include <iostream>using namespace std;
int main() {
    int&& j = 42;int x = 3,y=5; int&& z = x + y; cout << z << endl;
    z = 10; cout << z << endl;j=20;cout << j << endl;
}
```

Rvalue references are indicted by two `&&`. The following program will clearly demonstrate the use of rvalue references while invoking functions:

```
//------- RvaluerefCall.cpp
#include <iostream>
using namespace std;
void TestFunction( int & a ) {cout << a << endl;}
void TestFunction( int && a ){
    cout << "rvalue references" << endl;
    cout << a << endl;
}
int main() {
int&& j = 42;
int x = 3,y=5;
int&& z = x + y;
    TestFunction(x + y ); // Should call rvalue reference function
```

```
        TestFunction(j); // Calls Lvalue Refreence function
}
```

The real power of rvalue references is visible in the case of memory management. The C++ programming language has got the notion of Copy constructor and Assignment operators. They mostly copy the source object contents. With the help of rvalue references, one can avoid expensive copying by swapping pointers, as rvalue references are temporaries or intermediate expressions. The following section demonstrates this.

Move semantics

The C++ programming language implicitly warrants a Copy Constructor, Assignment Operator, and a Destructor (some times virtual) with every class designed by us. This is meant to do resource management while cloning an object or while assigning to an existing object. Sometimes it is very expensive to copy an object and the movement of ownership (through pointers) helps in writing fast code. Modern C++ has got a facility to provide a Move Constructor and a Move assignment operator to help developers avoid copying large objects, during the creation of a new object or assignment to a new object. Rvalue references can act as a hint to the compiler that, when temporary objects are involved, a move version of a constructor or a move version of assignment is better suited for the context:

```cpp
//----- FloatBuffer.cpp
#include <iostream>
#include <vector>
using namespace std;
class FloatBuffer {
    double *bfr; int count;
public:
    FloatBuffer():bfr(nullptr),count(0){}
    FloatBuffer(int pcount):bfr(new double[pcount]),count(pcount){}
        // Copy constructor.
    FloatBuffer(const FloatBuffer& other) : count(other.count)
        , bfr(new double[other.count])
    { std::copy(other.bfr, other.bfr + count, bfr); }
    // Copy assignment operator - source code is obvious
    FloatBuffer& operator=(const FloatBuffer& other) {
        if (this != &other) {
          if ( bfr != nullptr)
            delete[] bfr; // free memory of the current object
            count = other.count;
            bfr = new double[count]; //re-allocate
            std::copy(other.bfr, other.bfr + count, bfr);
        }
        return *this;
```

```
        }
        // Move constructor to enable move semantics
        // The Modern STL containers supports move sementcis
        FloatBuffer(FloatBuffer&& other) : bfr(nullptr) , count(0) {
        cout << "in move constructor" << endl;
        // since it is a move constructor, we are not copying elements from
        // the source object. We just assign the pointers to steal memory
        bfr = other.bfr;
        count = other.count;
        // Now that we have grabbed our memory, we just assign null to
        // source pointer
        other.bfr = nullptr;
        other.count = 0;
        }
    // Move assignment operator.
    FloatBuffer& operator=(FloatBuffer&& other) {
        if (this != &other)
        {
            // Free the existing resource.
            delete[] bfr;
            // Copy the data pointer and its length from the
            // source object.
            bfr = other.bfr;
            count = other.count;
            // We have stolen the memory, now set the pinter to null
            other.bfr = nullptr;
            other.count = 0;
        }
        return *this;
    }

};
int main() {
    // Create a vector object and add a few elements to it.
    // Since STL supports move semantics move methods will be called.
    // in this particular case (Modern Compilers are smart)
    vector<FloatBuffer> v;
    v.push_back(FloatBuffer(25));
    v.push_back(FloatBuffer(75));
}
```

The std::move function can be used to indicate (while passing parameters) that the candidate object is movable and the compiler will invoke appropriate methods (move assignment or move constructor) to optimize the cost associated with memory management. Basically, std::move is a static_cast to an rvalue reference.

Smart pointers

Managing object lifetimes has been a problematic area for the C++ programming language. If the developer is not careful, the program can leak memory and will slow down performance. Smart pointers are wrapper classes around a raw pointer where operators such as dereferencing (*) and referencing (->) are overloaded. Smart pointers can do object lifetime management, act as a limited form of garbage collection, free memory, and so on. The Modern C++ language has:

- `unique_ptr<T>`
- `shared_ptr<T>`
- `weak_ptr<T>`

A `unique_ptr<T>` is a wrapper for a raw pointer where there is exclusive ownership with the wrapper. The following code snippet will demonstrate the use of `<unique_ptr>`:

```
//---- Unique_Ptr.cpp
#include <iostream>
#include <deque>#include <memory>
using namespace std;
int main( int argc , char **argv ) {
    // Define a Smart Pointer for STL deque container...
    unique_ptr< deque<int> > dq(new deque<int>() );
    //------ populate values , leverages -> operator
    dq->push_front(10); dq->push_front(20);
    dq->push_back(23); dq->push_front(16);
    dq->push_back(41);
    auto dqiter = dq->begin();
    while ( dqiter != dq->end())
    { cout << *dqiter << "\n"; dqiter++; }
    //------ SmartPointer will free reference
    //------ and it's dtor will be called here
    return 0;
}
```

`std::shared_ptr` is a smart pointer that uses reference counting to keep track of references made to a particular instance of an object. The underlying object is destroyed when the last remaining `shared_ptr` pointing to it is destroyed or reset:

```
//----- Shared_Ptr.cpp
#include <iostream>
#include <memory>
#include <stdio.h>
using namespace std;
/////////////////////////////////////////////////
```

```
// Even If you pass shared_ptr<T> instance
// by value, the update is visible to callee
// as shared_ptr<T>'s copy constructor reference
// counts to the orginial instance
//

void foo_byvalue(std::shared_ptr<int> i) { (*i)++; }

//////////////////////////////////////////
// passed by reference,we have not
// created a copy.
//
void foo_byreference(std::shared_ptr<int>& i) { (*i)++; }
int main(int argc, char **argv )
{
    auto sp = std::make_shared<int>(10);
    foo_byvalue(sp);
    foo_byreference(sp);
    //--------- The output should be 12
    std::cout << *sp << std::endl;
}
```

std:weak_ptr is a container for a raw pointer. It is created as a copy of a shared_ptr. The existence or destruction of weak_ptr copies of a shared_ptr have no effect on the shared_ptr or its other copies. After all copies of a shared_ptr have been destroyed, all weak_ptr copies become empty. The following program demonstrates a mechanism that helps us to detect defunct pointers using weak_ptr:

```
//------- Weak_Ptr.cpp
#include <iostream>
#include <deque>
#include <memory>

using namespace std;
int main( int argc , char **argv )
{
    std::shared_ptr<int> ptr_1(new int(500));
    std::weak_ptr<int> wptr_1 = ptr_1;
    {
        std::shared_ptr<int> ptr_2 = wptr_1.lock();
        if(ptr_2)
        {
            cout << *ptr_2 << endl; // this will be exeucted
        }
    //---- ptr_2 will go out of the scope
    }
    ptr_1.reset(); //Memory is deleted.
```

```
std::shared_ptr<int> ptr_3= wptr_1.lock();
//-------- Always else part will be executed
//-------- as ptr_3 is nullptr now
if(ptr_3)
    cout << *ptr_3 << endl;
else
    cout << "Defunct Pointer" << endl;
return 0;
}
```

Classic C++ had a smart pointer type called `auto_ptr` and it has been removed from the language standard. One needs to use `unique_ptr` instead.

Lambda functions

One of the major additions to the C++ language is Lambda functions and Lambda expressions. They are anonymous functions that the programmer can define at the call site to perform some logic. This simplifies the logic and code readability also increases in a remarkable manner.

Rather than defining what a Lambda function is, let us write a piece of code that helps us count the number of positive numbers in a `vector<int>`. In this case, we need to filter out the negative values and count the rest. We will use an STL `count_if` to write the code:

```
//LambdaFirst.cpp
#include <iostream>
#include <iterator>
#include <vector>
#include <algorithm>
using namespace std;
int main() {
    auto num_vect =
        vector<int>{ 10, 23, -33, 15, -7, 60, 80};
    //---- Define a Lambda Function to Filter out negatives
    auto filter = [](int const value) {return value > 0; };
    auto cnt= count_if(
        begin(num_vect), end(num_vect),filter);
    cout << cnt << endl;
}
```

In the preceding code snippet, the variable filter is assigned an anonymous function and we are using the filter in the `count_if` STL function. Now, let us write a simple Lambda function that we will specify at the function call site. We will be using STL accumulate to aggregate the values inside a vector:

```cpp
//-------------- LambdaSecond.cpp
#include <iostream>
#include <iterator>
#include <vector>
#include <algorithm>
#include <numeric>
using namespace std;
int main() {
    auto num_vect =
        vector<int>{ 10, 23, -33, 15, -7, 60, 80};
    //-- Define a BinaryOperation Lambda at the call site
    auto accum = std::accumulate(
        std::begin(num_vect), std::end(num_vect), 0,
        [](auto const s, auto const n) {return s + n;});
    cout << accum << endl;
}
```

Functors and Lambdas

In classic C++, while using STL, we extensively use Function Objects or Functors by overloading Function Operators to write transformation filters and perform reduction on STL containers:

```cpp
//----- LambdaThird.cpp
#include <iostream>
#include <numeric>
using namespace std;
////////////////////////////
// Functors to add and multiply two numbers
template <typename T>
struct addition{
    T operator () (const T& init, const T& a ) { return init + a; }
};
template <typename T>
struct multiply {
    T operator () (const T& init, const T& a ) { return init * a; }
};
int main()
{
    double v1[3] = {1.0, 2.0, 4.0}, sum;
    sum = accumulate(v1, v1 + 3, 0.0, addition<double>());
```

```
      cout << "sum = " << sum << endl;
      sum = accumulate(v1,v1+3,0.0, [] (const double& a ,const double& b    )
{
          return a +b;
      });
      cout << "sum = " << sum << endl;
      double mul_pi = accumulate(v1, v1 + 3, 1.0, multiply<double>());
      cout << "mul_pi = " << mul_pi << endl;
      mul_pi= accumulate(v1,v1+3,1, [] (const double& a , const double& b ){
          return a *b;
      });
      cout << "mul_pi = " << mul_pi << endl;
}
```

The following program clearly demonstrates the usage of Lambda by writing a toy sort program. We will show how we can use Function Objects and Lambdas to write equivalent code. The code is written in a generic manner, but it makes an assumption that numbers are expected (`double`, `float`, `integer`, or a user defined equivalent):

```
//////////////////
//-------- LambdaFourth.cpp
#include <iostream>
#include <vector>
#include <algorithm>
using namespace std;
//--- Generic functions for Comparison and Swap
template <typename T>
bool Cmp( T& a , T&b ) {return ( a > b ) ? true: false;}
template <typename T>
void Swap( T& a , T&b ) { T c = a;a = b;b = c;}
```

`Cmp` and `Swap` are generic functions that will be used to compare adjacent elements and swap elements, respectively, while performing the sort operation:

```
template <typename T>
void BubbleSortFunctor( T *arr , int length ) {
    for( int i=0; i< length-1; ++i )
        for(int j=i+1; j< length; ++j )
            if ( Cmp( arr[i] , arr[j] ) )
                Swap(arr[i],arr[j] );
}
```

Armed with Cmp and Swap, writing a bubble sort is a simple affair. We need to have a nested loop where we will compare two elements and if Cmp returns true, we will invoke Swap to exchange values:

```
template <typename T>
```

```
void BubbleSortLambda( T *arr , int length ) {
    auto CmpLambda = [] (const auto& a , const auto& b )
    { return ( a > b ) ? true: false; };
    auto SwapLambda = [] ( auto& a , auto& b )
    { auto c = a;a = b;b = c;};
    for( int i=0; i< length-1; ++i )
        for(int j=i+1; j< length; ++j )
            if ( CmpLambda( arr[i] , arr[j] ) )
                SwapLambda (arr[i],arr[j] );
}
```

In the preceding routine, we define the comparison and swap function as Lambdas. The Lambda function is a mechanism to specify a piece of code or expression inline, often called anonymous functions. The definition can be given in a syntax specified by the C++ language, and can be assigned to a variable, passed as a parameter, or returned from a function. In the preceding function, the variables `CmpLambda` and `SwapLambda` are examples of anonymous functions specified in Lambda syntax. The body of the Lambda functions is not much different from the preceding function version. To learn more about Lambda functions and expression, you can consult the page at `http://en.cppreference.com/w/cpp/language/lambda`.

```
template <typename T>
void Print( const T& container){
    for(auto i = container.begin() ; i != container.end(); ++i )
        cout << *i << "\n" ;
}
```

The `Print` routine just cycles through the elements in the container and prints the contents to the console:

```
int main( int argc , char **argv ){
    double ar[4] = {20,10,15,-41};
    BubbleSortFunctor(ar,4);
    vector<double> a(ar,ar+4);
    Print(a);
    cout << "==========================================" << endl;
    ar[0] = 20;ar[1] = 10;ar[2] = 15;ar[3] = -41;
    BubbleSortLambda(ar,4);
    vector<double> a1(ar,ar+4);
    Print(a1);
    cout << "==========================================" << endl;
}
```

Composition, currying, and partial function application

One advantage of Lambdas is you can compose two functions together to create a composition of functions as you do in mathematics (read about function composition in the context of mathematics and functional programming using favorite search engine). The following program demonstrates the idea. This is a toy implementation and writing a general-purpose implementation is beyond the scope of this chapter:

```
//------------ Compose.cpp
//----- g++ -std=c++1z Compose.cpp
#include <iostream>
using namespace std;
//---------- base case compile time recursion
//---------- stops here
template <typename F, typename G>
auto Compose(F&& f, G&& g)
{ return [=](auto x) { return f(g(x)); };}
//----- Performs compile time recursion based
//----- on number of parameters
template <typename F, typename... R>
auto Compose(F&& f, R&&... r){
    return [=](auto x) { return f(Compose(r...)(x)); };
}
```

`Compose` is a variadic template function and the compiler generates code by recursively expanding the `Compose` arguments until all the arguments are processed. In the preceding code, we have used `[=]` to indicate to the compiler that we should capture all variables referenced in the body of the Lambda by value. You can study more about Closure and Variable Capture in the context of functional programming. The C++ language gives flexibility to `Capture` variables by value (as well as using `[&]`) or by specifying variables to be captured explicitly (such as `[&var]`).

The functional programming paradigm is based on a mathematical formalism called Lambda calculus invented by Alonzo Church, an American mathematician. The Lambda calculus supports only unary functions and currying is a technique that breaks a multiple argument function into a series of function evaluations that take one argument at a time.

Using Lambdas and writing functions in a specific manner, we can simulate currying in C++:

```
auto CurriedAdd3(int x) {
    return [x](int y) { //capture x
        return [x, y](int z){ return x + y + z; };
    };
};
```

The partial function application involves the conversion of functions with multiple arguments into a fixed number of arguments. If the fixed number of arguments is less than the arity (parameter count) of the function, a new function will be returned that expects the rest of the parameters. When all parameters are received, the function will be invoked. We can treat the partial application as some form of memorization where parameters are cached until we receive all of them to invoke them.

In the following code snippets, we have used constructs like template parameter pack and variadic templates. A template parameter pack is a template parameter that accepts zero or more template arguments (non-types, types, or templates). A function parameter pack is a function parameter that accepts zero or more function arguments. A template with at least one parameter pack is called a variadic template. A good idea about parameter pack and variadic templates is necessary for understanding `sizeof...` constructs.

```
template <typename... Ts>
auto PartialFunctionAdd3(Ts... xs) {
    //---- http://en.cppreference.com/w/cpp/language/parameter_pack
    //---- http://en.cppreference.com/w/cpp/language/sizeof...
    static_assert(sizeof...(xs) <= 3);
    if constexpr (sizeof...(xs) == 3){
        // Base case: evaluate and return the sum.
        return (0 + ... + xs);
    }
    else{
        // Recursive case: bind `xs...` and return another
        return [xs...](auto... ys){
            return PartialFunctionAdd3(xs..., ys...);
        };
    }
}
int main() {
    // ------------- Compose two functions together
    //----https://en.wikipedia.org/wiki/Function_composition
    auto val = Compose(
        [](int const a) {return std::to_string(a); },
        [](int const a) {return a * a; })(4); // val = "16"
    cout << val << std::endl; //should print 16
```

```
// ----------------- Invoke the Curried function
auto p = CurriedAdd3(4)(5)(6);
cout << p << endl;
//------------- Compose a set of function together
auto func = Compose(
    [](int const n) {return std::to_string(n); },
    [](int const n) {return n * n; },
    [](int const n) {return n + n; },
    [](int const n) {return std::abs(n); });
cout << func(5) << endl;
//----------- Invoke Partial Functions giving different arguments
PartialFunctionAdd3(1, 2, 3);
PartialFunctionAdd3(1, 2)(3);
PartialFunctionAdd3(1)(2)(3);
}
```

Function wrappers

Function wrappers are classes that can wrap any functions, function objects, or Lambdas into a copiable object. The type of the wrapper depends upon the function prototype of the class. `std::function(<prototype>)` from the `<functional>` header represents a function wrapper:

```
//--------------- FuncWrapper.cpp Requires C++ 17 (-std=c++1z )
#include <functional>
#include <iostream>
using namespace std;
//------------- Simple Function call
void PrintNumber(int val){ cout << val << endl; }
// ----------------- A class which overloads function operator
struct PrintNumber {
    void operator()(int i) const { std::cout << i << '\n';}
};
//------------ To demonstrate the usage of method call
struct FooClass {
    int number;
    FooClass(int pnum) : number(pnum){}
    void PrintNumber(int val) const { std::cout << number + val<< endl; }
};
int main() {
    // ---------------- Ordinary Function Wrapped
    std::function<void(int)>
    displaynum = PrintNumber;
    displaynum(0xF000);
    std::invoke(displaynum,0xFF00); //call through std::invoke
    //------------- Lambda Functions Wrapped
```

```
std::function<void()> lambdaprint = []() { PrintNumber(786); };
    lambdaprint();
    std::invoke(lambdaprint);
    // Wrapping member functions of a class
    std::function<void(const FooClass&, int)>
    class display = &FooClass::PrintNumber;
    // creating an instance
    const FooClass fooinstance(100);
    class display (fooinstance,100);
}
```

We will be using `std::function` in our code extensively in the coming sections, as it helps to drag function calls as data.

Composing functions together with the pipe operator

The Unix operating system's command line shell allows the standard output of one function to be piped into the another to form a filter chain. Later, this feature became part of every command line shell offered as part of most operating systems. While writing functional style code, when we combine methods through functional composition, the code becomes hard to read because of deep nesting. Now, with Modern C++ we can overload the pipe (|) operator to allow chaining several functions together, like we do commands in a Unix shell or **Windows PowerShell** console. That is why someone re-christened the LISP language as Lots of Irritating and Silly Parentheses. The RxCpp library uses the | operator extensively to compose functions together. The following code helps us understand how one can create pipeable functions. We will take a look at how this can be implemented in principle. The code given here is only good for expository purposes:

```
//---- PipeFunc2.cpp
//-------- g++ -std=c++1z PipeFunc2.cpp
#include <iostream>
using namespace std;

struct AddOne {
    template<class T>
    auto operator()(T x) const { return x + 1; }
};
```

```
struct SumFunction {
    template<class T>
    auto operator()(T x,T y) const { return x + y;} // Binary Operator
};
```

The preceding code creates a set of Callable classes and it will be used as part of a compositional chain of functions. Now, we need to create a mechanism to convert an arbitrary function to a closure:

```
//-------------- Create a Pipable Closure Function (Unary)
//-------------- Uses Variadic Templates Paramter pack
template<class F>
struct PipableClosure : F{
    template<class... Xs>
    PipableClosure(Xs&&... xs) : // Xs is a universal reference
    F(std::forward<Xs>(xs)...) // perfect forwarding
    {}
};
//---------- A helper function which converts a Function to a Closure
template<class F>
auto MakePipeClosure(F f)
{ return PipableClosure<F>(std::move(f)); }
// ------------ Declare a Closure for Binary
//------------- Functions
//
template<class F>
struct PipableClosureBinary {
    template<class... Ts>
    auto operator()(Ts... xs) const {
        return MakePipeClosure([=](auto x) -> decltype(auto)
        { return F()(x, xs...);}); }
};
//------- Declare a pipe operator
//------- uses perfect forwarding to invoke the function
template<class T, class F> //---- Declare a pipe operator
decltype(auto) operator|(T&& x, const PipableClosure<F>& pfn)
{ return pfn(std::forward<T>(x)); }

int main() {
    //-------- Declare a Unary Function Closure
    const PipableClosure<AddOne> fnclosure = {};
    int value = 1 | fnclosure| fnclosure;
    std::cout << value << std::endl;
```

```
//--------- Decalre a Binary function closure
const PipableClosureBinary<SumFunction> sumfunction = {};
int value1 = 1 | sumfunction(2) | sumfunction(5) | fnclosure;
std::cout << value1 << std::endl;
}
```

Now, we can create an instance of `PipableClosure` with a unary function as a parameter and chain (or compose) together a series of invocations to the closure. The preceding code snippet should print three on the console. We have also created a `PipableBinaryClosure` instance to string together both unary and binary functions.

Miscellaneous features

So far, we have covered the most important semantic changes to the language beginning with the C++ 11 standard. The purpose of this chapter is to highlight key changes that might be useful in writing idiomatic Modern C++ programs. The C++ 17 standard added some more stuff into the language. We will be highlighting a few more features of the language to wrap up this discussion.

Fold expressions

The C++ 17 standard added support for fold expressions to ease the generation of variadic functions. The Compiler does pattern matching and generates the code by inferring the intent of the programmer. The following code snippet demonstrates the idea:

```
//---------------- Folds.cpp
//--------------- Requires C++ 17 (-std=c++1z )
//--------------- http://en.cppreference.com/w/cpp/language/fold
#include <functional>
#include <iostream>

using namespace std;
template <typename... Ts>
auto AddFoldLeftUn(Ts... args) { return (... + args); }
template <typename... Ts>
auto AddFoldLeftBin(int n,Ts... args){ return (n + ... + args);}
template <typename... Ts>
auto AddFoldRightUn(Ts... args) { return (args + ...); }
template <typename... Ts>
auto AddFoldRightBin(int n,Ts... args) { return (args + ... + n); }
template <typename T,typename... Ts>
auto AddFoldRightBinPoly(T n,Ts... args) { return (args + ... + n); }
template <typename T,typename... Ts>
```

```
auto AddFoldLeftBinPoly(T n,Ts... args) { return (n + ... + args); }

int main() {
    auto a = AddFoldLeftUn(1,2,3,4);
    cout << a << endl;
    cout << AddFoldRightBin(a,4,5,6) << endl;
    //---------- Folds from Right
    //---------- should produce "Hello  World C++"
    auto b = AddFoldRightBinPoly("C++ "s,"Hello "s,"World "s );
    cout << b << endl;
    //---------- Folds (Reduce) from Left
    //---------- should produce "Hello World C++"
    auto c = AddFoldLeftBinPoly("Hello "s,"World "s,"C++ "s );
    cout << c << endl;
}
```

The expected output on the console is as follows

```
10
 25
Hello World C++
Hello World C++
```

Variant type

A geeky definition of variant would be "type safe union". We can give a list of types as a template argument while defining variants. At any given time, the object will hold only one type of data out of the template argument list. `std::bad_variant_access` will be thrown if we try to access an index that does not hold the current value. The following code does not handle this exception:

```
//------------ Variant.cpp
//------------ g++ -std=c++1z Variant.cpp
#include <variant>
#include <string>
#include <cassert>
#include <iostream>
using namespace std;

int main(){
    std::variant<int, float,string> v, w;
    v = 12.0f; // v contains now contains float
    cout << std::get<1>(v) << endl;
    w = 20; // assign to int
    cout << std::get<0>(w) << endl;
    w = "hello"s; //assign to string
```

```
            cout << std::get<2>(w) << endl;
}
```

Other important topics

Modern C++ supports features such as language-level concurrency, memory guarantees, and asynchronous executions, which are covered in the next two chapters. The language offers support for optional data types and the `std::any` type. One of the most important feature is parallel versions of most of the STL algorithms.

Range-based for loops and observables

In this section, we will implement range-based for loops on a custom type written by us to help you understand how all the things mentioned earlier in this chapter can be put together to write programs that support modern idioms. We will implement a class that returns a series of numbers within a bound and will implement infrastructure support for the iteration of the values based on range-based for loops. First, we write the "Iterable/Iterator" (aka "Enumerable/Enumerable") version by leveraging the range-based for loops. After some tweaks, the implementation will be transformed to Observable/Observer (the key interface of Reactive Programming) patterns: The implementation of Observable/Observer pattern here is just for elucidation purpose and should not be considered as an Industrial strength implementation of these patterns.

The following `iterable` class is a nested class:

```
// Iterobservable.cpp
// we can use Range Based For loop as given below (see the main below)
// for (auto l : EnumerableRange<5, 25>()) { std::cout << l << ' '; }
// std::cout << endl;
#include <iostream>
#include <vector>
#include <iterator>
#include <algorithm>
#include <functional>
using namespace std;

template<long START, long END>
class EnumerableRange {
public:
    class iterable : public std::iterator<
        std::input_iterator_tag, // category
        long, // value_type
```

```
long, // difference_type
const long*, // pointer type
long> // reference type
{
    long current_num = START;
    public:
        reference operator*() const { return current_num; }
        explicit iterable(long val = 0) : current_num(val) {}
        iterable& operator++() {
            current_num = ( END >= START) ? current_num + 1 :
                current_num - 1;
        return *this;
    }
    iterable operator++(int) {
        iterable retval = *this; ++(*this); return retval;
    }
    bool operator==(iterable other) const
        { return current_num == other.current_num; }
    bool operator!=(iterable other) const
        { return !(*this == other); }
};
```

The preceding code implements an inner class derived from `std::iterator` to take care of the requirements for a type to be enumerable through range-based for loops. We will now write two public methods, (`begin()` and `end()`), so consumers of the class can use range-based for loops:

```
iterable begin() { return iterable(START); }
    iterable end() { return iterable(END >= START ? END + 1 :
        END - 1); }
};
```

Now, we can write code to consume the preceding class as follows:

```
for (long l : EnumerableRange<5, 25>())
    { std::cout << l << ' '; }
```

In the previous chapter, we defined the `IEnumerable<T>` interface. The idea was to stick with the documentation of Reactive eXtensions. The iterable class is very similar to the `IEnumerable<T>` implementation in the previous chapter. As outlined in the previous chapter, the preceding class can be made push based, if we tweak the code a bit. Let us write an OBSERVER class that contains three methods. We will be using Function Wrappers available with standard library to define the methods:

```
struct OBSERVER {
    std::function<void(const long&)> ondata;
    std::function<void()> oncompleted;
```

```
        std::function<void(const std::exception &)> onexception;
};
```

The `ObservableRange` class given here contains a `vector<T>` that stores the list of
subscribers. When a new number is generated, the event will be notified to all subscribers.
If we dispatch the notification call from an asynchronous method, the consumer is
decoupled from the producer of the range stream. We have not implemented
the `IObserver/IObserver<T>` interface for the following class, but we can subscribe to
notifications through subscribe methods:

```
template<long START, long END>
class ObservableRange {
    private:
        //---------- Container to store observers
        std::vector<
            std::pair<const OBSERVER&,int>> _observers;
        int _id = 0;
```

We will store the list of subscribers in an `std::vector` as an `std::pair`. The first value in
the `std::pair` is the reference to the `OBSERVER` and the second value in the `std::pair` is
an integer that uniquely identifies the subscriber. Consumers are supposed to unsubscribe
by using the ID returned by the subscribe method:

```
//----- The following implementation of iterable does
//----- not allow to take address of the pointed value [ &(*it)
//----- Eg- &(*iterable.begin()) will be ill-formed
//----- Code is just for demonstrate Obervable/Observer
class iterable : public std::iterator<
    std::input_iterator_tag, // category
    long, // value_type
    long, // difference_type
    const long*, // pointer type
    long> // reference type
{
    long current_num = START;
public:
    reference operator*() const { return current_num; }
    explicit iterable(long val = 0) : current_num(val) {}
    iterable& operator++() {
        current_num = ( END >= START) ? current_num + 1 :
            current_num - 1;
        return *this;
    }
    iterable operator++(int) {
        iterable retval = *this; ++(*this); return retval;
    }
    bool operator==(iterable other) const
```

```
                { return current_num == other.current_num; }
        bool operator!=(iterable other) const
            { return !(*this == other); }
        };
    iterable begin() { return iterable(START); }
    iterable end() { return iterable(END >= START ? END + 1 : END - 1); }
// generate values between the range
// This is a private method and will be invoked from the generate
// ideally speaking, we should invoke this method with std::asnyc
void generate_async()
{
    auto& subscribers = _observers;
    for( auto l : *this )
        for (const auto& obs : subscribers) {
            const OBSERVER& ob = obs.first;
            ob.ondata(l);
        }
}

//----- The public interface of the call include generate which triggers
//----- the generation of the sequence, subscribe/unsubscribe pair
public:
    //-------- the public interface to trigger generation
    //-------- of thevalues. The generate_async can be executed
    //--------- via std::async to return to the caller
    void generate() { generate_async(); }
    //---------- subscribe method. The clients which
    //----------- expects notification can register here
    int subscribe(const OBSERVER& call) {
        // https://en.cppreference.com/w/cpp/container/vector/emplace_back
        _observers.emplace_back(call, ++_id);
        return _id;
    }
    //------------ has just stubbed unsubscribe to keep
    //------------ the listing small
    void unsubscribe(const int subscription) {}

};

int main() {
    //------ Call the Range based enumerable
    for (long l : EnumerableRange<5, 25>())
        { std::cout << l << ' '; }
    std::cout << endl;
    // instantiate an instance of ObservableRange
    auto j = ObservableRange<10,20>();
    OBSERVER test_handler;
    test_handler.ondata = [=](const long & r)
```

```
    {cout << r << endl; };
    //---- subscribe to the notifiactions
    int cnt = j.subscribe(test_handler);
    j.generate(); //trigget events to generate notifications
    return 0;
}
```

Summary

In this chapter, we learned about programming language features that a C++ programmer should be comfortable with while writing Reactive programs, or for that matter any kind of programs. We talked about type inference, Variadic templates, rvalue references and move semantics, Lambda functions, elementary Functional programming, pipeable operators, and implementation of Iterators and observers. In the next chapter, we will learn about concurrent programming support provided by the C++ programming language.

3
Language-Level Concurrency and Parallelism in C++

C++ has had excellent support for concurrent programming ever since the C++ 11 language standard came out. Until then, threading was an affair that was handled by platform-specific libraries. The Microsoft Corporation had its own threading libraries, and other platforms (GNU Linux/macOS X) supported the POSIX threading model. A threading mechanism as part of the language has helped C++ programmers write portable code that runs on multiple platforms.

The original C++ standard was published in 1998, and the language design committee firmly believed that threading, filesystems, GUI libraries, and so on are better left to the platform-specific libraries. Herb Sutter published an influential article in the Dr. Dobbs Journal titled, *The Free Lunch Is Over*, where he advocated programming techniques to exploit multiple cores available in the processors of those days. While writing parallel code, functional programming models are well-suited for the task. Features such as threads, Lambda functions and expressions, move semantics, and memory guarantee helps people write concurrent or parallel code without much hassle. This chapter aims to enable developers to leverage thread libraries and their best practices.

In this chapter, we will cover the following topics:

- What is concurrency?
- A characteristic Hello World program using multiple threads
- How to manage the lifetime and resources of threads
- Sharing data between threads
- How to write a thread-safe data structure

What is concurrency?

At a basic level, concurrency stands for more than one activity happening at the same time. We can correlate concurrency to many of our real-life situations, such as eating popcorn while we watch a movie or using two hands for separate functions at the same time, and so on. Well then, what is concurrency in a computer?

Computer systems were enabled to do task switching decades ago, and multitasking operating systems have been in existence for a long time. Why is there renewed interest in concurrency all of a sudden in the computing realm? The microprocessor manufacturers were increasing computing power by cramming more and more silicon into a processor. At a certain stage in the process, they could not cram more things into the same area as they reached fundamental physical limits. The CPUs of those eras had a single path of execution at a time and they were running multiple paths of instructions by switching tasks (stream of instructions). At the CPU level, only one instruction stream was getting executed, and as things happen very fast (compared to human perception), the users felt actions were happening at the same time.

Around the year 2005, Intel announced their new multicore processors (which support multiple paths of execution at the hardware level), which was a game changer. Instead of one processor doing every task by switching between them, multicore processors came as a solution to actually perform them in parallel. But this introduced another challenge to the programmers; to write their code to leverage hardware-level concurrency. Also, the issue of the actual hardware concurrency behaving differently compared to the illusion created by the task switches arose. Until the multicore processors came to light, the chip manufacturers were in a race to increase their computing power, expecting that it might reach 10 GHz before the end of the first decade of the 21st century. As Herb Sutter said in *The Free Lunch is Over* (http://www.gotw.ca/publications/concurrency-ddj.htm), *"If software is to take advantage of this increased computing power, it must be designed to run multiple tasks concurrently"*. Herb warned the programmers that those who ignored concurrency must also take that into account while writing a program.

The modern C++ standard libraries provide a set of mechanisms to support concurrency and parallelism. First and foremost, `std::thread`, along with the synchronization objects (such as `std::mutex`, `std::lock_guards`, `std::unique_lock`, `std::condition_variables`, and so on) empowers the programmers to write a concurrent multithreaded code using standard C++. Secondly, to use task-based parallelism (as in .NET and Java), C++ introduced the classes `std::future` and `std::promise`, which work in pairs to separate the function invocation and wait for results.

Finally, to avoid the additional overhead of managing threads, C++ introduced a class called `std::async`, which will be covered in detail in the following chapter where the focus of discussion will be writing lock-free concurrent programs (well, at least minimizing locks, wherever possible).

 Concurrency is when two or more threads or execution paths can start, run, and complete in overlapping time periods (in some kind of interleaved execution). Parallelism means two tasks can run at the same time (like you see on a multicore CPU). Concurrency is about response time and parallelism is mostly about exploiting available resources.

Hello World of concurrency (using std::thread)

Now, let's get started with our first program using the `std::thread` library. You are expected to have C++ 11 or later to compile the programs we are going to discuss in this chapter. Let's take a simple, classic Hello World example as a reference before going into a multi-threaded Hello World:

```
//---- Thanks to Dennis Ritchie and Brian Kernighan, this is a norm for all
languages
#include <iostream>
int main()
{
    std::cout << "Hello World\n";
}
```

This program simply writes Hello World into the standard output stream (mainly the console). Now, let's see another example that does the same stuff, but using a background thread (often called a worker thread instead):

```
#include <iostream>
#include <thread>
#include <string>
//---- The following function will be invoked by the thread library
void thread_proc(std::string msg)
{
    std::cout << "ThreadProc msg:" << msg;
}
int main()
{
    // creates a new thread and execute thread_proc on it.
    std::thread t(thread_proc, "Hello World\n");
```

```
    // Waiting for the thread_proc to complete its execution
    // before exiting from the program
    t.join();
}
```

The first difference with traditional code is the inclusion of the <thread> standard header file. All of the multithreading support functions and classes are declared in this new header. But to achieve synchronization and shared data protection, the supporting classes are available in other headers. If you are familiar with platform-level threads in Windows or POSIX systems, all threads require an initial function. The same concept is what the standard library is also following. In this example, the thread_proc function is the initial function of a thread that's declared in the main function. The initial function (through the function pointer) is specified in the constructor of the std::thread object t, and construction starts the execution of the thread.

The most notable difference is that now the application writes the message into a standard output stream from a new thread (background thread), which results in having two threads or a path of execution in this application. Once the new thread has been launched, the main thread continues its execution. If the main thread is not waiting for the newly started thread to finish, the main() function would end and thus that would be the end of the application—even before the new thread has had the chance to finish its execution. This is the reason for calling join() before the main thread finishes, in order to wait for the new thread, t, which is started here.

Managing threads

At runtime, the execution starts at the user entry point main() (after the execution of the start-up code), and it will be executing in a default thread that's been created. So, every program will have at least one thread of execution. During the execution of the program, an arbitrary number of threads can be created through a standard library or platform-specific libraries. These threads can run in parallel if the CPU cores are available to execute them. If the number of threads are more than the number of CPU cores, even though there is parallelism, we cannot run all of the threads simultaneously. So, thread switching happens here as well. A program can launch any number of threads from the main thread, and those threads run concurrently on the initial thread. As we can see, the initial function for a program thread is main(), and the program ends when the main returns from its execution. This terminates all the parallel threads. Therefore, the main thread needs to wait until all the children threads finish execution. So, let's see how the launch and join of threads occurs.

Thread launch

In the previous example, we saw that the initialization function is passed as an argument to the std::thread constructor, and the thread gets launched. This function runs on its own thread. The thread launch happens during the thread object's construction, but the initialization functions can have other alternatives as well. A function object is another possible argument in a thread class. The C++ standard library ensures that the std::thread works with any callable type.

The modern C++ standard supports threads to be initialized through:

- Function pointers (as in the previous section)
- An object that implements the call operator
- Lambdas

Any callable entity is a candidate for initializing a thread. This enables the std::thread to accept a class object with an overloaded function call operator:

```
class parallel_job
{
public:
void operator() ()
{
    some_implementation();
}
};
parallel_job job;
std::thread t(job);
```

Here, the newly created thread copies the object into its storage, hence the copy behavior must be ensured. Here, we can also use std::move to avoid problems related to copying:

```
std::thread t(std::move(job));
```

If you pass temporary (an rvalue) instead of a function object, the syntax is as follows:

```
std::thread t(parallel_job());
```

This code can be interpreted by the compiler as a declaration of a function that accepts a function pointer and returns a std::thread object. However, we can avoid this by using the new uniform initialization syntax, as follows:

```
std::thread t{ parallel_job() };
```

An extra set of parenthesis, as given in the following code snippet, can also avoid the interpretation of `std::thread` object declaration into a function declaration:

```
std::thread t((parallel_job()));
```

Another interesting way to launch a thread is by giving the C++ Lambdas as an argument into a `std::thread` constructor. Lambdas can capture local variables and thus avoid unnecessary usage of any arguments. Lambdas are very useful when it comes to writing anonymous functions, but that doesn't mean that they should be used everywhere.

The Lambda function can be used along with a thread declaration as follows:

```
std::thread t([]{
    some_implementation();
});
```

Thread join

In the Hello World example, you might have noticed the use of `t.join()` at the end of `main()` before leaving from the function. The call to `join()` on the associated thread instance ensures that the launched function will wait until the background thread completes its execution. In the absence of join, the thread will be terminated before the thread starts until the current context is finished (their child threads will also be terminated).

`join()` is a direct function, either waiting for the thread to finish or not. To get more control over the thread, we have other mechanisms such as mutex, condition variables, and futures, and they will be discussed in the later sections of this chapter and the next chapter. The call to `join()` cleans up the storage associated with the thread, and so it ensures that the object is no longer associated with the thread that was launched. This asserts that the `join()` function can only be called once per thread; the call to `joinable()` will always return false after a call to `join()`. The previous example with a function object can be modified as follows to understand `join()`:

```
class parallel_job
{
    int& _iterations;

public:
    parallel_job(int& input): _iterations(input)
    {}

    void operator() ()
```

```
    {
        for (int i = 0; i < _iterations; ++i)
        {
            some_implementation(i);
        }
    }
};
void func()
{
    int local_Val = 10000;
    parallel_job job(local_Val);
    std::thread t(job);
    if(t.joinable())
        t.join();
}
```

In this case, at the end of the `func()` function, the thread object is verified to confirm whether the thread is still in execution. We call `joinable()` to see its return value before we place the join call.

To prevent the wait on `func()`, there is a mechanism that was introduced by the standard to continue execution, even if the parent function finishes its execution. This can be achieved using another standard function, `detach()`:

```
if(t.joinable())
        t.detach();
```

There are a couple of things that we need to consider before detaching a thread; the `t` thread will probably still be running when `func()` exits. As per the implementation given in the preceding example, the thread is using the reference of a local variable created in `func()`, which is not a good idea since the old stack variables can be overwritten at any time on most architectures. These situations must always be addressed while using `detach()` in your code. The most common way of handling this situation is making a thread self-contained and copying the data into the thread instead of sharing it.

Passing arguments into a thread

So, we have figured out how to launch and wait over a thread. Now, let's see how to pass arguments into a thread initialization function. Let's look at an example to find the factorial of a number:

```
class Factorial
{
private:
```

```
        long long myFact;
public:
        Factorial() : myFact(1)
        {
        }
        void operator() (int number)
        {
            myFact = 1;
            for (int i = 1; i <= number; ++i)
            {
                myFact *= i;
            }
            std::cout << "Factorial of " << number << " is " << myFact;
        }
};

int main()
{
    Factorial fact;
    std::thread t1(fact, 10);
    t1.join();
}
```

From this example, it is clear that passing arguments into a thread function or a thread callable object can be achieved by passing additional arguments into an `std::thread()` declaration. One thing we must keep in mind; *the arguments passed are copied into the thread's internal storage for further execution.* It is important for a thread's execution to have its own copy of arguments, as we have seen the problems associated with local variables going out of scope. To discuss passing arguments into a thread further, let's go back to our first Hello World example from this chapter:

```
void thread_proc(std::string msg);

std::thread t(thread_proc, "Hello World\n");
```

In this case, the `thread_proc()` function takes `std::string` as an argument, but we are passing a `const char*` as an argument to the thread function. Only in the case of a thread is the argument passed, converted, and copied into the thread's internal storage. Here, `const char*` will be converted to `std::string`. The type of argument supplied to a thread must be chosen while keeping this in mind. Let's see what happens if a pointer is supplied to the thread as an argument:

```
void thread_proc(std::string msg);
void func()
{
    char buf[512];
```

```
    const char* hello = "Hello World\n";
    std::strcpy(buf, hello);

    std::thread t(thread_proc, buf);
    t.detach();
}
```

In the preceding code, the argument supplied to the thread is a pointer to the local variable buf. There is a probable chance that the func() function will exit before the conversion of buf to an std::string happens on the thread. This could lead to an undefined behavior. This problem can be resolved by casting the buf variable into std::string in the declaration itself, as follows:

```
std::thread t(thread_proc, std::string(buf));
```

Now, let's look at the cases where you want a reference to get updated in the thread. In a typical scenario, the thread copies the value supplied to the thread to ensure a safe execution, but the standard library has also provided a means to pass the argument by reference to a thread. In many practical systems, you might have seen that a shared data structure is getting updated inside a thread. The following example shows how to achieve pass by reference in a thread:

```
void update_data(shared_data& data);

void another_func()
{
    shared_data data;
    std::thread t(update_data, std::ref(data));
    t.join();
    do_something_else(data);
}
```

In the preceding code, wrapping the arguments passed into the std::thread constructor with std::ref ensures that the variable supplied inside the thread is referenced to the actual parameters. You might have noticed that the function prototype of the thread initialization function is accepting a reference to the shared_data object, but why do you still need an std::ref() wrapping for thread invocation? Consider the following code for thread invocation:

```
std::thread t(update_data, data);
```

In this case, the `update_data()` function expects the `shared_data` argument to be treated as a reference to actual parameters. But when used as a thread initialization function, arguments are simply copied internally. When the call to `update_data()` happens, it will pass a reference to the internal copies of arguments and not a reference to the actual parameters.

Using Lambdas

Now, let's see the usefulness of Lambda expressions for multithreading. In the following code, we are going to create five threads and put those into a vector container. Each thread will be using a Lambda function as the initialization function. The threads initialized in the following code are capturing the loop index by value:

```
int main()
{
    std::vector<std::thread> threads;

    for (int i = 0; i < 5; ++i)
    {
        threads.push_back(std::thread( [i]() {
            std::cout << "Thread #" << i << std::endl;
        }));
    }

    std::cout << "nMain function";

    std::for_each(threads.begin(), threads.end(), [](std::thread &t) {
        t.join();
    });
}
```

The vector container threads store five threads that have been created inside the loop. They are joined at the end of the `main()` function once the execution is over. The output for the preceding code may look as follows:

```
Thread # Thread # Thread # Thread # Thread #
Main function
0
4
1
3
2
```

The output of the program could be different for each run. This program is a good example to showcase the non-determinism associated with concurrent programming. In the following section, we will discuss the move properties of a `std::thread` object.

Ownership management

From the examples discussed so far in this chapter, you might have noticed that the function that launches the thread has to wait for the thread to complete its execution using the `join()` function, otherwise it will call `detach()` with a cost of the program losing control over the thread. In modern C++, many standard types are movable, but cannot be copied; `std::thread` is one of them. This means that the ownership of a thread's execution can be moved between `std::thread` instances with the help of move semantics.

There are many situations where we want to move the ownership to another thread, for example, if we want the thread to run in the background without waiting for it on the function that created the thread. This can be achieved by passing the thread ownership to a calling function rather than waiting for it to complete in the created function. In another instance, pass the ownership to some other function, which will wait for the thread to complete its execution. Both of these cases can be achieved by passing the ownership from one thread instance to another.

To explain further, let us define two functions to use as the thread functions:

```
void function1()
{
    std::cout << "function1()n";
}

void function2()
{
    std::cout << "function2()n";
}
```

Let's look into the main function that spawns threads from previously declared functions:

```
int main()
{
    std::thread t1(function1);
    // Ownership of t1 is transferred to t2
    std::thread t2 = std::move(t1);
```

In the preceding code, a new thread started with `t1` in the first line of `main()`. Ownership is then transferred to `t2` using the `std::move()` function, which is invoking the move constructor of `std::thread`, which is associated with `t2`. Now, the t1 instance has no associated thread of execution. The initialization function `function1()` is now associated with `t2`:

```
t1 = std::thread(function2);
```

Then, a new thread is started using an rvalue, which invokes the move assignment operator of `std::thread`, which is associated with `t1`. Since we are using an rvalue, an explicit call to `std::move()` is not required:

```
// thread instance Created without any associated thread execution
std::thread t3;
// Ownership of t2 is transferred to t3
t3 = std::move(t2);
```

`t3` was instantiated without any thread of execution, which means it is invoking the default constructor. The ownership currently associated with `t2` is then transferred to `t3` by the move assignment operator, by explicitly calling the `std::move()` function:

```
// No need to join t1, no longer has any associated thread of execution
if (t1.joinable())  t1.join();
if (t3.joinable())  t3.join();
return 0;
}
```

Finally, the `std::thread` instances with an associated thread of execution are joined before the program exits. Here, `t1` and `t3` are the instances with an associated thread of execution.

Now, let's assume that the following code is present before the threads `join()` in the preceding example:

```
t1 = std::move(t3);
```

Here, the instance `t1` is already associated with a running function (`function2`). When `std::move()` attempts to transfer the ownership of `function1` back to `t1`, `std::terminate()` is called to terminate the program. This guarantees the consistency of the `std::thread` destructor.

The move support in `std::thread` helps in transferring the ownership of a thread out of a function. The following example demonstrates such a scenario:

```
void func()
{
    std::cout << "func()n";
}

std::thread thread_creator()
{
    return std::thread(func);
}

void thread_wait_func()
{
    std::thread t = thread_creator();
    t.join();
}
```

Here, the `thread_creator()` function returns the `std::thread` associated with the `func()` function. The `thread_wait_func()` function calls `thread_creator()`, and then returns the thread object, which is an rvalue that is assigned to an `std::thread` object. This transfers the ownership of the thread into the `std::thread` object t, and object t is waiting for the completion of thread execution in the transferred function.

Sharing data between threads

We have seen how to start a thread and different methods of managing them. Now, let's discuss how to share data between threads. One key feature of concurrency is its ability to share data between the threads in action. First, let's see what the problems associated with threads accessing common (shared) data are.

There won't be a problem if the data shared between threads is immutable (read-only), because the data read by one thread is unaffected by whether the other threads are reading the same data or not. The moment threads start modifying shared data is when problems begin to emerge.

For example, if the threads are accessing a common data structure, the invariants associated with the data structure are broken if an update is happening. In this case, the number of elements is stored in the data structure, which usually requires the modification of more than one value. Consider the delete operation of a self-balancing tree or a doubly linked list. If you don't do anything special to ensure otherwise, if one thread is reading the data structure, while another is removing a node, it is quite possible for the reading thread to see the data structure with a partially removed node, so the invariant is broken. This might end up corrupting the data structure permanently and could lead to the program crashing.

 An invariant is a set of assertions that must always be true during the execution of a program or lifetime of an object. Placing proper assertion within the code to see whether invariants have been violated will result in robust code. This is a great way to document software as well as a good mechanism to prevent regression bugs. More can be read about this in the following Wikipedia article: `https://en.wikipedia.org/wiki/Invariant_(computer_science)`.

This often leads to a situation called *race condition*, which is the most common cause of bugs in concurrent programs. In multithreading, race condition means that the threads race to perform their respective operations. Here, the outcome depends on the relative ordering of the execution of an operation in two or more threads. Usually, the term race condition means a problematic race condition; normal race conditions don't cause any bugs. Problematic race conditions usually occur where the completion of an operation requires modification of two or more bits of data, such as deletion of a node in a tree data structure or a doubly linked list. Because the modification must access separate pieces of data, these must be modified in separate instructions when another thread is trying to access the data structure. This occurs when half of the previous modifications have been completed.

Race conditions are often very hard to find and hard to duplicate because they occur in a very short window of execution. For software that uses concurrency, the major complexity of implementation comes from avoiding problematic race conditions.

There are many ways to deal with problematic race conditions. The common and simplest option is to use *synchronization primitives*, which are lock-based protection mechanisms. This wraps the data structure by using some locking mechanisms to prevent the access of other threads during its execution. We will discuss the available synchronization primitives and their uses in detail in this chapter.

Another option is to alter the design of your data structure and its invariants so that the modification guarantees the sequential consistency of your code, even across multiple threads. This is a difficult way of writing programs and is commonly referred to as *lock-free programming*. Lock-free programming and the C++ memory model will be covered in Chapter 4, *Asynchronous and Lock-Free Programming in C++*.

Then, there are other mechanisms such as handling the updates to a data structure as a transaction, as updates to databases are done within transactions. Currently, this topic is not in the scope of this book, and therefore it won't be covered.

Now, let's consider the most basic mechanism in C++ standard for protecting shared data, which is the *mutex*.

Mutexes

A mutex is a mechanism used in concurrency control to prevent race conditions. The function of a mutex is to prevent a thread of execution to enter its *critical section* at the same time another concurrent thread enters its own critical section. It is a lockable object designed to signal when the critical sections of code need exclusive access, thereby restricting other concurrent threads with the same protection in execution as well as memory access. The C++ 11 standard introduced an std::mutex class into the standard library to achieve data protection across concurrent threads.

The std::mutex class consist of the lock() and unlock() functions to create a critical section in code. One thing to keep in mind while using the member functions to create critical sections is that you should never skip an unlock function associated with a lock function to mark the critical section in code.

Now, let's discuss the same code we used for discussing Lambdas with threads. There, we observed that the output of the program was scrambled due to a race condition with a common resource, std::cout, and std::ostream operators. That code is now being rewritten using std::mutex to print the thread index:

```
#include <iostream>
#include <thread>
#include <mutex>
#include <vector>
std::mutex m;
int main()
{
    std::vector<std::thread> threads;

    for (int i = 1; i < 10; ++i)
```

```
    {
        threads.push_back(std::thread( [i]() {
            m.lock();
            std::cout << "Thread #" << i << std::endl;
            m.unlock();
        }));
    }
    std::for_each(threads.begin(), threads.end(), [](std::thread &t) {
        t.join();
    });
}
```

The output for the preceding code may look as follows:

```
Thread #1
Thread #2
Thread #3
Thread #4
Thread #5
Thread #6
Thread #7
Thread #8
Thread #9
```

In the preceding code, the mutex is used to protect the shared resource, which is the
std::cout and cascaded std::ostream operators. Unlike the older example, the addition
of a mutex in the code now avoids the scrambled output, but it will appear in a random
order. The use of lock() and unlock() functions in the std::mutex class guarantees the
output is not garbled. However, the practice to call member functions directly is not
recommended, because you need to call unlock on every code path in the function,
including the exception scenarios as well. Instead, C++ standard introduced a new template
class, std::lock_guard, which implemented the **Resource Acquisition Is Initialization
(RAII)** idiom for a mutex. It locks the supplied mutex in the constructor and unlocks it in
the destructor. The implementation of this template class is available in the <mutex>
standard header library. The previous example can be rewritten using std::lock_guard
as follows:

```
std::mutex m;
int main()
{
    std::vector<std::thread> threads;
    for (int i = 1; i < 10; ++i)
    {
        threads.push_back(std::thread( [i]() {
            std::lock_guard<std::mutex> local_lock(m);
            std::cout << "Thread #" << i << std::endl;
```

```
        })));
    }
    std::for_each(threads.begin(), threads.end(), [](std::thread &t) {
        t.join();
    });
}
```

In the preceding code, the mutex that protects the critical section is at global scope and the `std::lock_guard` object is local to the Lambda each time thread execution happens. This way, as soon as the object is constructed, the mutex acquires the lock. It unlocks the mutex with the call to destructor when the Lambda execution is over.

 RAII is a C++ idiom where the lifetime of entities such as database/file handles, socket handles, mutexes, dynamically allocated memory on the heap, and so on are bounded to the life cycle of the object holding it. You can read more about RAII at the following Wikipedia page: `https://en.wikipedia.org/wiki/Resource_acquisition_is_initialization`.

Avoiding deadlock

While dealing with mutexes, the biggest problem that can arise is a deadlock. To understand what deadlock is, just imagine an iPod. For an iPod to achieve its purpose, it requires both an iPod as well as an earpiece. If two siblings share one iPod, there are situations where both want to listen to music at the same time. Imagine one person got their hands on the iPod and the other got the earpiece, and neither of them is willing to share the item they possess. Now they are stuck, unless one of them tries to be nice and lets the other person listen to music.

Here, the siblings are arguing over an iPod and an earpiece, but coming back to our situation, threads argue over the locks on mutexes. Here, each thread has one mutex and is waiting for the other. No mutex can proceed here, because each thread is waiting for the other thread to release its mutex. This scenario is called **deadlock**.

Avoiding deadlock is sometimes quite straightforward because different mutexes serve different purposes, but there are instances where handling such situations is not that obvious. The best advice I can give you to avoid deadlock is to always lock multiple mutexes in the same order. Then, you will never get deadlock situations.

Consider an example of a program with two threads; each thread is intended to print odd numbers and even numbers alone. Since the intentions of the two threads are different, the program uses two mutexes to control each thread. The shared resource between the two threads is `std::cout`. Let's look at the following program with a deadlock situation:

```
// Global mutexes
std::mutex evenMutex;
std::mutex oddMutex;
// Function to print even numbers
void printEven(int max)
{
    for (int i = 0; i <= max; i +=2)
    {
        oddMutex.lock();
        std::cout << i << ",";
        evenMutex.lock();
        oddMutex.unlock();
        evenMutex.unlock();
    }
}
```

The `printEven()` function is defined to print all the positive even numbers into the standard console which are less than the `max` value. Similarly, let us define a `printOdd()` function to print all the positive odd numbers less than `max`, as follows:

```
// Function to print odd numbers
void printOdd(int max)
{
    for (int i = 1; i <= max; i +=2)
    {
        evenMutex.lock();
        std::cout << i << ",";
        oddMutex.lock();
        evenMutex.unlock();
        oddMutex.unlock();
    }
}
```

Now, let's write the `main` function to spawn two independent threads to print odd and even numbers using the previously defined functions as the thread functions for each operation:

```
int main()
{
    auto max = 100;
    std::thread t1(printEven, max);
    std::thread t2(printOdd, max);
```

```
        if (t1.joinable())
            t1.join();
        if (t2.joinable())
            t2.join();
    }
```

In this example, std::cout is protected with two mutexes, printEven and printOdd, which perform locking in a different order. With this code, we always ends up in deadlock, since each thread is clearly waiting for the mutex locked by the other thread. Running this code would result in a hang. As mentioned previously, deadlock can be avoided by locking them in the same order, as follows:

```
    void printEven(int max)
    {
        for (int i = 0; i <= max; i +=2)
        {
            evenMutex.lock();
            std::cout << i << ",";
            oddMutex.lock();
            evenMutex.unlock();
            oddMutex.unlock();
        }
    }
    void printOdd(int max)
    {
        for (int i = 1; i <= max; i +=2)
        {
            evenMutex.lock();
            std::cout << i << ",";
            oddMutex.lock();
            evenMutex.unlock();
            oddMutex.unlock();
        }
    }
```

But this code is clearly not clean. You already know that using a mutex with the RAII idiom makes the code cleaner and safer, but to ensure the order of locking, the C++ standard library has introduced a new function, std::lock—a function that can lock two or more mutexes in one go without deadlock risk. The following example shows how to use this for our previous odd-even program:

```
    void printEven(int max)
    {
        for (int i = 0; i <= max; i +=2)
        {
            std::lock(evenMutex, oddMutex);
            std::lock_guard<std::mutex> lk_even(evenMutex, std::adopt_lock);
```

```
            std::lock_guard<std::mutex> lk_odd(oddMutex, std::adopt_lock);
            std::cout << i << ",";
    }
}
void printOdd(int max)
{
    for (int i = 1; i <= max; i +=2)
    {
        std::lock(evenMutex, oddMutex);
        std::lock_guard<std::mutex> lk_even(evenMutex, std::adopt_lock);
        std::lock_guard<std::mutex> lk_odd(oddMutex, std::adopt_lock);
        std::cout << i << ",";
    }
}
```

In this case, as soon as the thread execution enters the loop, the call to `std::lock` locks the two mutexes. Two `std::lock_guard` instances are constructed for each mutex. The `std::adopt_lock` parameter is supplied in addition to the mutex instance to `std::lock_guard` to indicate that the mutexes are already locked, and they should just adopt the ownership of the existing lock on the mutex rather than attempt to lock the mutex in the constructor. This guarantees safe unlocking, even in exceptional cases.

However, `std::lock` can help you to avoid deadlocks in cases where the program demands the locking of two or more mutexes at the same time; it doesn't help if they are acquired separately. Deadlocks are one of the hardest problems that can occur in a multithreaded program. It ultimately relies on the discipline of a programmer to not get into any deadlock situations.

Locking with std::unique_lock

Compared to `std::lock_guard`, `std::unique_lock` provides a bit more flexibility in operations. An `std::unique_lock` instance doesn't always own a mutex associated with it. Firstly, you can pass `std::adopt_lock` as a second argument to the constructor to manage a lock on a mutex similar to `std::lock_guard`. Secondly, the mutex can remain unlocked during construction by passing `std::defer_lock` as a second argument to the constructor. So, later in the code, a lock can be acquired by calling `lock()` on the same `std::unique_lock` object. But the flexibility available with `std::unique_lock` comes with a price; it is a bit slower than `lock_guard` in regards to storing this extra information and is in need of an update. Therefore, it is recommended to use `lock_guard` unless there is a real need for the flexibility that `std::unique_lock` offers.

Another interesting feature about `std::unique_lock` is its ability to transfer ownership. Since `std::unique_lock` must own its associated mutexes, this results in the ownership transfer of mutexes. Similar to `std::thread`, the `std::unique_lock` class is also a move only type. All of the move semantic language nuances and rvalue reference handling available in the C++ standard library applies to `std::unique_lock` as well.

The availability of member functions such as `lock()` and `unlock()`, similar to `std::mutex`, increases the flexibility of its use in code compared to `std::lock_guard`. The ability to release the lock before an `std::unique_lock` instance is destroyed, meaning that you can optionally release it anywhere in the code if it's obvious that the lock is no longer required. Holding down the lock unnecessarily can drop the performance of the application drastically, since the threads waiting for locks are prevented from executing for longer than is necessary. Hence, `std::unique_lock` is a very handy feature introduced by the C++ standard library, which supports RAII idiom, and it can effectively minimize the size of a critical section of the applicable code:

```
void retrieve_and_process_data(data_params param)
{
    std::unique_lock<std::mutex> local_lock(global_mutex, std::defer_lock);
    prepare_data(param);

    local_lock.lock();
    data_class data = get_data_to_process();
    local_lock.unlock();

    result_class result = process_data(data);

    local_lock.lock();
    strore_result(result);
}
```

In the preceding code, you can see the fine-grained locking achieved by leveraging the flexibility of `std::unique_lock`. As the function starts its execution, an `std::unique_lock` object is constructed with `global_mutex` in an unlocked state. Immediately, data is prepared with params, which don't require exclusive access; it is executing freely. Before retrieving the prepared data, the `local_lock` is marking the beginning of a critical section using the lock member function in `std::unique_lock`. As soon as the data retrieval is over, the lock is released, marking the end of the critical section. Followed by that, a call to the `process_data()` function, which again does not require exclusive access, is getting executed freely. Finally, before the execution of the `store_result()` function, the mutex is locked to protect the write operation, which updates the processed result. When exiting the function, the lock gets released when the local instance of `std::unique_lock` is destroyed.

Condition variables

We already know that mutexes can be used to share common resources and synchronize operations between threads. But synchronization using mutexes is a little complex and deadlock-prone if you are not careful. In this section, we will discuss how to wait for events with condition variables and how to use them for synchronization in an easier way.

When it comes to synchronization using mutexes, if the waiting thread has acquired a lock over a mutex, it can't be locked by any other thread. Also, waiting for one thread to complete its execution by checking on a status flag periodically that is protected by a mutex is a waste of CPU resources. This is because these resources can be effectively utilized by other threads in the system rather than having to wait for a longer time.

To address these problems, the C++ standard library has provided two implementations of conditional variables: `std::condition_variable` and `std::condition_variable_any`. Both are declared inside the `<condition_variable>` library header, and both the implementations need to work with a mutex to synchronize threads. The implementation of `std::condition_variable` is limited to working with `std::mutex`. On the other hand, `std::condition_variable_any` can work with anything that meets mutex-like criteria (mutex-like semantics), hence `suffix` `_any`. Because of its generic behavior, `std::condition_variable_any` ends up consuming more memory and degrades performance. It is not recommended unless a real, tailored requirement is in place.

The following program is an implementation of odd-even threads that we discussed when we talked about mutexes, which is now being re-implemented using condition variables:

```
std::mutex numMutex;
std::condition_variable syncCond;
auto bEvenReady = false;
auto bOddReady  = false;
void printEven(int max)
{
    for (int i = 0; i <= max; i +=2)
    {
        std::unique_lock<std::mutex> lk(numMutex);
        syncCond.wait(lk, []{return bEvenReady;});
        std::cout << i << ",";
        bEvenReady = false;
        bOddReady  = true;
        syncCond.notify_one();
    }
}
```

The program starts with the declaration of a mutex, a conditional variable, and two Boolean flags globally so that we can synchronize them between two threads. The `printEven` function gets executed in a worker thread and prints only even numbers starting from 0. Here, when it enters the loop, the mutex is protected with `std::unique_lock` instead of `std::lock_guard`; we will see the reason for that in a moment. The thread then calls the `wait()` function in `std::condition_variable`, passing the lock object and a Lambda predicate function that expresses the condition being waited for. This can be replaced with any callable object that returns bool. In this function, the predicate function returns the `bEvenReady` flag, so that the function continues execution when it becomes true. If the predicate returns false, the `wait()` function will unlock the mutex and wait for another thread to notify it, hence the `std::unique_lock` object comes handy here with the provided flexibility to lock and unlock.

As soon as `std::cout` prints the loop index, the `bEvenReady` flag is raised to false and `bOddReady` is raised to true. Then, the call to the `notify_one()` function associated with `syncCond` signals the waiting odd thread to write an odd number into the standard output stream:

```
void printOdd(int max)
{
    for (int i = 1; i <= max; i +=2)
    {
        std::unique_lock<std::mutex> lk(numMutex);
        syncCond.wait(lk, []{return bOddReady;});
        std::cout << i << ",";
        bEvenReady = true;
        bOddReady  = false;
        syncCond.notify_one();
    }
}
```

The `printOdd` function gets executed in another worker thread and prints only odd numbers starting from 1. Like the `printEven` function, a loop iterates and prints the index that is protected by the globally declared conditional variable and mutex. Unlike the `printEven` function, the predicate used in the `wait()` function of a condition variable returns `bOddReady`, and the `bEvenReady` flag is raised to `true` and the `bOddReady` flag is raised to `false`. Followed by that, calling the `notify_one()` function associated with `syncCond` signals the waiting even thread to write an even number into the standard output stream. This interleaved printing of even and odd numbers continues until the max value:

```
int main()
{
    auto max = 10;
```

```
    bEvenReady = true;
    std::thread t1(printEven, max);
    std::thread t2(printOdd, max);
    if (t1.joinable())
        t1.join();
    if (t2.joinable())
        t2.join();
}
```

The main function launches two background threads, t1, which is associated with the printEven function and t2, which is associated with the printOdd function. The output starts when even parity is confirmed by raising the bEvenReady flag to true before the threads are launched.

A thread-safe stack data structure

So far, we have discussed how to launch and manage a thread, and how to synchronize the operations between concurrent threads. But, when it comes to actual systems, the data is represented in the form of data structures, which must be chosen appropriately for the situation to guarantee the performance of the program. In this section, we are going to discuss how to design a concurrent stack using conditional variables and mutexes. The following program is a wrapper to std::stack, which is declared under the library header <stack>, and the stack wrapper will be available with different overloads for pop and push functionalities (this has been done to keep the listing small, and this also demonstrates how we can adapt a sequential data structure to work in a concurrent context):

```
template <typename T>
class Stack
{
private:
    std::stack<T> myData;
    mutable std::mutex myMutex;
    std::condition_variable myCond;
public:
    Stack() = default;
    ~Stack() = default;
    Stack& operator=(const Stack&) = delete;
    Stack(const Stack& that)
    {
        std::lock_guard<std::mutex> lock(that.myMutex);
        myData = that.myData;
    }
```

The `Stack` class contains an object to the template class `std::stack`, along with member variables for `std::mutex` and `std::condition_variable`. The constructor and destructor of the class are marked as default, letting the compiler generate a default implementation for those, and the copy assignment operator is marked as delete to prevent the invocation of the assignment operator of this class at compile time itself. The copy constructor is defined, which copies the `std::stack` member object `myData`, by invoking its own copy assignment operator, which is protected by the right-hand side object's mutex:

```
void push(T new_value)
{
    std::lock_guard<std::mutex> local_lock(myMutex);
    myData.push(new_value);
    myCond.notify_one();
}
```

The member function `push()` is wrapping the `push` function of `std::stack container`. As you can see, the mutex member variable, `myMutex`, is locked by an `std::lock_guard` object to safeguard the `push` operation that follows in the next line. Followed by that, the `notify_one()` function is invoked using the member `std::condition_variable` object to raise an event to notify the waiting threads over this same condition variable. There are two overloads of the `pop` operation that you will see in the following code listings, which wait over this condition variable to get signaled:

```
bool try_pop(T& return_value)
{
    std::lock_guard<std::mutex> local_lock(myMutex);
    if (myData.empty()) return false;
    return_value = myData.top();
    myData.pop();
    return true;
}
```

The `try_pop()` function takes a template argument as a reference. Since the implementation never waits for the stack to fill at least one element, this uses the `std::lock_guard` object to protect the thread. The function returns `false` if the stack is empty, otherwise it returns `true`. Here, the output is assigned to input a reference argument by invoking the `top()` function of `std::stack`, which returns the topmost element in the stack, followed by the `pop()` function to clear the topmost element from the stack. All overloads for the `pop` function invoke the `top()` function followed by a call to the `pop()` function of `std::stack`:

```
std::shared_ptr<T> try_pop()
{
    std::lock_guard<std::mutex> local_lock(myMutex);
```

```
        if (myData.empty()) return std::shared_ptr<T>();
        std::shared_ptr<T> return_value(std::make_shared<T>(myData.top()));
        myData.pop();
        return return_value;
    }
```

This is another overload of the `try_pop()` function, which returns an instance of `std::shared_ptr` (smart pointer) of the template type. As you have already seen, the `try_pop` function overloads, and never waits for a stack to fill at least one element; therefore, this implementation uses `std::lock_guard`. If the internal stack is empty, the function returns an instance of `std::shared_ptr` and holds no element of the stack. Otherwise, a `std::shared_ptr` instance that holds the top element of the stack is returned:

```
    void wait_n_pop(T& return_value)
    {
        std::unique_lock<std::mutex> local_lock(myMutex);
        myCond.wait(local_lock, [this]{ return !myData.empty(); });
        return_value = myData.top();
        myData.pop();
    }
    std::shared_ptr<T> wait_n_pop()
    {
        std::unique_lock<std::mutex> local_lock(myMutex);
        myCond.wait(local_lock, [this]{ return !myData.empty(); });
        std::shared_ptr<T> return_value(std::make_shared<T>(myData.top()));
        return return_value;
    }
};
```

So far, the overloads of the `pop` function are not waiting for the stack to fill at least one element if it is empty. To achieve that, two more overloads of the `pop` function are added, which uses the wait function associated with `std::condition_variable`. The first implementation returns the template value as an output argument, and the second one returns an `std::shared_ptr` instance. Both functions use `std::unique_lock` to control the mutex in order to supply the `wait()` function of `std::condition_variable`. In the `wait` function, the `predicate` function is checking whether the stack is empty or not. If the stack is empty, then the `wait()` function unlocks the mutex and continues to wait until a notification is received from the `push()` function. As soon as the push is called, the predicate will return true, and `wait_n_pop` continues its execution. The function overload takes the template reference and assigns the top element into the input argument, and the latter implementation returns an `std::shared_ptr` instance, holding the top element.

Summary

In this chapter, we discussed the threading library available in C++ standard libraries. We saw how to launch and manage a thread, and discussed different aspects of the threading library, such as how to pass arguments into a thread, ownership management of a thread object, sharing of data between threads, and so on. The C++ standard threading library can execute most callable objects as threads! We have seen the importance of all the available callable objects in association with threads, such as `std::function`, Lambdas, and functors. We discussed the synchronization primitives available in the C++ standard library, starting with the simple `std::mutex`, the use of the RAII idiom to protect mutexes from unhandled exit cases to avoid explicit unlock, and using classes such as `std::lock_guard` and `std::unique_lock`. We also discussed condition variables (`std::condition_variable`) in the context of thread synchronization. This chapter lays a good foundation for concurrency support introduced in modern C++ to kickstart the journey of this book into functional idioms.

In the following chapter, we will be covering more concurrency library features in C++, such as task-based parallelism and lock-free programming.

4
Asynchronous and Lock-Free Programming in C++

In the previous chapter, we looked at the threading library introduced by Modern C++ and various ways to create, manage, and synchronize threads. The way of writing code with threads is a rather low level and is prone to potential errors associated with concurrent code (deadlock, live-lock, and so on). Even though it is not noticed by many programmers, the Modern C++ language provides a standard memory model that helps to write concurrent code better. To be a concurrent programming language from the ground up, a language has to provide certain guarantees to the developer regarding memory access and the order in which things will be executed during runtime. If we are using constructs such as mutexes, condition variables, and futures to signal events, one doesn't need to be aware of the memory model. But awareness of the memory model and its guarantees will help us write faster concurrent code using lock-free programming techniques. Locks can be simulated using something called atomic operations, and we will look at this technique in depth.

As we discussed in `Chapter 2`, *A Tour of Modern C++ and its Key Idioms*, zero-cost abstraction remains one of the most fundamental principles of the C++ programming language. C++ is always a system programmer's language, and the standard committee managed to strike a good balance between higher-level abstraction mechanisms supported by the language and the ability to access lower-level resources to write system programs. C++ exposes atomic types and a set of associated operations to have fine-grained control over the execution of programs. The standard committee has published detailed semantics of the memory model, and the language has a set of libraries that help programmers to exploit them.

In the previous chapter, we learned how to synchronize actions in separate threads using condition variables. This chapter discusses the facilities provided by the standard library to perform task-based parallelism using *futures*. In this chapter, we will cover:

- Task-based parallelism in C++
- The C++ memory model
- Atomic types and atomic operations
- Synchronizing operations and memory ordering
- How to write a lock-free data structure

Task-based parallelism in C++

A *task* is a computation that can be potentially executed concurrently with other computations. A thread is a system-level representation of a task. In the previous chapter, we learned how to execute a task concurrently with other tasks launched by constructing an `std::thread` object with the task as its argument to the constructor. A task can be any callable object such as a function, Lambda, or a functor. But this approach of executing a function concurrently using `std::thread` is called a *thread-based approach*. The preferred choice for concurrent execution is a *task-based approach*, and this will be discussed in this chapter. The advantage of a task-based approach over a thread-based approach is to operate at the (higher) conceptual level of tasks rather than directly at the lower level of threads and locks. Task-based parallelism is achieved by following standard library features:

- Future and promise for returning a value from a task associated with a separate thread
- `packaged_task` to help launch tasks and provide a mechanism for returning a result
- `async()` for launching a task similar to a function call

Future and promise

The C++ tasks often behave like a data channel of sorts. The sending end, often called promise, sends data to a receiving end, often called the **future**. The important notion about futures and promises is that they enable a transfer of values between two tasks without the explicit use of a lock. The transfer of values is handled by the system (runtime) itself. The basic concept behind **future** and **promise** is simple; when a task wants to pass a value into another, it puts the value into a **promise**.

A standard library makes sure that the future associated with this promise gets this value. The other task can read this value from this **future** (the following diagram has to be read from the right to the left):

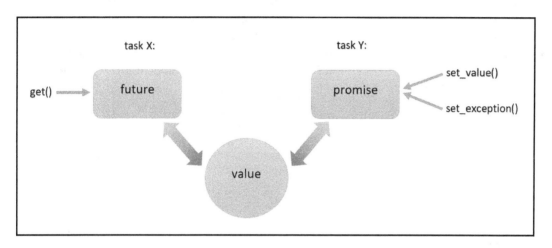

The future comes in handy if a calling thread needs to wait for a specific *one-off event*. The future representing this event makes itself available to the calling thread, and the calling thread can access the value once the future is ready (when a value is set to a corresponding promise). During its execution, a future may have data associated with it or not. Once the event occurs, data will be available in the future and it can't be reset.

The template classes associated with task-based parallelism are declared inside the library header <future>. There are two sorts of futures available in the standard library: unique futures (std::future<>) and shared futures (std::shared_future<>). You can correlate these with the smart pointers std::unique_ptr<> and std::shared_ptr<>, respectively. The std::future instance refers to the one and only instance of the associated event. On the contrary, multiple instances of std::shared_future may point to the same event. In the case of shared_future, all the instances associated with a common event will become ready at the same time and they may access the data associated with the event. The template parameter is the associated data, and the std::future<void> and std::shared_future<void> template specifications should be used if there is no data associated with it. Even though data communication between threads is managed internally by futures, the future objects themselves don't provide synchronized access. If multiple threads need to access a single std::future object, they must be protected with mutexes or other synchronization mechanisms.

The classes `std::future` and `std::promise` work in pairs to separate task invocation and wait for results. For an `std::future<T>` object `f`, we can access the value `T` associated with it using the `std::future` class function `get()`. Similarly for an `std::promise<T>`, there are two put operation functions available with it (`set_value()` and `set_exception()`) to match the future's `get()`. For a promise object, you can either give it a value by using `set_value()` or pass an exception to it using `set_exception()`. For example, the following pseudo code helps you see how the values are set in the promise (in `func1`) and how things are consumed in the function where invocation to `future<T>::get()` is invoked (`func2`):

```
// promise associated with the task launched
void func1(std::promise<T>& pr)
{
    try
    {
        T val;
        process_data(val);
        pr.set_value(val); // Can be retrieved by future<T>::get()
    }
    catch(...)
    {
        // Can be retrieved by future<T>::get()
        // At the future level, when we call get(), the
        // get will propagate the exception
        pr.set_exception(std::current_exception());
    }
}
```

In the preceding case, the *val* of type `T` is set to promise *pr* after processing and obtaining a result. If any exception happens during the execution, the exception is also set to promise. Now, let's see how to access the value you set:

```
// future corresponding to task already launched
void func2(std::future<T>& ft)
{
    try
    {
        // An exception will be thrown here, if the corresponding
        // promise had set an exception ..otherwise, retrieve the
        // value sets by the promise.
        T result = ft.get()
    }
    catch(...)
```

```
    {
        // Handle exception
    }
}
```

Here, the value set in the corresponding promise is accessed using the future passed as an argument. The `get()` function associated with `std::future()` retrieves the value stored during the execution of the task. The call to `get()` must be prepared to catch the exception transmitted through the future and handle it. After explaining `std::packaged_task`, we will show a complete example where futures and promises work together in action.

std::packaged_task

Now, let's discuss how we get a return value associated with a future into your code that needs results. The `std::packaged_task` is a template class that is available in the standard library to achieve task-based parallelism with the help of futures and promises. By setting up futures and promises in threads, it simplifies setting up a task without any explicit locks for sharing the result. A `packaged_task` instance provides a wrapper over `std::thread` to put the return value or exception caught into a promise. The member function `get_future()` in `std::packaged_task` will give you the future instance associated with the corresponding promise. Let's look at an example that uses a packaged task to find the sum of all elements in a vector (the working of promise is deep inside the implementation of `packaged_task`):

```
// Function to calculate the sum of elements in an integer vector
int calc_sum(std::vector<int> v)
{
    int sum = std::accumulate(v.begin(), v.end(), 0);
    return sum;
}

int main()
{
    // Creating a packaged_task encapsulates a function
    std::packaged_task<int(std::vector<int>)> task(calc_sum);
    // Fetch associated future from packaged_task
    std::future<int> result = task.get_future();
    std::vector<int> nums{1,2,3,4,5,6,7,8,9,10};
    // Pass packaged_task to thread to run asynchronously
    std::thread t(std::move(task), std::move(nums));
    t.join();
```

```
            // Fetch the result of packaged_task, the value returned by calc_sum()
            int sum = result.get();
            std::cout << "Sum = " << sum << std::endl;
            return 0;
    }
```

The `packaged_task` object takes the type of task as its template argument and the function pointer (`calc_sum`) as a constructor argument. The future instance is obtained through the call to the `get_future()` function of the task object. The explicit `std::move()` is used since the `packaged_task` instances cannot be copied. This is because it is a resource handle and is responsible for whatever resources its task may own. Then, a call to the `get()` function picks up the result from the task and prints it.

Now, let's see how `packaged_task` can be used along with Lambdas:

```
            std::packaged_task<int(std::vector<int>)> task([](std::vector<int>
            v) {
                return std::accumulate(v.begin(), v.end(), 0);
            });
```

Here, instead of a function pointer, a Lambda is passed into the constructor of `packaged_task`. As you have already seen in previous chapters, for a small block of code to run concurrently, Lambdas come in handy. The primary notion behind futures is to be able to get results without having any concern for the mechanisms for managing communication. Also, these two operations are running in two different threads and thus are parallel.

std::async

Modern C++ provides a mechanism to execute a task like a function that might or might not execute in parallel. Here, we are referring to `std::async`, which manages the threading detail internally. `std::async` takes a callable object as its argument and returns an `std::future` that will store the result or exception from the task that has been launched. Let's rewrite our previous example to calculate the sum of all elements from a vector using `std::async`:

```
    // Function to calculate the sum of elements in a vector
    int calc_sum(std::vector<int> v)
    {
        int sum = std::accumulate(v.begin(), v.end(), 0);
        return sum;
    }
```

```
int main()
{
    std::vector<int> nums{1,2,3,4,5,6,7,8,9,10};
    // task launch using std::async
    std::future<int> result(std::async(std::launch::async, calc_sum,
std::move(nums)));
    // Fetch the result of async, the value returned by calc_sum()
    int sum = result.get();
    std::cout << "Sum = " << sum << std::endl;
    return 0;
}
```

Primarily, when using `std::async` for task-based parallelism, the launch of a task and fetching result from the task are following straightforward syntax and well-separated with task execution. In the preceding code, `std::async` is taking three arguments:

- The `async` flag determines the launch policy of the `async` task and `std::launch::async`, meaning that `async` executes the task on a new thread of execution. The `std::launch::deferred` flag doesn't spawn a new thread, but *lazy evaluation* is performed. If both the flags are set as in `std::launch::async` and `std::launch::deferred`, it is up to the implementation as to whether to perform an asynchronous execution or lazy evaluation. If you explicitly don't pass any launch policy into `std::async`, it is again up to the implementation to choose the method of execution.
- The second argument to the `std::async` is a callable object, and it can be a function pointer, function object, or a Lambda. In this example, the `calc_sum` function is the task that gets executed in a separate thread.
- The third argument is the input parameter to the task. Generally, that is a variadic argument and it can pass the number of parameters required for a task callable object.

Now, let's see how `async` and Lambda go together for the same example:

```
// Fetch associated future from async
std::future<int> result( async([](std::vector<int> v) {
return std::accumulate(v.begin(), v.end(), 0);
}, std::move(nums)));
```

In this example, the callable object argument has a Lambda function inside it, which returns the result of `std::accumulate()`. As always, simple operations along with the Lambda beautify the code's overall appearance and improve readability.

Using `async`, you don't have to think about threads and locks. But just think in terms of tasks that do the computations asynchronously, and that you don't know how many threads will be used because that's up to the internal implementation to decide based on the system resources available at the time of calling. It checks for the idle cores (processors) that are available before deciding how many threads to use. This points to the obvious limitation with `async` in that it needs to be employed for tasks that share resources needing locks.

C++ memory model

The classic C++ was essentially a single threaded language. Even though people were writing multithread programs in C++, they were using respective platform threading facilities to write them. Modern C++ can be considered a concurrent programming language. The language standard provides a standard thread and task mechanism (as we have already seen) with the help of standard libraries. Since it is a part of the standard library, the language specification has defined how things should behave across the platform in a precise manner. Having a consistent platform-agnostic behavior for threads, tasks, and so on is a massive challenge that the standard committee handled really well. The committee designed and specified a standard memory model for achieving consistent behavior while the program is running. The memory model consists of two aspects:

- **Structural** aspects, which relate to how data is laid out in memory
- **Concurrency** aspects, which deal with the concurrent access of memory

For a C++ program, all data is made up of *objects*. The language defines an object as a *region of storage*, which is defined with its type and lifetime. Objects can be an instance of a fundamental type such as an int or double, or instances of user-defined types. Some objects may have sub objects, but others don't. The key point is that every variable is an object, including the members' objects of other objects, and every object occupies at least some memory location. Now, let's take a look at what this has to do with concurrency.

Memory access and concurrency

For multithread applications, everything hangs on those memory locations. If multiple threads access different memory locations, everything works fine. But if two threads access the same memory location, then you must be very careful. As you have seen in Chapter 3, *Language-Level Concurrency and Parallelism in C++*, multiple threads trying to read from the same memory location introduce no trouble, but as soon as any thread tries to modify data in a common memory location, chances for *race conditions* to occur come into the frame.

The problematic race conditions can only be avoided by enforced ordering between the access in multiple threads. As discussed in Chapter 3, *Language-Level Concurrency and Parallelism in C++*, lock-based memory access using mutexes is a popular option. The other way is to leverage the synchronization properties of *atomic operations* by enforcing ordering between the access in two threads. In later sections of this chapter, you will see the use of atomic operations to enforce ordering.

Atomic operation appears to the rest of the system and occurs at once without being interrupted (no task switch happens during atomic operation) in concurrent programming. Atomicity is a guarantee of isolation from interrupts, signals, concurrent processes, and threads. More can be read on this topic at the Wikipedia article at https://en. wikipedia.org/wiki/Linearizability.

If there is no enforced ordering between multiple accesses to a single memory location from different threads, one or both accesses are not atomic. If there is a write involved, then it can cause a data race and could lead to an undefined behavior. The data race is a serious bug, and it must be avoided at all costs. The undefined behavior can be avoided by atomic operations, but it doesn't prevent the race situation. The atomic operation makes sure that thread switching never happens when the operation is going on. This is a guarantee against interleaved access to memory. The atomic operations guarantee the preclusion of the interleaved memory access (serial ordering), but cannot prevent race conditions (as there is potential to overwrite updates).

The modification contract

While a program or process is in execution, all the threads in the system should agree on the modification order (for the memory). Every program is executed in an environment, which involves the instruction stream, memory, registers, heap, stack, caches, virtual memory, and so on. This modification order is a contract, between the programmer and system, that is defined by the memory model. The system consists of the compiler (and linker), which morphs the program into executable code, the processor, which executes the instruction set specified in the stream, the cache, and associated states of the program. The contract requires mandating the programmer to obey certain rules, which enables the system to generate a fully optimized program. This set of rules (or heuristics) that a programmer has to conform to while writing code to access memory is achieved with the help of atomic types and atomic operations that were introduced in the standard library.

These operations are not only atomic, but they create synchronization and order constraints on the program's execution. Compared to higher-level lock-based synchronization primitives (mutexes and condition variables), discussed in `Chapter 3`, *Language-Level Concurrency and Parallelism in C++*, you can tailor synchronizations and order constraints to your needs. The important take away from the C++ memory model is this: even though the language has adopted a lot of modern programming idioms and language features, C++, as a system programmer's language, has given more low-level control to your memory resources to optimize the code as you desire.

Atomic operations and types in C++

Generally, a non-atomic operation might be seen as half-done by other threads. As discussed in `Chapter 3`, *Language-Level Concurrency and Parallelism in C++*, in such cases, the invariance associated with the shared data structure will be broken. This happens when the modification to a shared data structure requires modification of more than one value. The best example of this is a partially removed node of a binary tree. If another thread tries to read from this data structure at the same time, the invariant will be broken and could result in undefined behavior.

Using an *atomic operation*, you can't observe an operation that's half-done from any thread in the system, because atomic operations are indivisible. If any operation (such as read) associated with an object is atomic, then all of the modifications to the object are also atomic. C++ has provided atomic types so that you can use atomicity as you require.

Atomic types

All atomic types defined by the standard library can be found in the `<atomic>` header library. The system guarantees the atomicity to these types and all the related operations with these types. Some operations may not be atomic, but the system creates the illusion of atomicity in such cases. The standard atomic types use a member function, `is_lock_free()`, that allows the user to determine whether operations on a given type are done directly with atomic instructions (`is_lock_free()` returns `true`) or done using internal locks by the compiler and library (`is_lock_free()` returns `false`).

`std::atomic_flag` is different among all atomic types. The operations on this type are required to be atomic as per the standard. Hence, this doesn't provide the `is_lock_free()` member function. This is a very simple type with a minimal set of allowed operations such as `test_and_set()` (they can be either queried or set) or `clear()` (clears the value).

The remaining atomic types follow a similar signature as per the specifications of the `std::atomic<>` class template. These types, compared to `std::atomic_flag`, are a bit more fully featured, but not all operations are always atomic. The atomicity of *operations* highly depends on the platform as well. On popular platforms, the atomic variants of built-in types are indeed lock-free, but this is not guaranteed everywhere.

Instead of using `std::atomic<>` template classes, you can use the direct types supplied by the implementation, as given in the following table:

Atomic type	Corresponding specialization
atomic_bool	std::atomic<bool>
atomic_char	std::atomic<char>
atomic_schar	std::atomic<signed char>
atomic_uchar	std::atomic<unsigned char>
atomic_int	std::atomic<int>
atomic_uint	std::atomic<unsigned>
atomic_short	std::atomic<short>
atomic_ushort	std::atomic<unsigned short>
atomic_long	std::atomic<long>
atomic_ulong	std::atomic<unsigned long>
atomic_llong	std::atomic<long long>
atomic_ullong	std::atomic<unsigned long long>
atomic_char16_t	std::atomic<char16_t>

`atomic_char32_t`	`std::atomic<char32_t>`
`atomic_wchar_t`	`std::atomic<wchar_t>`

Along with all of these basic atomic types, the C++ standard library has also provided a set of `typedefs` for atomic types compared to the `typedefs` available in the standard library such as `std::size_t`. There is a simple pattern to identify the corresponding atomic version of `typedefs`: for any standard `typedef` T, use the `atomic_` prefix: `atomic_T`. The following table lists the standard atomic `typedefs` and their corresponding built-in `typedefs`:

Atomic `typedef`	**Standard library** `typedef`
`atomic_size_t`	`size_t`
`atomic_intptr_t`	`intptr_t`
`atomic_uintptr_t`	`uintptr_t`
`atomic_ptrdiff_t`	`ptrdiff_t`
`atomic_intmax_t`	`intmax_t`
`atomic_uintmax_t`	`uintmax_t`
`atomic_int_least8_t`	`int_least8_t`
`atomic_uint_least8_t`	`uint_least8_t`
`atomic_int_least16_t`	`int_least16_t`
`atomic_uint_least16_t`	`uint_least16_t`
`atomic_int_least32_t`	`int_least32_t`
`atomic_uint_least32_t`	`uint_least32_t`
`atomic_int_least64_t`	`int_least64_t`
`atomic_uint_least64_t`	`uint_least64_t`
`atomic_int_fast8_t`	`int_fast8_t`
`atomic_uint_fast8_t`	`uint_fast8_t`
`atomic_int_fast16_t`	`int_fast16_t`
`atomic_uint_fast16_t`	`uint_fast16_t`
`atomic_int_fast32_t`	`int_fast32_t`
`atomic_uint_fast32_t`	`uint_fast32_t`
`atomic_int_fast64_t`	`int_fast64_t`
`atomic_uint_fast64_t`	`uint_fast64_t`

The `std::atomic<>` class templates are not just a set of specializations; they have a primary template to expand and an atomic variant of the user-defined type. Being a generic template class, the operations supported are limited to `load()`, `store()`, `exchange()`, `compare_exchange_weak()`, and `compare_exchange_strong()`. Each of the operations on atomic types has an optional argument to specify the memory-ordering semantics that are required. The concepts of memory ordering will be covered in detail in a later section of this chapter. For now, just keep in mind that all atomic operations can be divided into three categories:

- **Store operations:** These operations can have `memory_order_relaxed`, `memory_order_release`, or `memory_order_seq_cst` ordering
- **Load operations:** These can have `memory_order_relaxed`, `memory_order_consume`, `memory_order_acquire`, or `memory_order_seq_cst` ordering
- **Read-modify-write operations:** These operations can have `memory_order_relaxed`, `memory_order_consume`, `memory_order_acquire`, `memory_order_release`, `memory_order_acq_rel`, or `memory_order_seq_cst` ordering

The default memory ordering for all atomic operations is `memory_order_seq_cst`.

Compared to conventional standard C++ types, standard atomic types are not *copiable* or *assignable*. This means that they have no copy constructors or copy assignment operators. Apart from direct member functions, they support from and implicit conversions to the corresponding built-in types. All operations on atomic types are defined as atomic, and assignment and copy-construction involve two objects. An operation involving two distinct objects cannot be atomic. In both operations, the value must read from one object and be written to the other. Therefore, these operations cannot be considered atomic.

Now, let's look at the operations that you can actually perform on each of the standard atomic types, beginning with `std::atomic_flag`.

std::atomic_flag

`std::atomic_flag` represents a Boolean flag, and it is the simplest among all the atomic types in the standard library. This is the only type where all operations on it are required to be *lock-free* in every platform. This type is very basic, hence it is intended as a building block only.

A `std::atomic_flag` object must always be initialized with `ATOMIC_FLAG_INIT` to set the state to *clear*:

```
std::atomic_flag flg = ATOMIC_FLAG_INIT;
```

This is the only atomic type that requires such initialization, irrespective of the scope of its declaration. Once it is initialized, there are only three operations permissible with this type: destroy it, clear it, or set a query for the previous value. These correspond to the destructor, the `clear()` member function, and the `test_and_set()` member function, respectively. `clear()` is a *store* operation, whereas `test_and_set()` is a read-modify-write operation, as discussed in the previous section:

```
flg.clear()
bool val = flg.test_and_set(std::memory_order_relaxed);
```

In the preceding code snippet, the `clear()` function call requests that the flag is cleared with default memory order, which is `std:: memory_order_seq_cst`, while the call to `test_and set()` uses the relaxed semantics (more on this in the *Relaxed ordering*), which are explicitly used for setting the flag and retrieving the old value.

The primitive implementation of `std::atomic_flag` makes it ideal for the spin-lock mutex. Let's see an example spin-lock:

```
class spin_lock
{
    std::atomic_flag flg;
    public:
    spin_lock() : flg(ATOMIC_FLAG_INIT){}
    void lock() {
        // simulates a lock here... and spin
        while (flg.test_and_set(std::memory_order_acquire));
        //----- Do some action here
        //----- Often , the code to be guarded will be sequenced as
        // sp.lock() ...... Action_to_Guard() .....sp.unlock()
    }
    void unlock() {
        //------ End of Section to be guarded
        flg.clear(std::memory_order_release); // release lock
    }
};
```

In the preceding code snippet, the instance variable `flg` (of the `std::atomic_flag` type) is cleared initially. In the lock method, it tries to set the flag by testing the `flg` to see whether the value is cleared.

If the value is cleared, the value will be set and we will exit the loop. The value in the flag will only be reset when the flag is cleared by the `unlock()` method. In other words, this implementation achieves mutual exclusion with a busy wait in `lock()`.

Because of its limitation, `std::atomic_ flag` cannot be used as a Boolean atomic type, and it doesn't support any *non-modifying query* operations. So, let's look into `std::atomic<bool>` to compensate the requirement of atomic Boolean flags.

std::atomic<bool>

`std::atomic<bool>` is a full-featured atomic Boolean type compared to `std::atomic_flag`. But neither copy-construction nor assignment is possible with this type. The value of an `std::atomic<bool>` object can initially be either `true` or `false`. The objects of this type can be constructed or assigned values from a non-atomic `bool`:

```
std::atomic<bool> flg(true);
flg = false;
```

One thing needs to be noted about the assignment operator of atomic types, which is that the operator returns the value of non-atomic types rather than the conventional scheme of returning references. If a reference is returned instead of a value, it would create a situation where the result of assignment gets the result of a modification by another thread, that is, if it depends on the result of the assignment operator. While returning the result of the assignment operator as a non-atomic value, this additional load can be avoided, and you can infer that the value obtained is the value that has actually been stored.

Now, let's move on to the operations supported by `std::atomic<bool>`. First and foremost, the `store()` member function, which is available in `std::atomic<bool>`, is used for write operations (either `true` or `false`), and it replaces the corresponding restrictive `clear()` function of `std::atomic_flag`. Also, the `store()` function is an atomic store operation. Similarly, the `test_and_set()` function has been effectively replaced with a more generic `exchange()` member function that allows you to replace the stored value with a chosen new one and retrieves the original value. This is an atomic *read-modify-write* operation. Then, `std::atomic<bool>` supports a simple non-modifying query of the value with an explicit call to `load()`, which is an atomic load operation:

```
std::atomic<bool> flg;
flg.store(true);
bool val = flg.load(std::memory_order_acquire);
val = flg.exchange(false, std::memory_order_acq_rel);
```

Apart from `exchange()`, `std::atomic<bool>` introduces an operation to perform a read-modify-write operation, which executes the popular atomic **compare-and-swap (CAS)** instructions. This operation stores a new value if the current value is equal to an expected value. This is called a compare/exchange operation. There are two implementations of this operation that are available in standard library atomic types: `compare_exchange_weak()` and `compare_exchange_strong()`. This operation compares the value of the atomic variable with a supplied expected value and stores the supplied value if they are equal. If these values are not equal, the expected value is updated with the actual value of the atomic variable. The return type of the compare/exchange function is a *bool*, which is `true` if the store was performed; otherwise, it is `false`.

For `compare_exchange_weak()`, the store might not be successful, even if the expected value and original value are equal. In such cases, the exchange of value will not happen and the function will return `false`. This most often happens on a platform that lacks single compare-and-swap instructions, which means that the processor cannot guarantee that the operation will be executed atomically. In such machines, the thread performing the operation might get switched out halfway through executing the sequence of instructions associated with the operation, and another thread will be scheduled in its place by the operating system with a given condition of more threads running than the number of available processors. This condition is called **spurious failure**.

Since `compare_exchange_weak()` can cause spurious failure, it should be used in a loop:

```
bool expected = false;
atomic<bool> flg;
...
while (!flg.compare_exchange_weak(expected, true));
```

In the preceding code, the loop continues to iterate as long as expected is `false`, and it denotes that spurious failure is happening to the `compare_exchange_weak()` call. On the contrary, `compare_exchange_strong()` is guaranteed to return `false` if the actual value isn't equal to the expected value. This can avoid the need for loops as in the previous situations where you want to know the status of variables with respect to running threads.

The compare/exchange functions can take two memory-ordering parameters in order to allow the memory-ordering semantics to differ in success and failure cases. Those memory-ordering semantics are only valid for store operations and cannot be used for failure cases, since a store operation won't occur:

```
bool expected;
std::atomic<bool> flg;
```

```
b.compare_exchange_weak(expected, true, std::memory_order_acq_rel,
std::memory_order_acquire);
b.compare_exchange_weak(expected, true, std::memory_order_release);
```

If you won't specify any memory-ordering semantics, the default `memory_order_seq_cst` will be taken for both success and failure cases. If you don't specify any ordering for failure, then it's assumed to be the same as for success, except that the release part of the ordering is omitted. `memory_order_acq_rel` becomes `memory_order_acquire` and `memory_order_release` becomes `memory_order_relaxed`.

The specifications and consequences of memory ordering will be discussed in detail in the *Memory ordering* section of this chapter. Now, let's see the use of atomic integral types as a group.

Standard atomic integral types

Similar to `std::atomic<bool>`, standard atomic integral types can be neither copy-constructible nor copy-assignable. However, they can be constructed and assigned from the corresponding non-atomic standard variant. Apart from the mandatory `is_lock_free()` member function, the standard atomic integral types, such as `std::atomic<int>` or `std::atomic<unsigned long long>`, also have `load()`, `store()`, `exchange()`, `compare_exchange_weak()`, and `compare_exchange_strong()` member functions, with similar semantics to those of `std::atomic<bool>`.

The integral variants of atomic types do support mathematical operations such as `fetch_add()`, `fetch_sub()`, `fetch_and()`, `fetch_or()` and `fetch_xor()`, compound-assignment operators (+=, -=, &=, |= and ^=), and both post- and pre-increment and decrement operators with ++ and --.

The named functions, such as `fetch_add()` and `fetch_sub()`, atomically perform their operations and return the old value, but the compound-assignment operators return the new value. Pre- and post-increment/decrement work as per usual C/C++ conventions: the post-increment/decrement performs the operation, but returns the old value, and pre-increment/decrement operators perform the operation and return the new value. The following simple example can easily demonstrate the specifications of these operations:

```
int main()
{
std::atomic<int> value;

std::cout << "Result returned from Operation: " << value.fetch_add(5) <<
'n';
std::cout << "Result after Operation: " << value << 'n';
```

```
    std::cout << "Result returned from Operation: " << value.fetch_sub(3) <<
    'n';
    std::cout << "Result after Operation: " << value << 'n';

    std::cout << "Result returned from Operation: " << value++ << 'n';
    std::cout << "Result after Operation: " << value << 'n';

    std::cout << "Result returned from Operation: " << ++value << 'n';
    std::cout << "Result after Operation: " << value << 'n';

    value += 1;
    std::cout << "Result after Operation: " << value << 'n';

    value -= 1;
    std::cout << "Result after Operation: " << value << 'n';
    }
```

The output for this code should look as follows:

```
Result returned from Operation: 0
Result after Operation: 5
Result returned from Operation: 5
Result after Operation: 2
Result returned from Operation: 2
Result after Operation: 3
Result returned from Operation: 4
Result after Operation: 4
Result after Operation: 5
Result after Operation: 4
```

Except for `std::atomic_flag` and `std::atomic<bool>`, all of the other listed atomic types in the first table are atomic integral types. Now, let's look into the atomic pointer specialization, `std::atomic<T*>`.

std::atomic<T*> – pointer arithmetic

Along with the usual set of operations such as `load()`, `store()`, `exchange()`, `compare_exchange_weak()`, and `compare_exchange_strong()`, the atomic pointer type is loaded with the pointer arithmetic operations. The member functions `fetch_add()` and `fetch_sub()` provide operation support for the type to do atomic addition and subtraction on the stored address, and the operators += and -=, and both pre- and post-increment/decrement, use the ++ and -- operators.

The operators work in the same way as standard non-atomic pointer arithmetic works. If `obj` is an `std::atomic<some_class*>`, an object points to the first entry of an array of `some_class` objects. The `obj+=2` changes it to point to the third element in the array and returns a raw pointer to `some_class*` that points to the third element in the array. As discussed in the *Standard atomic integral types* section, the named functions such as `fetch_add()` and `fetch_sub` execute the operation on atomic types, but return the pointer to the first element in the array.

The function forms of atomic operations also allow the memory-ordering semantics to be specified in an additional argument to the function call:

```
obj.fetch_add(3, std::memory_order_release);
```

Since both `fetch_add()` and `fetch_sub` are read-modify-write operations, they can use any memory ordering semantics in a standard atomic library. But, for the operator forms, memory ordering cannot be specified, so these operators will always have `memory_order_seq_cst` semantics.

std::atomic<> primary class template

The primary class template in the standard library allows the user to create an atomic variant of a **user-defined type** (**UDT**). To use a user-defined type as an atomic type, you have to follow some criteria before implementing the class. For a user-defined class UDT, `std::atomic<UDT>` is possible if this type has a trivial copy-assignment operator. This means that the user-defined class should not contain any virtual functions or virtual base classes and must use the compiler-generated default copy-assignment operator. Also, every base class and non-static data member of the user-defined class must have a trivial copy-assignment operator. This allows the compiler to execute `memcpy()` or an equivalent operation for assignment operations, since there is no user-written code to execute.

Along with the requirements on assignment operators, the user-defined types must be *bitwise equality comparable*. This means that you must be able to compare the instances for equality using `memcmp()`. This guarantee is required to ensure that the compare/exchange operation will work.

For an instance of the standard atomic type with the user-defined type `T`, that is, `std::atomic<T>`, the interface is limited to the operations available for `std::atomic<bool>`: `load()`, `store()`, `exchange()`, `compare_exchange_weak()`, `compare_exchange_strong()`, and the assignment from and conversion to an instance of type `T`.

Memory ordering

We have already learned about the atomic types and atomic operators available in the standard library. While performing operations on atomic types, we need to specify memory ordering for certain operations. Now, we will talk about the significance and use cases for the different memory-ordering semantics. The key idea behind atomic operations is to provide synchronization in data access across multiple threads, and this is achieved by enforcing the order of execution. For example, if writing to the data happens before the read from the data, things will be fine. Otherwise, you are in trouble! There are six memory-ordering options available with the standard library that can be applied to operations on atomic types: `memory_order_relaxed`, `memory_order_consume`, `memory_order_acquire`, `memory_order_release`, `memory_order_acq_rel`, and `memory_order_seq_cst`. For all atomic operations on atomic types, `memory_order_seq_cst` is the memory order by default unless you specify something else.

These six options can be classified into three categories:

- **Sequentially consistent ordering**: `memory_order_seq_cst`
- **Acquire-release ordering**: `memory_order_consume`, `memory_order_release`, `memory_order_acquire`, and `memory_order_acq_rel`
- **Relaxed ordering**: `memory_order_relaxed`

The cost of execution varies with different CPUs for different memory-ordering models. The availability of distinct memory-ordering models allows an expert to take advantage of the increased performance of more fine-grained ordering relationships compared to blocking sequentially consistent ordering, but to choose the appropriate memory model as required, one should understand how these options affect the behavior of the program. Let's look into the sequentially consistent model first.

Sequential consistency

The concept of sequential consistency was defined by Leslie Lamport in 1979. Sequential consistency provides two guarantees in the execution of a program. First and foremost, memory ordering the instructions of a program are executed in source code order, or an illusion of source code order will be guaranteed by the compiler. Then, there is a global order of all atomic operations in all threads.

For a programmer, the global ordering behavior of sequential consistency in which all operations in all threads take place in a global clock is an interesting high ground, but is also a disadvantage.

The interesting thing about sequential consistency is that the code works as per our intuition of multiple concurrent threads, but with the cost of a lot of background work being done by the system. The following program is a simple example to give us an edge into sequential consistency:

```
std::string result;
std::atomic<bool> ready(false);

void thread1()
{
    while(!ready.load(std::memory_order_seq_cst));
    result += "consistency";
}

void thread2()
{
    result = "sequential ";
    ready=true;
}

int main()
{
    std::thread t1(thread1);
    std::thread t2(thread2);
    t1.join();
    t2.join();
    std::cout << "Result : " << result << 'n';
}
```

The preceding program synchronizes the threads thread1 and thread2 with the help of sequential consistency. Because of sequential consistency, the execution is totally *deterministic*, so the output of this program is always as follows:

```
Result : sequential consistency
```

Here, thread1 waits in the while loop until the atomic variable ready is true. As soon as *ready* becomes true in thread2, thread1 continues its execution, hence the result always gets updated with strings in the same order. The usage of sequential consistency allows both threads to see the operations in other threads in the same order, hence both threads follow the same global time clock. The loop statement also helps to hold the time clock for the synchronization of both threads.

The details of *acquire-release semantics* will follow in the next section.

Acquire-release ordering

Now, let's dive deep into memory-ordering semantics provided by the C++ standard library. This is the area where the programmer's intuition about ordering in multithread code begins to fade, because there is no global synchronization between threads in acquire-release semantics of atomic operations. These semantics only allow synchronization between atomic operations on the same atomic variable. To elaborate, the load operation on an atomic variable performing in one thread can be synchronized with store operation happening on the same atomic variable in some other thread. A programmer must extract this feature that establishes a *happen-before* relationship between atomic variables to synchronize between threads. This makes working with an acquire-release model a bit difficult, but at the same time more thrilling. The acquire-release semantics shorten the journey towards lock-free programming, because you don't need to bother about synchronization of threads, but synchronization of the same atomic variables in different threads is the one we need to reason about.

As we explained previously, the key idea of acquire-release semantics is the synchronization between a release operation with an acquire operation on the same atomic variable and establishing an *ordering constant* in addition to this. Now, as the name implies, an acquire operation involves acquiring a lock, which includes the operations used to read an atomic variable, such as the `load()` and `test_and_set()` functions. Consequently, the releasing of a lock is a release operation, which consists of atomic operations such as `store()` and `clear()`.

In other words, the lock of a *mutex* is an acquire operation, whereas the unlock is a release operation. Thus, in a *critical-section*, the operation on a variable cannot be taken outside in either direction. However, a variable can be moved inside a critical-section, because the variable moves from an unprotected area to a protected area. This is represented in the following diagram:

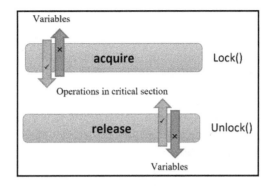

The critical-section contains one-way barriers: an acquire barrier and a release barrier. The same reasoning can be applied for starting a thread and placing a join-call on a thread, and the operations related to all other synchronization primitives available with the standard library.

Since synchronization takes place at atomic variable level rather than at thread level, let's revisit the spin-lock that's been implemented using `std::atomic_flag`:

```
class spin_lock
{
    std::atomic_flag flg;
public:
    spin_lock() : flg(ATOMIC_FLAG_INIT)
    {}
    void lock()
    {
        // acquire lock and spin
        while (flg.test_and_set(std::memory_order_acquire));
    }
    void unlock()
    {
        // release lock
        flg.clear(std::memory_order_release);
    }
};
```

In this code, the `lock()` function is an `acquire` operation. Instead of using the default sequentially consistent memory ordering that was used in the previous example, an explicit acquire memory ordering flag is used now. Also, the `unlock()` function, which is a release operation that was also using default memory order, has now been replaced with explicit release semantics. So, the heavyweight synchronization with sequential consistency of two threads is replaced by the lightweight and performant acquire-release semantics.

As the number of threads using the `spin_lock` increases more than two threads, the general acquire semantics using `std::memory_order_acquire` will not be sufficient, because the lock method becomes an acquire-release operation. Therefore, the memory model has to be changed to `std::memory_order_acq_rel`.

So far, we have seen that sequentially consistent ordering ensures synchronization between threads, while acquire-release ordering establishes ordering between read and write operations on the same atomic variable on multiple threads. Now, let's see the specifications of relaxed memory ordering.

Relaxed ordering

Operations on atomic types performed with relaxed memory ordering using the tag `std::memory_order_relaxed` are not synchronization operations. In contrast with other ordering options that are available in the standard library, they do not impose an order among concurrent memory access. The relaxed memory ordering semantics only guarantee that the operations on the same atomic type inside the same thread cannot be reordered, and this guarantee is called **modification order consistency**. In fact, relaxed ordering only guarantees atomicity and modification order consistency. Therefore, other threads can see these operations in different orders.

Relaxed memory ordering can be used effectively in places where synchronization or ordering is not required, and atomicity can be an added advantage for performance boosting. One typical example would be incrementing counters, such as reference counters of **std::shared_ptr**, where they only require atomicity. But decrementing the reference count needs acquire-release synchronization with the destructor of this template class.

Let's see a simple example to count the number of threads that were spawned with relaxed ordering:

```
std::atomic<int> count = {0};

void func()
{
    count.fetch_add(1, std::memory_order_relaxed);
}

int main()
{
    std::vector<std::thread> v;
    for (int n = 0; n < 10; ++n)
    {
        v.emplace_back(func);
```

```
    }
    for (auto& t : v)
    {
        t.join();
    }
    std::cout << "Number of spawned threads : " << count << 'n';
}
```

In this code, ten threads are spawned from the `main()` function with a thread function `func()`, where on each thread the atomic integer value is incremented by one using the atomic operation `fetch_add()`. In contrast to compound assignment operators and post- and pre-increment operators, available with `std::atomic<int>`, the `fetch_add()` function can accept the memory ordering argument and it is `std::memory_order_relaxed`.

The program prints the number of threads spawned in the program as follows:

Number of spawned threads : 10

The output of the program remains the same for any other relevant memory-ordering tags, but the relaxed memory ordering ensures atomicity and thus performance.

Until now, we have discussed the levels of the different memory models, and their effect on atomic and non-atomic operations. Now, let's dive into an implementation of a lock-free data structure using atomic operations.

A lock-free data structure queue

As we already know, the data in an actual system is often represented in the form of a data structure, and when it comes to concurrent operations on a data structure, performance is a big deal. In Chapter 3, *Language-Level Concurrency and Parallelism in C++*, we learned how to write a thread-safe stack. However, we used locks and condition variables to implement it. To explain how to write a lock-free data structure, let's write a very basic queue system using a producer/consumer paradigm without using locks or condition variables. This will improve the performance of the code for sure. Rather than using a wrapper over a standard data type, we will roll it out from scratch. We have made an assumption that there is a single producer and a single consumer in this case:

```
template<typename T>
class Lock_free_Queue
{
private:
    struct Node
```

```
    {
        std::shared_ptr<T> my_data;
        Node* my_next_node;
        Node() : my_next_node(nullptr)
        {}
    };
    std::atomic<Node*> my_head_node;
    std::atomic<Node*> my_tail_node;
    Node* pop_head_node()
    {
        Node* const old_head_node = my_head_node.load();
        if(old_head_node == my_tail_node.load())
        {
            return nullptr;
        }
        my_head_node.store(old_head_node->my_next_node);
        return old_head_node;
    }
```

The `Lock_free_stack` class contains a structure to represent a queue node (named `Node`) with data members to represent the data of a node (`my_data`) and a pointer to the next node. Then, the class contains two instances of an atomic pointer to the user-defined structure `Node`, which is already defined inside the class. One instance stores the pointer to the head node of the queue, while the other points to the tail node. Finally, a `private pop_head_node()` function is used to retrieve the head node of the queue by calling an atomic *store* operation, but only if the queue contains at least one element. Here, the atomic operation follows the default sequentially consistent memory-ordering semantics:

```
public:
Lock_free_Queue() : my_head_node(new Node),
my_tail_node(my_head_node.load())
    {}
    Lock_free_Queue(const Lock_free_Queue& other) = delete;
    Lock_free_Queue& operator= (const Lock_free_Queue& other) = delete;
    ~Lock_free_Queue()
    {
        while(Node* const old_head_node = my_head_node.load())
        {
            my_head_node.store(old_head_node->my_next_node);
            delete old_head_node;
        }
    }
```

The head node is instantiated and the tail points to that memory when the queue object is constructed. The copy constructor and copy assignment operators are marked as deleted to prevent them from being used. Inside the destructor, all of the elements in the queue are deleted iteratively:

```cpp
std::shared_ptr<T> dequeue()
{
    Node* old_head_node = pop_head_node();
    if(!old_head_node)
    {
        return std::shared_ptr<T>();
    }
    std::shared_ptr<T> const result(old_head_node->my_data);
    delete old_head_node;
    return result;
}
void enqueue(T new_value)
{
    std::shared_ptr<T> new_data(std::make_shared<T>(new_value));
    Node* p = new Node;
    Node* const old_tail_node = my_tail_node.load();
    old_tail_node->my_data.swap(new_data);
    old_tail_node->my_next_node = p;
    my_tail_node.store(p);
}
};
```

The preceding code snippet implements standard queue operations, which are Enqueue and Dequeue. Here, we have ensured that there is a *happens before* relationship between Enqueue and Dequeue using the swap and store atomic operations.

Summary

In this chapter, we have discussed facilities provided by the standard library to write task-based parallelism. We saw how to use futures and promises with `std::packaged_task` and `std::async`. We discussed the new multi-threading-aware memory model that is available with the Modern C++ language. After that, we covered atomic types, and operations associated with them. The most important thing that we learned about are the various memory-ordering semantics of the language. In a nutshell, this particular chapter and the previous one will enable us to reason about the concurrency aspects of the reactive programming model.

In the following chapter, we will shift our attention from language and concurrency to the standard interface of the reactive programming model. We will be covering Observables!

Introduction to Observables

5

In the last three chapters, we learned about the linguistic features of modern C++: multithreading, lock-free programming models, and so on. The topics covered there can be considered as sort of prerequisites to start learning about the reactive programming model. The reactive programming model warrants skills in functional programming, concurrent programming, schedulers, object/functional programming, design patterns, and event Stream processing, to name a few. We have already covered or touched upon functional programming, object/functional programming, and some topics that are related to scheduling in the previous chapter. This time, we will cover the wonderful world of design patterns to appreciate the crux of reactive programming in general and Observables in particular. In the next chapter, we will deal with the topic of event Stream programming before we jump into the RxCpp library. The design pattern movement reached critical mass with the publication of a book titled *Design Patterns: Elements of Reusable Object Oriented Software* by the **Gang of Four** (**GoF**). who cataloged a set of 23 patterns grouped into creational, structural, and behavioral families. The GoF catalog defined the Observer pattern in the category of behavioral patterns. A key message we want to deliver here is that the reactive programming model can be understood through knowledge of the venerable GoF patterns. In this chapter, we will cover:

- The GoF Observer pattern
- Limitations of the GoF Observer pattern
- A holistic look at design patterns and Observables
- Modeling real-world hierarchies using composite design patterns
- Behavioral processing of composites using visitors
- Flattening the composite and navigating through the Iterator pattern
- Transformation from Iterator to Observable/Observer by reversing the gaze!

The GoF Observer pattern

The GoF Observer pattern is also referred to as a *publish-subscribe pattern* in the GoF book. The idea is simple. EventSource (classes that emits events) will have a one-to-many relationship with event sinks (classes that listen to the event notification). Every EventSource will have a mechanism for the event sinks to subscribe to, in order to get different types of notification. A single EventSource might emit multiple events. An EventSource can send notifications to thousands of subscribers (event sinks or listeners) when there is a change in state or something significant happens in its realm. The EventSource will walk through the list of subscribers and notify them one by one. The GoF book was written at a time when the world was mostly doing sequential programming. Topics such as concurrency were mostly related to platform-specific libraries or the POSIX thread library. We will write a simple C++ program to demonstrate the whole idea of the Observer pattern. The purpose is to quickly understand the Observer pattern, and ideas such as robustness have been given secondary priority. The listing is self-contained and easily understandable:

```cpp
//-------------------- Observer.cpp
#include <iostream>
#include  <vector>
#include <memory>
using namespace std;
//---- Forward declaration of event sink
template<class T>
class EventSourceValueObserver;
//----------A toy implementation of EventSource
template<class T>
class EventSourceValueSubject{
   vector<EventSourceValueObserver<T> *> sinks;
   T State; // T is expected to be a value type
  public:
   EventSourceValueSubject() { State = 0; }
   ~EventSourceValueSubject() {
       sinks.clear();
   }
   bool Subscribe( EventSourceValueObserver<T> *sink ) {
sinks.push_back(sink);}
   void NotifyAll() { for (auto sink : sinks) { sink->Update(State); }}
   T GetState() { return State; }
   void SetState(T pstate) { State = pstate; NotifyAll(); }
};
```

The previous code snippet implements a trivial `EventSource`, which can potentially store an integral value as the state. In modern C++, we can use type traits to detect whether the consumer has instantiated this class with an integral type. Since our focus is on elucidation, we have not added assertions pertaining to type constraints. In the next C++ standards, there is a notion called **concept** (known as Constraints in other languages) that will help in enforcing that directly (without type traits). In a real-life scenario, an `EventSource` might store lots of variables or Streams of values. Any changes in them will be broadcast to all subscribers. In the `SetState` method, when a consumer of the `EventSource` class (the event sink itself is the consumer in this class) mutates the state, the `NotifyAll()` method will get triggered. The `NotifyAll()` method works through the list of sinks and invokes the `Update()` method. Then, event sinks can do the tasks that are specific to their context. We have not implemented methods such as unsubscribe to focus on the core issues:

```cpp
//--------------------- An event sink class for the preceding EventSources
template <class T>
class EventSourceValueObserver{
    T OldState;
  public:
    EventSourceValueObserver() { OldState = 0; }
    virtual ~EventSorceValueObserver() {}
    virtual void Update( T State ) {
        cout << "Old State " << OldState << endl;
        OldState = State;
        cout << "Current State " << State << endl;
    }
};
```

The `EventSourceValueObserver` class has implemented the `Update` method to do a task that is relevant for its context. Here, it just prints the values of the old state and current state onto the console. In real life, sinks might modify a UX element or relay the propagation of state to other objects through notifications. Let's also write another event sink, which will inherit from `EventSourceValueObserver`:

```cpp
//------------ A simple specialized Observe
class AnotherObserver : public EventSourceValueObserver<double> {
  public:
    AnotherObserver():EventSourceValueObserver() {}
    virtual ~AnotherObserver() {}
    virtual void Update( double State )
    { cout << " Specialized Observer" << State <<  endl; }
};
```

We have implemented a specialized version of the Observer for demonstration purposes. This has been done to show that we can have subscribers that are instances of two classes (which can be inherited from `EventSourceObserver<T>`). Here also, we do not do much when we get a notification from the `EventSource`:

```
int main() {
    unique_ptr<EventSourceValueSubject<double>>
                    evsrc(new EventSourceValueSubject<double>());
    //---- Create Two instance of Observer and Subscribe
    unique_ptr<AnotherObserver> evobs( new AnotherObserver());
    unique_ptr<EventSourceValueObserver<double>>
                    evobs2( new EventSourceValueObserver<double>());
    evsrc->Subscribe( evobs.get() );
    evsrc->Subscribe( evobs2.get());
    //------ Change the State of the EventSource
    //------ This should trigger call to Update of the Sink
    evsrc->SetState(100);
}
```

The previous code snippet instantiates an `EventSource` object and adds two subscribers. When we change the state of the `EventSource`, the notification will be received by the subscribers. This is the crux of the Observer pattern. In a normal OOP program, the consumption of objects is done in the following way:

1. Instantiate the object
2. Call a method to compute some value or change state
3. Do something useful based on the return value or a change in the state

Here, in the case of the Observer, we have done the following:

1. Instantiate the object (`EventSource`)
2. Subscribe for the notification by implementing Observers (for event listening)
3. When something changes at the `EventSource`, you will be notified
4. Do something with the value received through the notification

The `Method` function outlined here helps in the separation of concerns, and modularity has been achieved. This is a good mechanism to implement event-driven code. Rather than polling for events, you are asking to be notified. Most GUI toolkits today use similar paradigms.

The limitations of the GoF Observer pattern

The GoF pattern book was written at a time when the world was really doing sequential programming. The architecture of Observer pattern implementation had lot of anomalies, judging from the current programming model world view. Here are some of them:

- The close coupling between Subjects and Observers.
- The lifetime of the `EventSource` is controlled by the Observers.
- Observers (sinks) can block the `EventSource`.
- The implementation is not thread-safe.
- Event filtering is done at the sink level. Ideally speaking, the data should be filtered at the place where the data is (at the subject level, before notification).
- Most of the time, Observers do not do much and the CPU cycles will be wasted.
- The `EventSource` should ideally publish the value to the environment. The environment should notify all the subscribers. This level of indirection can facilitate techniques such as event aggregation, event transformation, event filtering, and canonicalizing the event data to name a few.

With the advent of functional programming techniques such as immutable variables, functional composition, functional style transformation, lock-free concurrent programming, and so on, we can circumvent the limits of the classic Observer pattern. The solution outlined by the industry is the notion of Observables.

In the classic Observer pattern, a diligent reader might have seen the potential for the asynchronous programming model to be incorporated. The `EventSource` can make asynchronous calls to the Subscribers method, rather than looping the subscribers sequentially. By using a fire and forget mechanism, we can decouple the `EventSource` from its sinks. The invocation can be done from a background thread, async task, or packaged task, or a suitable mechanism for the context. The asynchronous invocation of notification methods has the added advantage that if any of the client blocks (by getting into an infinite loop or a crash), others can still get the notification. The asynchronous method works on the following schema:

1. Define methods for handling data, exceptions, and the end of the data (on the event sink side)
2. An Observer (event Sink) interface should have `OnData`, `OnError`, and `OnCompleted` methods
3. Every event sink should implement the Observer interface
4. Every `EventSource` (Observable) should have subscribe and unsubscribe methods

5. The event sink should subscribe to an instance of Observable through Subscribe methods

6. When an event happens, the Observer will be notified by the Observable

Some of these things were already mentioned in `Chapter 1`, *Reactive Programming Model – Overview and History*. We did not cover the asynchronous part then. In this chapter, we will revisit those ideas. Based on the experience which authors had based on the technical presentations and interaction with developers, jumping right into the Observable/Observer model of programming does not help in comprehension. Most developers are confused regarding Observable/Observer because of the fact that they do not know what particular problem this pattern solves. The classic GoF Observer implementation given here is to set the context for discussions on Observable Streams.

A holistic look at GoF patterns

The design pattern movement started at a time when the World was struggling to come to terms with complexities of object-oriented software design methods. The GoF book and the associated pattern catalog gave developers a set of techniques for designing large-scale systems. Topics such as concurrency and parallelism were not in the minds of the people who designed the catalog. (At least, their work did not reflect this!)

We have seen that event handling through the classic Observer pattern has some limitations, which might be a problem in some cases. What is the way out? We need to take a fresh look at the problem of event handling by taking a step back. We will digress into the subject of philosophy a bit to have a different outlook on the problem that the reactive programming model (programming with Observable Streams!) is trying to solve. Our Journey will help us to transition nicely from GOF patterns to the world of Reactive programming using functional programming constructs.

The following content in this section is bit abstract and has been given here to provide a conceptual background from which authors of this book have approached the subject covered in this chapter. Our approach to explaining Observables starts from the GoF Composite/Visitor pattern and iteratively reaches the topic of Observables. The idea of this approach came from a book on Advaita Vedanta, a mystical philosophical tradition that originated in India. The topic has been explained in Western Philosophical terms. If a matter seems bit abstract, feel free to gloss over it.

Nataraja Guru (1895-1973) was an Indian philosopher who was a proponent of the Advaita Vedanta Philosophy, an Indian philosophical school based on the non-dualism of a supreme force that governs all of us. According to this philosophical school, whatever we see around , be it humans, animals, or plants, are manifestations of the Absolute (called Brahman in Sanskrit) and its only positive affirmation is SAT-CHIT-ANAND (Vedanta philosophy uses negation and proof by contradiction to depict Brahman). This can be translated into the English language as existence, essence, and bliss (the implied meaning of bliss is "good" here). In a book titled *The Unitive Philosophy* published by DK Print World, New Delhi, he gives a mapping of SAT-CHIT-ANAND to Ontology, Epistemology, and Axiology (the three primary branches of philosophy). The Ontology, Epistemology, and Axiology are the theories of existence, knowledge, and values respectively. The following table gives possible mappings of SAT-CHIT-ANAND to other entities that mean more or less the same:

SAT	CHIT	ANAND
Existence	Essence	Bliss
Ontology	Epistemology	Axiology
Who am I?	What can I know?	What should I do?
Structure	Behavior	Function

In Vedanta (the Advaita school) philosophy, the whole World is viewed as existence, essence, and bliss. From the table, we will map the problems in the software design world into the problem of structure, behavior, and function. Every system in the world can be viewed from the structural, behavioral, and functional perspectives. The canonical structure for a OOP programs is hierarchies. We will model the world we are interested in as hierarchies and process them in a canonical manner. The GOF pattern catalog has got Composite pattern (structural) for modelling hierarchies and Visitor pattern (behavioral) to process them.

The OOP programming model and hierarchies

This section is bit conceptual in nature and those of you who have not dabbled with GoF design patterns will find it a bit difficult. The best strategy could be to skip this section and focus on the running example. Once you have understood the running example, this particular section can be revisited.

Object-oriented programming is very good at modeling hierarchies. In fact, the hierarchy can be considered the canonical data model for the object-oriented processing of data. In the GoF pattern world, we model hierarchies using the Composite pattern. The Composite pattern is categorized as a structural pattern. Whenever there is a Composite pattern used, the Visitor pattern will also be part of the system. The Visitor pattern is good for processing composites to add behavior to the structure. The Visitor/Composite patterns come as a pair in real-life contexts. Of course, one instance of the Composite can be processed by different visitors. In a Compiler project, the **Abstract Syntax Tree** (**AST**) will be modeled as a composite and there will be Visitor implementations for type checking, code optimization, code generation, and static analysis to name a few.

One of the problems with the Visitor pattern is the fact that it has to have some notion of the structure of the Composite to do the processing. Moreover, it will result in code bloat in the context where it needs to process a filtered subset of the available data in the Composite hierarchy. We might require different visitors for each filter criterion. The GoF pattern catalog has another pattern that falls into the behavioral category, called Iterator, something that every C++ programmer is familiar with. The Iterator pattern is good at processing data in a structure-agnostic manner. Any kind of hierarchical structure has to be linearized or flattened to be in a shape amenable to be processed by an Iterator. An example could be a tree, which can be processed using a BFS Iterator or a DFS Iterator. For the application programmer, all of a sudden the tree appears as a linear structure. We need to flatten the hierarchies to be in a state where the structure is amenable to Iterators. The process will be implemented by the person who has implemented the API. There are some limitations to the Iterator pattern (which is pull-based) and we will reverse the gaze and make the system push-based using a pattern called Observerable/Observer, an enhanced version of the Observer pattern. This section is a bit abstract, but after going through the entire chapter, you can come back and make sense of what is happening. In a nutshell, we can sum up the whole thing as follows:

- We can model hierarchical structures using the Composite pattern
- We can process the Composite using the Visitor pattern
- We can flatten or linearize the Composite to navigate it through Iterators
- Iterators follow a pull method and we need to reverse the gaze for a push-based scheme
- Now, we have managed to reach the Observable/Observer way of implementing things
- Observables and Iterators are binary opposites (one man's push is another man's pull!)

We will implement all of the preceding points to have a firm grounding on Observables.

A Composite/Visitor pattern for expression processing

To demonstrate the journey from the GoF pattern catalog to Observables, we will model a four-function calculator as a running example. Since expression trees or AST are hierarchical in nature, they will be a good example to model as a Composite pattern. We have purposefully omitted writing a parser to keep the code listing small:

```
#include <iostream>
#include <memory>
#include <list>
#include <stack>
#include <functional>
#include <thread>
#include <future>
#include <random>
#include "FuncCompose.h" // available int the code base
using namespace std;
//--------------------List of operators supported by the evaluator
enum class OPERATOR{ ILLEGAL,PLUS,MINUS,MUL,DIV,UNARY_PLUS,UNARY_MINUS };
```

We have defined an enum type to represent the four binary operators (+ , - , * , /) and two unary operators (+ , -). Other than the standard C++ headers, we have included a custom header (FuncCompose.h), which is available at the GitHub repo associated with this book. It contains code for the Compose function and pipe operator (|) for functional composition. We can use Unix pipeline style composition to tie together a collection of transformations:

```
//------------ forward declarations for the Composites
class Number;   //----- Stores IEEE double precision floating point number
class BinaryExpr; //--- Node for Binary Expression
class UnaryExpr;  //--- Node for Unary Expression
class IExprVisitor; //---- Interface for the Visitor
//---- Every node in the expression tree will inherit from the Expr class
class Expr {
  public:
    //---- The standard Visitor double dispatch method
    //---- Normally return value of accept method are void.... and Concrete
    //---- classes store the result which can be retrieved later
    virtual double accept(IExprVisitor& expr_vis) = 0;
    virtual ~Expr() {}
};
//----- The Visitor interface contains methods for each of the concrete node
//----- Normal practice is to use
struct IExprVisitor{
```

```
    virtual   double Visit(Number& num)  = 0;
    virtual   double Visit(BinaryExpr& bin) = 0;
    virtual   double Visit(UnaryExpr& un)=0 ;
};
```

The Expr class will act as the base class for all the nodes that are part of the Expression Tree. Since our purpose is to demonstrate the Composite/Visitor GoF pattern, we support only constants, binary expressions, and unary expressions. The accept method in the Expr class accepts a Visitor reference as a parameter and the body of the method will be the same for all the nodes. The method will redirect the call to the appropriate handler on the Visitor implementation. To gain more insight into the whole subject covered in this section, read about *double dispatch* and *Visitor pattern* by searching the web using your favorite search engine.

The Visitor interface (`IExprVisitor`) contains methods to process all the node types supported by the hierarchy. In our case, there are methods for processing constant numbers, binary operators, and unary operators. Let's see the code for the Node types. We start with the Number class:

```
//---------A class to represent IEEE 754 interface
class Number : public Expr {
   double NUM;
  public:
   double getNUM() { return NUM; }
   void setNUM(double num)    { NUM = num;  }
   Number(double n) { this->NUM = n; }
   ~Number() {}
   double accept(IExprVisitor& expr_vis){ return expr_vis.Visit(*this);}
};
```

The Number class wraps an IEEE double precision floating point number. The code is obvious and all we need to bother about is the content of the `accept` method. The method receives a parameter of type visitor (`IExprVisitor&`). The routine just reflects the call back to the appropriate node on the Visitor implementation. In this case, it will call `Visit(Number&)` on `IExpressionVisitor`:

```
//-------------- Modeling Binary Expresison
class BinaryExpr : public Expr {
   Expr* left; Expr* right; OPERATOR OP;
  public:
   BinaryExpr(Expr* l,Expr* r , OPERATOR op ) { left = l; right = r; OP =
op;}
   OPERATOR getOP() { return OP; }
   Expr& getLeft() { return *left; }
   Expr& getRight() { return *right; }
   ~BinaryExpr() { delete left; delete right;left =0; right=0; }
```

```
    double accept(IExprVisitor& expr_vis) { return expr_vis.Visit(*this);}
};
```

The `BinaryExpr` class models a binary operation with left and right operands. The operands can be any of the classes in the hierarchy. The candidate classes are `Number`, `BinaryExpr`, and `UnaryExpr`. This can go to an arbitrary depth. The terminal node is Number in our case. The previous code has support for four binary operators:

```
//-----------------Modeling Unary Expression
class UnaryExpr : public Expr {
    Expr * right; OPERATOR op;
  public:
    UnaryExpr( Expr *operand , OPERATOR op ) { right = operand;this-> op =
op; }
    Expr& getRight( ) { return *right; }
    OPERATOR getOP() { return op; }
    virtual ~UnaryExpr() { delete right; right = 0; }
    double accept(IExprVisitor& expr_vis){ return expr_vis.Visit(*this);}
};
```

The `UnaryExpr` method models a unary expression with an operator and a right side expression. We support unary plus and unary minus for this implementation. The right side expression can in turn be a `UnaryExpr`, `BinaryExpr`, or `Number`. Now that we have implementations for all the node types supported, let's focus on the implementation of the Visitor Interface. We will write a Tree Walker and Evaluator to compute the value of the expression:

```
//--------An Evaluator for Expression Composite using Visitor Pattern
class TreeEvaluatorVisitor : public IExprVisitor{
  public:
    double Visit(Number& num){ return num.getNUM();}
    double Visit(BinaryExpr& bin) {
      OPERATOR temp = bin.getOP(); double lval =
bin.getLeft().accept(*this);
      double rval = bin.getRight().accept(*this);
      return (temp == OPERATOR::PLUS) ? lval + rval: (temp == OPERATOR::MUL)
?
        lval*rval : (temp == OPERATOR::DIV)? lval/rval : lval-rval;
    }
    double Visit(UnaryExpr& un) {
      OPERATOR temp = un.getOP(); double rval = un.getRight().accept(*this);
      return (temp == OPERATOR::UNARY_PLUS)  ? +rval : -rval;
    }
};
```

This does a depth-first walk of the AST and recursively evaluates the node. Let's write an expression processor (an implementation of `IExprVisitor`) that will print the expression tree to the console in **Reverse Polish Notation (RPN)** form:

```
//-------------A Visitor to Print Expression in RPN
class ReversePolishEvaluator : public IExprVisitor {
    public:
    double Visit(Number& num){cout << num.getNUM() << " " << endl; return
42;}
    double Visit(BinaryExpr& bin){
        bin.getLeft().accept(*this); bin.getRight().accept(*this);
        OPERATOR temp = bin.getOP();
        cout << ( (temp==OPERATOR::PLUS) ? " + " :(temp==OPERATOR::MUL) ?
        " * " : (temp == OPERATOR::DIV) ? " / ": " - " ) ; return 42;
    }
    double Visit(UnaryExpr& un){
        OPERATOR temp = un.getOP();un.getRight().accept(*this);
        cout << (temp == OPERATOR::UNARY_PLUS) ?" (+) " : " (-) "; return
42;
    }
};
```

The RPN notation is also called the postfix notion, where the operator comes after the operands. They are suitable for processing using an evaluation stack. They form the basis of the stack-based virtual machine architecture leveraged by the Java Virtual Machine and the .NET CLR. Now, let's write a main function to put everything together:

```
int main( int argc, char **argv ){
    unique_ptr<Expr>
            a(new BinaryExpr( new Number(10) , new Number(20) ,
OPERATOR::PLUS));
    unique_ptr<IExprVisitor> eval( new TreeEvaluatorVisitor());
    double result = a->accept(*eval);
    cout << "Output is => " << result << endl;
    unique_ptr<IExprVisitor>  exp(new ReversePolishEvaluator());
    a->accept(*exp);
}
```

This code snippet creates an instance of a composite (an instance of `BinaryExpr`) and also instantiates an instances of `TreeEvaluatorVisitor` and `ReversePolshEvaluator`. Then, the `accept` method of Expr is called to start processing. We will see the value of the expression and an RPN equivalent of the expression on the console. In this section, we learned how to create a Composite and process the Composite using a Visitor interface. Other potential examples for Composites/Visitors are storing directory contents and their traversal, XML processing, document processing, and so on. Popular opinion says that, if you know the Composite/Visitor duo, you have understood the GoF pattern catalog well.

We have seen that the Composite pattern and Visitor pattern act as a pair to take care of the structural and behavioral aspects of a system and provide some functionality. The Visitor has to be written in a manner that presupposes the cognizance of the structure of the Composite. This can be a potential problem from an abstraction perspective. An implementer of a hierarchy can provide a mechanism to flatten the hierarchy into a list (which is possible in most cases). This will enable the API implementer to provide an Iterator-based API. The Iterator-based API is good for functional-style processing as well. Let's see how it works.

Flattening the composite for iterative processing

We have already learned that the Visitor pattern has to know the structure of the composite for someone to write an instance of the Visitor interface. This can create an anomaly called *abstraction leak*. The GoF pattern catalog has a pattern that will help us to navigate the contents of a tree in a structure-agnostic manner. Yes, you might have guessed it correctly: the Iterator pattern is the candidate! For the Iterator to do its job, the composite has to be flattened into a list sequence or Stream. Let's write some code to flatten the expression tree that we modeled in the previous section. Before we write the logic to flatten a Composite, let's create a data structure to store the contents of an AST as a list. Every node in the list has to store either an operator or value, depending upon whether we need to store operators or operands. We describe a data structure called `EXPR_ITEM` for this purpose:

```
///////////////////////////
// A enum to store discriminator -> Operator or a Value?
enum class ExprKind{ ILLEGAL_EXP, OPERATOR , VALUE };
// A Data structure to store the Expression node.
// A node will either be a Operator or Value
struct EXPR_ITEM {
    ExprKind knd; double Value; OPERATOR op;
    EXPR_ITEM():op(OPERATOR::ILLEGAL),Value(0),knd(ExprKind::ILLEGAL_EXP){}
    bool SetOperator( OPERATOR op )
```

```
        {  this->op = op;this->knd = ExprKind::OPERATOR; return true; }
        bool SetValue(double value)
        {  this->knd = ExprKind::VALUE;this->Value = value;return true;}
        string toString() {DumpContents();return "";}
    private:
        void DumpContents() { //---- Code omitted for brevity }
};
```

The `list<EXPR_ITEM>` data structure will store the contents of the composite as a linear structure. Let's write a class that will flatten the composite:

```
//---- A Flattener for Expressions
class FlattenVisitor : public IExprVisitor {
        list<EXPR_ITEM>  ils;
        EXPR_ITEM MakeListItem(double num)
        { EXPR_ITEM temp; temp.SetValue(num); return temp; }
        EXPR_ITEM MakeListItem(OPERATOR op)
        { EXPR_ITEM temp;temp.SetOperator(op); return temp;}
    public:
        list<EXPR_ITEM> FlattenedExpr(){ return ils;}
        FlattenVisitor(){}
        double Visit(Number& num){
            ils.push_back(MakeListItem(num.getNUM()));return 42;
        }
        double Visit(BinaryExpr& bin) {
            bin.getLeft().accept(*this);bin.getRight().accept(*this);
            ils.push_back(MakeListItem(bin.getOP()));return 42;
        }
        double Visit(UnaryExpr& un){
            un.getRight().accept(*this);
            ils.push_back(MakeListItem(un.getOP())); return 42;
        }
};
```

The `FlattenerVistor` class will flatten the composite `Expr` node to a list of EXPR_ITEM. Once the composite has been linearized, it is possible to process items using the Iterator pattern. Let's write a small global function to convert an `Expr` tree to `list<EXPR_ITEM>`:

```
list<EXPR_ITEM> ExprList(Expr* r) {
    unique_ptr<FlattenVisitor> fl(new FlattenVisitor());
    r->accept(*fl);
    list<EXPR_ITEM> ret = fl->FlattenedExpr();return ret;
}
```

The global subroutine `ExprList` will flatten an arbitrary expression tree of a list of EXPR_ITEM. Once we have flattened the composite, we can use an iterator to process the content. After linearizing the structure as a list, we can use a stack data structure to evaluate the expression data to produce the output:

```
//--------- A minimal stack to evaluate RPN expression
class DoubleStack : public stack<double> {
    public:
    DoubleStack() { }
    void Push( double a ) { this->push(a);}
    double Pop() { double a = this->top(); this->pop(); return a; }
};
```

`DoubleStack` is a wrapper around the STL stack container. This can be considered as some kind of helper routine to keep the listing terse. Let's write an evaluator for the flattened expression. We will iterate through list<EXPR_ITEM> and push the value to the stack, if a value is encountered. If an operator is encountered, we will pop the values from the stack and apply the operation. The result is pushed into the stack once again. At the end of the iteration, the existing element in the stack will be the value associated with the expression:

```
//------Iterator through eachn element of Expression list
double Evaluate( list<EXPR_ITEM> ls) {
    DoubleStack stk; double n;
    for( EXPR_ITEM s : ls ) {
        if (s.knd == ExprKind::VALUE) { stk.Push(s.Value); }
        else if ( s.op == OPERATOR::PLUS) { stk.Push(stk.Pop() + stk.Pop());}
        else if (s.op == OPERATOR::MINUS ) { stk.Push(stk.Pop() - stk.Pop());}
        else if ( s.op ==  OPERATOR::DIV) { n = stk.Pop(); stk.Push(stk.Pop()
/ n);}
        else if (s.op == OPERATOR::MUL) { stk.Push(stk.Pop() * stk.Pop()); }
        else if ( s.op == OPERATOR::UNARY_MINUS) { stk.Push(-stk.Pop()); }
    }
    return stk.Pop();
}
//----- Global Function Evaluate an Expression Tree
double Evaluate( Expr* r ) { return Evaluate(ExprList(r)); }
```

Let's write a main program that will call this function to evaluate the expression. The code listing in the evaluator is easy to understand because we are reducing a list. In the tree-based interpreter, things were not obvious:

```
int main( int argc, char **argv ){
    unique_ptr<Expr>
```

```
        a(new BinaryExpr( new Number(10) , new Number(20) ,
    OPERATOR::PLUS));
        double result = Evaluate( &(*a));
        cout << result << endl;
    }
```

Map and filter operations on the list

Map is a functional operator where a function will be applied to a list. Filter will apply a predicate to a list and return another list. They are the cornerstone of any functional processing pipeline. They are also called higher-order functions. We can write a generic Map function, using `std::transform` for `std::list` and the `std::vector`:

```
template <typename R, typename F>
R Map(R r , F&& fn) {
    std::transform(std::begin(r), std::end(r), std::begin(r),
        std::forward<F>(fn));
    return r;
}
```

Let's also write a function to filter a `std::list` (we assume only a list will be passed). The same can work on `std::vector`. We can compose a higher-order function using the pipe operator. The composite function can also be passed as a predicate:

```
template <typename R, typename F>
R Filter( R r , F&& fn ) {
    R ret(r.size());
    auto first = std::begin(r), last = std::end(r) , result =
std::begin(ret);
    bool inserted = false;
    while (first!=last) {
     if (fn(*first)) { *result = *first; inserted = true; ++result; }
     ++first;
    }
    if ( !inserted ) { ret.clear(); ret.resize(0); }
    return ret;
}
```

In this implementation of Filter, due to limitations in `std::copy_if`, we were forced to roll our own iteration logic. It is generally advised to use the STL implementation of functions to write wrappers. For this particular scenario, we need to detect whether a list is empty or not:

```
//------------------- Global Function to Iterate through the list
void Iterate( list<EXPR_ITEM>& s ){
    for (auto n : s ) { std::cout << n.toString()   << 'n';}
}
```

Let's write a main function to put everything together. The code will demonstrate how to use Map and Filter in the application code. The logic for functional composition and the pipe operator are available in the `FuncCompose.h`:

```
int main( int argc, char **argv ){
    unique_ptr<Expr>
        a(new BinaryExpr( new Number(10.0) , new Number(20.0) ,
OPERATOR::PLUS));
    //------ExprList(Expr *) will flatten the list and Filter will by
applied
    auto cd = Filter( ExprList(&(*a)) ,
            [](auto as) {  return as.knd !=   ExprKind::OPERATOR;} );
    //-----  Square the Value and Multiply by 3... used | as composition
Operator
    //---------- See FuncCompose.h for details
    auto cdr = Map( cd, [] (auto s ) {  s.Value *=3; return s; } |
                [] (auto s ) { s.Value *= s.Value; return s; } );
    Iterate(cdr);
}
```

The `Filter` routine creates a new `list<Expr>`, which contains only the values or operands used in the expression. The `Map` routine applies a composite function on the list of values to return a new list.

Reversing the gaze for Observables!

We have already learned that we can transform a composite to a list and traverse them through an Iterator. The Iterator pattern pulls data from the data source and manipulates the result at the consumer level. The most important problem we face is that we are coupling our `EventSource` and event sink. The GoF Observer pattern also does not help here.

Let's write a class that can act as an event hub, which the sinks will subscribe to. By having an event hub, we will now have an object that will act as an intermediary between the `EventSource` and event sink. One advantage of this indirection is readily obvious from the fact that our class can aggregate, transform, and filter out events before they reach the consumer. The consumer can even set transformation and filtering criteria at the event hub level:

```
//---------------- OBSERVER interface
struct  OBSERVER {
    int id;
    std::function<void(const double)> ondata;
    std::function<void()> oncompleted;
    std::function<void(const std::exception &)> onexception;
};
//--------------- Interface to be implemented by EventSource
struct OBSERVABLE {
    virtual bool Subscribe( OBSERVER * obs ) = 0;
    // did not implement unsuscribe
};
```

We have already covered the `OBSERVABLE` and `OBSERVER` in `Chapter 1`, *Reactive Programming Model – Overview and History* and `Chapter 2`, *A Tour of Modern C++ and its Key Idioms*. The `EventSource` implements `OBSERVABLE` and the event sinks implement the `OBSERVER` interface. A class derived from `OBSERVER` will implement the following methods:

- `ondata` (for receiving data)
- `onexception` (exception processing)
- `oncompleted` (end of the data)

The `EventSource` class will be derived from `OBSERVABLE` and has to implement:

- Subscribe (subscribe to notification)
- Unsubscribe (not implemented in our case)

```
//------------------A toy implementation of EventSource
template<class T,class F,class M, class Marg, class Farg >
class EventSourceValueSubject : public OBSERVABLE {
    vector<OBSERVER> sinks;
    T *State;
    std::function<bool(Farg)> filter_func;
    std::function<Marg(Marg)> map_func;
```

`map_func` and `filter_func` are functions that can help us to transform and filter the values before they are dispatched to the subscribers in an asynchronous manner. We give these values as parameters when we instantiate the `EventSource` class. Currently, we have written the code under the assumption that only the `Expr` object will be stored in the `EventSource`. We can have a list or vector of expressions and Stream the value to the subscribers. For this, implementation a scalar value can be pushed to the listeners:

```
public:
  EventSourceValueSubject(Expr *n,F&& filter, M&& mapper) {
      State = n; map_func = mapper; filter_func = filter; NotifyAll();
  }
  ~EventSourceValueSubject() {  sinks.clear(); }
  //------ used Raw Pointer ...In real life, a shared_ptr<T>
  //------ is more apt here
  virtual  bool Subscribe( OBSERVER  *sink ) { sinks.push_back(*sink);
return true; }
```

We have made some assumptions that the `Expr` objects will be owned by the caller. We have also omitted the implementation of the unsubscribe method. The constructor takes an `Expr` object, a `Filter` predicate (it can be a composite function using the | operator), and a `Mapping` function (it can be a composite function using the | operator):

```
void NotifyAll() {
    double ret = Evaluate(State);
    list<double> ls; ls.push_back(ret);
    auto result = Map( ls, map_func);; // Apply Mapping Logic
    auto resulttr = Filter( result,filter_func); //Apply Filter
    if (resulttr.size() == 0 ) { return; }
```

After evaluating the expression, the scalar value will be put into an STL list. Then, the Map function will be applied on the list to transform the value. In future, we will handle a list of values. Once we have mapped or transformed the values, we will apply a filter to the list. If there is no value in the list, the method returns without notifying the subscribers:

```
    double dispatch_number = resulttr.front();
    for (auto sink : sinks) {
        std::packaged_task<int()> task([&] ()
        { sink.ondata(dispatch_number); return 1;  });
        std::future<int> result = task.get_future();task();
        double dresult = result.get();
    }
}
```

In this code, we will call `packaged_task` to dispatch the data to the event sinks. Industrial-strength libraries use a piece of code called Scheduler to do this part of the task. Since we are using fire and forget, the sinks will not be able to block the `EventSource`. This is one of the most important use cases of Observables:

```
T* GetState() { return State; }
void SetState(T *pstate) { State = pstate; NotifyAll(); }
};
```

Now, let's write a method to emit random expressions based on the modern C++ random number generator with a uniform probability distribution. The choice of this distribution is rather arbitrary. We can try other distributions as well to see different results:

```
Expr *getRandomExpr(int start, int end) {
    std::random_device rd;
    std::default_random_engine reng(rd());
    std::uniform_int_distribution<int> uniform_dist(start, end);
    double mean = uniform_dist(reng);
    return  new
            BinaryExpr( new Number(mean*1.0) , new Number(mean*2.0) ,
OPERATOR::PLUS);
}
```

Now, let's write a main function to put everything together. We will instantiate the `EventSourceValueSubject` class with an `Expr`, a `Filter`, and a `Mapper`:

```
int main( int argc, char **argv ){
    unique_ptr<Expr>
        a(new BinaryExpr( new Number(10) , new Number(20) ,
OPERATOR::PLUS));
    EventSourceValueSubject<Expr,std::function<bool(double)>,
                std::function<double(double)>,double,double>
            temp(&(*a),[] (auto s ) {    return s > 40.0;  },
            []   (auto s ) { return s+ s ; }  |
            []   (auto s ) { return s*2;} );
```

While instantiating the object, we have used the pipe operator to compose two Lambdas. This is to demonstrate that we can compose an arbitrary list of functions to form a composite function. When we write RxCpp programs, we will exploit this technique a lot:

```
OBSERVER obs_one ;        OBSERVER obs_two ;
obs_one.ondata = [](const double  r) {  cout << "*Final Value " <<  r
<< endl;};
obs_two.ondata = [] ( const double r ){ cout << "**Final Value " << r
<< endl;};
```

In this code, we have instantiated two `OBSERVER` objects and assigned them to the ondata member using Lambda functions . We have not implemented other methods. This is for demonstration purposes only:

```
temp.Subscribe(&obs_one); temp.Subscribe(&obs_two);
```

We subscribed to event notification using the `OBSERVER` instances. We have only implemented the ondata method. Implementing `onexception` and `oncompleted` are trivial tasks:

```
Expr *expr = 0;
for( int i= 0; i < 10; ++i ) {
        cout << "---------------------------" <<  i << " "<< endl;
        expr = getRandomExpr(i*2, i*3 ); temp.SetState(expr);
        std::this_thread::sleep_for(2s); delete expr;
    }
}
```

We evaluated a series of random expressions by setting the expression to the `EventSource` object. After transformation and filtering, if there is a value left, the value will be notified to the `OBSERVER` and it will printed to the console. With this, we have managed to write a non-blocking `EventSource` using `packaged_taks`. We have demonstrated the following in this chapter:

- Modeling an expression tree using a Composite
- Processing a Composite through the Visitor interface
- Flattening the expression tree into a list and processing it through Iterators (pull)
- Reversing the gaze from `EventSource` to the event sink (push)

Summary

We have covered a lot of ground in this chapter, inching towards the reactive programming model. We learned about the GoF Observer pattern and understood its shortcomings. Then, we digressed into philosophy to understand the method of looking at the world from a structural, behavioral, and functional perspective. We learned about the GoF Composite/Visitor pattern in the context of modeling an expression tree. We learned how to flatten the hierarchy into a list and navigate them through the Iterator. Finally, we transformed the scheme of things a bit to reach Observables. Normally, Observables work with Streams, but in our case it was a scalar value. In the next chapter, we will learn about event Stream processing to complete our prerequisites for learning reactive programming.

6
Introduction to Event Stream Programming Using C++

This chapter will be the last in the series of pre-requisite chapters required for programming reactive systems using C++. The reason why we need to go through quite a number of concepts is due to the fact that the reactive programming model unifies a lot of computing concepts in realizing its robust programming model. To start thinking in a reactive way, a programmer has to be familiar with object-oriented programming, functional programming, language-level concurrency, lock-free programming, the asynchronous programming model, design patterns, scheduling algorithms, data flow programming model, declarative-style programming, and even a bit of graph theory! We started the book with a peek into the event-driven programming models of various GUI systems and ways to structure our code around them. We covered the core essence of Modern C++ Chapter 2, *A Tour of Modern C++ and its Key Idioms*. In Chapter 3, *Language-Level Concurrency and Parallelism in C++*, and Chapter 4, *Asynchronous and Lock-Free Programming in C++*, we covered the language-level concurrency supported by the C++ language and lock-free programming, respectively. In Chapter 5, *Introduction to Observables*, we focused on how to put the reactive programming model into perspective by dealing with it in the context of GOF patterns. What is left is event Stream programming. Now we will be focusing on the processing of event Streams or event Stream programming. In this chapter, we will look at the following:

- What is the Stream programming model?
- Advantages of the Stream programming model
- Stream programming using C++ with a public domain library
- Stream programming using Streamulus
- Event Stream programming

What is Stream programming model?

Before we get into the topic of the Stream programming model, we will take a step back to look at parallels with the POSIX shell programming model. In a typical command line shell program, every command is a program and every program is a command. We can pipe the output of one program to another program after achieving a computational objective or task. In effect, we can chain a series of commands to achieve bigger computational task. We can see it as a stream of data passing through a series of filters or transformations to fetch the output. We can also call the preceding process as *command composition*. There are real-life cases where huge programs are being replaced by small amount of shell code using *command composition* . The same process can be realized in a C++ program, by treating the input of a function as a stream, sequence, or list. The data can be passed from one function or function object (aka functor) to another as a standard data container.

Dr. Donald Knuth, the legendary computer scientist and Stanford University Professor was asked to write a program that:

- Reads a text file and determines *n* frequently used words
- Prints out a sorted list of words along with their frequencies

Knuth's solution was a ten-page Pascal program! Doug McIlroy realized the same with just the following shell script:

```
tr -cs A-Za-z ' n ' | tr A-Z a-z | sor t | uniq -c | sor
t -rn | sed ${1}q
```

So much for the power of command composition.

Advantages of the Stream programming model

Traditional OOP programs model hierarchies well, and processing hierarchies is mostly a difficult process compared to processing a linear collection. In the case of the Stream programming model, we can treat the input as a stream of entities put into a container and the output as a bag of entities, without modifying the input data stream. Using C++ generic programming techniques, we can write container-agnostic code to process streams. Some advantages of this model are:

- Stream programming simplifies program logic
- Streams can support lazy evaluation and functional style transforms
- Streams are better suited for the concurrent programming model (Source Streams are immutable)

- We can compose functions to create higher-order functions to process them
- Streams facilitate the declarative programming model
- They can aggregate, filter, and transform data from different sources
- They decouple data sources and the entities that process them
- They improve code readability (developers can comprehend code faster)
- They can exploit data parallelism and task parallelism
- We can leverage hundreds of well-defined Stream operators (algorithms) to process data

Applied Stream programming using the Streams library

In this section, we will introduce the topic of Stream programming using the `Streams` library ,a public domain library written by Jonah Scheinerman. The library is hosted at `https://github.com/jscheiny/Streams` and the API documentation is available from `http://jscheiny.github.io/Streams/api.html#`. An introduction has been given as following (taken from the library GitHub page):

> `Streams` is a C++ library that provides lazy evaluation and functional-style transformations on data, to ease the use of C++ standard library containers and algorithms. `Streams` supports many common functional operations such as map, filter, and reduce, as well as various other useful operations such as various set operations (union, intersection, difference), partial sum, and adjacent difference, as well as many others.

We can see that a programmer who is familiar with the **standard template library** (**STL**) will clearly be at ease with this library. The STL Containers are treated as Stream data source and the STL algorithms can be considered as transformations on the Stream data source. The library uses functional programming idioms supported by Modern C++ and also supports lazy evaluation. The concept of lazy evaluation is very significant here, as it is the corner stone of functional programming model and Rx programming model.

Lazy evaluation

In programming languages, there are two prominent ways to evaluate arguments to a function they are as follows:

- **Applicative-order evaluation (AO)**
- **Normal-order evaluation (NO)**

In the case of AO, arguments are evaluated in the calling context, before being passed to the callee. Most conventional programming languages follow this method. In the case of NO, the evaluation of the variables is deferred until the result of the computation is warranted in the context of the callee. Some functional programming languages, such as Haskell, F#, and ML, follow the NO model. In functional programming languages, most of the evaluation of functions is referentially transparent (the invocation of the functions does not produce side-effects); we need to evaluate the expression only once (for a particular value as argument) and the result can be shared, when the evaluation with the same function with the same arguments appears once again for execution. This is called **lazy evaluation**. Thus, lazy evaluation can be considered a NO coupled with sharing of the previously computed results. The C++ programming language does not provide support for lazy evaluation of function parameters by default, but can be emulated using different techniques available such as Variadic Templates and expression templates.

A simple Stream program

To get started with the Streams library, let's write a small program to generate a Stream of numbers and compute the square of the first ten numbers:

```
//--------- Streams_First.cpp
#include "Stream.h"
using namespace std;
using namespace Stream;
using namespace Stream::op;
int main(){
  //-------- counter(n) - Generate a series of value
  //-------- Map (Apply a Lambda)
  //-------- limit(n) -- Take first ten items
  //-------- Sum -- aggregate
  int total = MakeStream::counter(1)
    | map_([] (int x) { return x * x; } // Apply square on each elements
    | limit(10) //take first ten elements
```

```
       | sum();   // sum the Stream contents Streams::op::sum
       //---------- print the result
       cout << total << endl;
   }
```

The previous code snippet generates a list of values (using `MakeStream::counter(1)`) and the generated values will be transformed using the map function (in this case, computing the square). When ten elements are assembled (`limit(10)`) in the Stream, we call the operator sum on the Stream.

Aggregating values using the Stream paradigm

Now that we understand the basics of Stream programming as envisaged by the Stream library, let's write a piece of code that computes the average of numbers stored in a std::vector container:

```
//--------------- Streams_Second.cpp
// g++ -I./Streams-master/sources Streams_Second.cpp
//
#include "Stream.h"
#include <ioStream>
#include <vector>
#include <algorithm>
#include <functional>
using namespace std;
using namespace Stream;
using namespace Stream::op;
int main() {
   std::vector<double> a = { 10,20,30,40,50 };
   //------------ Make a Stream and reduce
   auto val =  MakeStream::from(a)  | reduce(std::plus<void>());
   //------ Compute the arithematic average
   cout << val/a.size() << endl;
}
```

The previous code snippet creates a Stream out of `std::vector` and applies a reduction process using the `std::plus` functor. It is tantamount to aggregating the values in the Stream. Finally, we divide the aggregated value with by the of elements in `std::vector`.

The STL and the Stream paradigm

The `Streams` library can work seamlessly with the STL containers. The following code snippets will map a function on Streams and resultant data is being transformed to a vector container:

```
//--------------- Streams_Third.cpp
// g++ -I./Streams-master/sources Streams_Third.cpp
//
#include "Stream.h"
#include <ioStream>
#include <vector>
#include <algorithm>
#include <functional>
#include <cmath>
using namespace std;
using namespace Stream;
using namespace Stream::op;
double square( double a ) { return a*a; }
int main() {
  std::vector<double> values = { 1,2,3,4,5 };
  std::vector<double> outputs = MakeStream::from(values)
              | map_([] (double a ) { return a*a;})
              | to_vector();
  for(auto pn : outputs )
  { cout << pn << endl; }
}
```

The previous code snippet converts `std::vector<double>` into a Stream, applies the square function, and converts the stuff back to `std:::vector<double>`. After that, the vector is iterated to print the content. The `Streams` library documentation is very elaborate and contains lot of code samples that you can use to write code for production-quality applications. Consult the API documentation, available at `http://jscheiny.github.io/Streams/api.html`.

A word about the Streams library

The `Streams` library is a well-designed piece of software with an intuitive programming model. Any programmer who has worked with a functional programming and Streams programming will really be comfortable with it in a matter of hours. Those of you who are familiar with STL will also find the library to be very intuitive as well. From a programming model perspective, the API can be divided into:

- Core methods (Stream initialization)

- Generators (Stream creators)
- Stateful intermediate operators (functional immutable transformations)
- Stateless intermediate operators
- Terminal operators

The previously mentioned documentation of the library sheds light on the each of the aspects of this wonderful library.

Event Stream programming

We have got some kind of understanding about the working of Stream programming model. When we process events as Streams, it can be categorized as Event Stream programming. In the programming community, event-driven architecture is being projected as a better model for crafting modern programs. A wonderful example of software that relies on Event Stream programming is version control systems. In a version control system, everything is treated as an event. Typical examples include checking out the code, commits, rollbacks, and branching.

Advantages of Event Stream programming

Aggregating events as a Stream and processing them in downstream systems has many advantages compared to the traditional Event programming model. Some of the key advantages are:

- Event source and Event sinks are not coupled
- Event sinks can process events without bothering with Event sources
- We can apply Stream processing operators to process and filter Streams
- The transformation and filtering can be done at the aggregation level
- The events can be propagated through a Stream-processing network
- Event processing can be parallelized easily (declarative parallelism)

The Streamulus library and its programming model

The Streamulus library, from Irit Katiel, is a library that makes the programming of event Streams easier with a programming model, which implements **domain-specific embedded language (DSEL)**. To understand the programming model, let's inspect a program that Streams data into a class that aggregates received data:

```
#include "Streamulus.h"
#include <ioStream>
using namespace std;
using namespace Streamulus;
struct print {
    static double temp;
    print() { }
    template<typename T>
    T operator()(const T& value) const {
        print::temp += value;
        std::cout << print::temp << std::endl;  return value;
    }
};
double print::temp = 0;
```

The preceding functor just accumulates the value passed into a static variable. For each invocation of the function by the `Streamify` template (`Streamify<print>(s)`), the value accumulated so far will be printed to the console. More on this can be understood by going through the listing as follows:

```
void hello_Stream() {
    using namespace Streamulus;
    // Define an input Stream of strings, whose name is "Input Stream"
    InputStream<double> s =
            NewInputStream<double>("Input Stream", true /* verbose */);
    // Construct a Streamulus instance
    Streamulus Streamulus_engine;
```

We create a Stream using the `NewInputStream<T>` template method. The function expects a parameter that determines whether logs should be printed to the console. By giving the second parameter as `false`, we can turn off verbose mode. We need to create an instance of the Streamulus engine to orchestrate the data flow. The Streamulus engine does a topological sort of the Stream expressions to determine the change propagation order:

```
    // For each element of the Stream:
    //     aggregate the received value into a running sum
```

```
//      print it
Streamulus_engine.Subscribe(Streamify<print>( s));
```

We use the `Streamify<f>` strop (Stream operator) to serialize calls to the print functor we just created. We can create our own Stream operators, and usually Streamify would suffice for us. Streamfiy creates a single event functor and a strop:

```
// Insert data to the input Stream
InputStreamPut<double>(s, 10);
InputStreamPut<double>(s, 20);
InputStreamPut<double>(s, 30);
}
int main() {  hello_Stream();   return 0; }
```

The previous code snippets emit some values into the Stream. We would be able to see the accumulated sum to be printed on the console three times. In the main function, we invoke the `hello_Stream` function to trigger all the actions.

Now that we have learned how the Streamulus systems work with a simple program, let's write a program that clarifies the semantics of the library much better. The following program Streams data through a host of single argument functors to demonstrate the functioning of the library. We also use Stream expressions liberally in the listings:

```
////////////////////////////
//  g++ -I"./Streamulus-master/src"  -I<PathToBoost>s Streamulus_second.cpp
#include "Streamulus.h"
#include <ioStream>
using namespace std;
using namespace Streamulus;
//------- Functors for doubling/negating and halfving values
struct twice {
    template<typename T>
    T operator()(const T& value) const {return value*2;}
};
struct neg {
    template<typename T>
    T operator()(const T& value) const{ return -value; }
};
struct half{
    template<typename T>
    T operator()(const T& value) const { return 0.5*value;}
};
```

The preceding set of functors is arithmetical in nature. The `twice` functor doubles the argument, the `neg` functor flips the sign of the argument, and the `half` functor scales the value by 0.5 to halve the value of the argument:

```cpp
struct print{
    template<typename T>
    T operator()(const T& value) const{
        std::cout << value << std::endl;
        return value;
    }
};
struct as_string {
    template<typename T>
    std::string operator()(const T& value) const {
        std::stringStream ss;
        ss << value;
        return ss.str();
    }
};
```

How the preceding two function objects work is obvious—the first one (print) just outputs the value to the console. `as_string` converts the argument to the string using the `std::stringStream` class:

```cpp
void DataFlowGraph(){
    // Define an input Stream of strings, whose name is "Input Stream"
    InputStream<double> s =
            NewInputStream<double>("Input Stream", false /* verbose */);
    // Construct a Streamulus instance
    Streamulus Streamulus_engine;
    // Define a Data Flow Graph for Stream based computation
    Subscription<double>::type val2 =
Streamulus_engine.Subscribe(Streamify<neg>
                        (Streamify<neg>(Streamify<half>(2*s))));
    Subscription<double>::type val3 = Streamulus_engine.Subscribe(
                        Streamify<twice>(val2*0.5));
Streamulus_engine.Subscribe(Streamify<print>(Streamify<as_string>(val3*2)))
;
    //------------------ Ingest data into the Stream
    for (int i=0; i<5; i++)
        InputStreamPut(s, (double)i);
}
```

`DataFlowGraph()` created `InputStream<T>` to process a double-valued Stream. After instantiating the `Streamulus` object (engine), we glued a series of functors through a `Streamify<f>` Stream operator. The operation can be considered a kind of functional composition with a single argument function. After setting up the mechanism, we injected data to the Stream using the `InputStreamPut` function:

```
int main(){
    DataFlowGraph(); //Trigger all action
    return 0;
}
```

The Streamulus library – a peek into its internals

The `Streamulus` library basically creates a change propagation graph to ease Stream processing. We can treat the node of a graph as computation, and the edges as buffers that take the data from one node to another. Almost all data flow systems follow the same semantics. The `Streamulus` library helps us to build a graph of dependent variables, which help us propagate the changes to child nodes. The order in which variables should be updated will be defined by doing a topological sort on the graph.

A graph is a data structure where a set of dependent entities is represented as nodes (or vertices) and their relationship (as edges) between them. In computer science, especially when it comes to scheduling and analyzing dependencies, a particular version of graph, called directed acyclic graphs, is preferred for its unique qualities. A DAG is a directed graph without cycles. We can perform an operation called a topological sort to determine the linear order in which the entities are dependent. The topological sorting can only be performed on a DAG and they are not unique. In the following graph, we can find multiple topological orders:

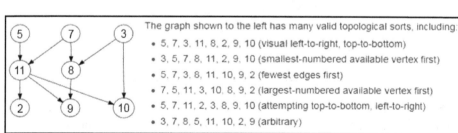

The graph shown to the left has many valid topological sorts, including:

* 5, 7, 3, 11, 8, 2, 9, 10 (visual left-to-right, top-to-bottom)
* 3, 5, 7, 8, 11, 2, 9, 10 (smallest-numbered available vertex first)
* 5, 7, 3, 8, 11, 10, 9, 2 (fewest edges first)
* 7, 5, 11, 3, 10, 8, 9, 2 (largest-numbered available vertex first)
* 5, 7, 11, 2, 3, 8, 9, 10 (attempting top-to-bottom, left-to-right)
* 3, 7, 8, 5, 11, 10, 2, 9 (arbitrary)

The Streamulus Library – a look into expression processing

We will take a look at how `Streamulus` processes expressions using a simple Stream expression:

```
InputStream<int>::type x = NewInputStream<int>("X");
Engine.Subscribe( -(x+1));
```

The `– (x+1)` Stream expression will produce the following graph. The term strop stands for Stream operators and each of the nodes is organized as a strop:

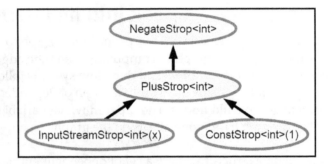

Once the node has been labeled correctly, a topological sort on the graph will be done to determine the execution order. The following diagram shows a topological sort (you can have multiple topological orders):

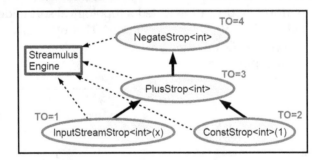

The Streamulus engine walks through the graph to find out the order in which Stream operators have to be applied on the data propagating through the network. The **TO** label stands for **topological order**. After topological sort, a linear list of Stream operators ranked by Topological order will be produced. The execution engine will execute the code in topological order.

The Streamulus engine performs its magic using the boost proto library. The latter manages expression trees for the Streamulus library. To really go through the source code of the library, you need to be comfortable with template meta programming, especially expression templates. Meta programming is a technique where we write code to generate or transform source code. It turned out that the C++ template mechanism was Turing complete by Erwin Unruh in the year 1994.

The spreadsheet Library — a change-propagation engine

An electronic spreadsheet is often touted as the quintessential example of a reactive system. In a spreadsheet, a page is organized as a matrix of cells. When there is a change in a cell, all dependent cells will be re-computed to reflect the change. This happens for every cell. In effect, modelling a spreadsheet is easy, if you have a library such as Streamulus. Fortunately, the designer of the library itself wrote another library that relies on Streamulus for change propagation.

 Spreadsheet is a C++ library that enables spreadsheet-programming, that is, setting up variables (cells) where each cell is assigned an expression that can contain the values of other cells. Changes are propagated to all dependent cells, as in a spreadsheet. Spreadsheet was developed to demonstrate the use of Streamulus. Spreadsheet is a header-only library. It uses boost and Streamulus. So put these three libraries in your include path. The details of the library can be found at `https://github.com/iritkatriel/spreadsheet`.

We will go through a sample program that leverages the `Spreadsheet` library, which is included in the project's GitHub repository (`main.cpp`):

```
#include "spreadsheet.hpp"
#include <ioStream>
int main (int argc, const char * argv[]) {
    using namespace spreadsheet;
    Spreadsheet sheet;
    Cell<double> a = sheet.NewCell<double>();
    Cell<double> b = sheet.NewCell<double>();
    Cell<double> c = sheet.NewCell<double>();
    Cell<double> d = sheet.NewCell<double>();
    Cell<double> e = sheet.NewCell<double>();
    Cell<double> f = sheet.NewCell<double>();
```

The previous code snippet creates a set of cells, which acts as a container for IEEE double-precision floating-point numbers. After we have initialized the cell, we will start mutating the values of the cell with the following set of expressions:

```
c.Set(SQRT(a()*a() + b()*b()));
a.Set(3.0);
b.Set(4.0);
d.Set(c()+b());
e.Set(d()+c());
```

Now, we will mutate the values with the preceding expressions. After each assignment through the Set method, a computational pass will get triggered through the cells. The Streamulus library manages the underlying flow:

```
std::cout << " a=" << a.Value()
          << " b=" << b.Value()
          << " c=" << c.Value()
          << " d=" << d.Value()
          << " e=" << e.Value()
          << std::endl;
```

The previous code snippet prints the value of the cells to the console. Once again, we will change the cells' expressions to trigger a computational flow graph:

```
c.Set(2*(a()+b()));
c.Set(4*(a()+b()));
c.Set(5*(a()+b()));
c.Set(6*(a()+b()));
c.Set(7*(a()+b()));
c.Set(8*(a()+b()));
c.Set(a());
std::cout << " a=" << a.Value()
          << " b=" << b.Value()
          << " c=" << c.Value()
          << " d=" << d.Value()
          << " e=" << e.Value()
          << std::endl;
std::cout << "Goodbye!n";
return 0;
}
```

The source code of the library can be perused to understand the internal workings of the library. A spreadsheet is a wonderful example of how the Streamulus library can be leveraged to write robust software.

RaftLib – another Stream-processing library

RaftLib is a library that is worth checking out for anyone (developers) who are interested in doing parallel programming or Stream-based programming. The library is available at `https://github.com/RaftLib/RaftLib` . The following description is available from the preceding site

> RaftLib is a C++ Library for enabling Stream/data-flow parallel computation. Using simple right-shift operators (just like the C++ Streams that you would use for string manipulation), you can link parallel compute kernels together. With RaftLib, we do away with explicit use of pthreads, std::thread, OpenMP, or any other parallel threading library. These are often mis-used, creating non-deterministic behavior. RaftLib's model allows lock-free FIFO-like access to the communications channels connecting each compute kernel. The full system has many auto-parallelization, optimization, and convenience features that enable relatively simple authoring of performant applications.

We won't be covering `RaftLib` in detail in this particular book, due to space constraints. A wonderful talk by the author of the library (Jonathan Beard) is available at `https://www.youtube.com/watch?v=IiQ787fJgmU`. Let's go through a code snippet that shows the working of this library:

```
#include <raft>
#include <raftio>
#include <cstdlib>
#include <string>

class hi : public raft::kernel
{
public:
    hi() : raft::kernel(){ output.addPort< std::string >( "0" ); }
    virtual raft::kstatus run(){
        output[ "0" ].push( std::string( "Hello Worldn" ) );
        return( raft::stop );
    }
};

int main( int argc, char **argv ) {
    /** instantiate print kernel **/
    raft::print< std::string > p;
    /** instantiate hello world kernel **/
    hi hello;
    /** make a map object **/
    raft::map m;
```

```
        /** add kernels to map, both hello and p are executed concurrently **/
        m += hello >> p;
        /** execute the map **/
        m.exe();
        return( EXIT_SUCCESS );
    }
```

As a programmer, you are supposed to define a kernel for custom computation and use the >> operator to Stream the data. In the preceding code, the `hi` class is such a kernel. Consult the `Raftlib` documentation (available at the preceding RaftLib URL) and source code examples to learn more about this wonderful library.

What do these things have to do with Rx programming?

Basically, the reactive programming model treats events as a Stream of data propagating through a change-propagation graph. For this to happen, we need to aggregate event elements to a container-based data structure and create a Stream out of that. Sometimes, we even apply statistical techniques to sample events, if there is plenty of data. The generated Stream can be filtered and transformed at the source level using functional transformation, before being notified to the observers who are waiting to get notified. The event source is supposed to take a fire-and-forget approach to event-Stream dispatch, to avoid the coupling between Event source sinks and the Event sinks . When to dispatch the event data will be determined by scheduling software which runs the functional transformation pipeline in an asynchronous manner. So, the key elements of reactive programming are:

- Observables (a Stream of data in which others are interested)
- Observer (entities which is interested in an Observable and Subscribe for notification)
- Scheduler (which determines when the Stream should be propagated down the network)
- Functional Operators (event filtering and transformation)

In a nutshell, the `Scheduler` (part of the Rx Engine) takes an `Observable` for filtering and transformation asynchronously before notifying the subscribers, as shown:

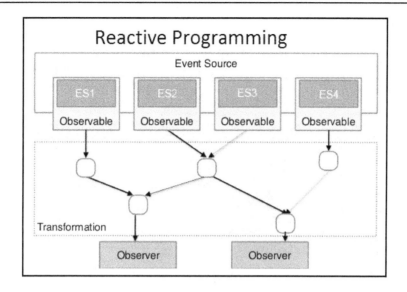

Summary

In this chapter, we covered the topic of event Stream programming. Treating events as Streams has many advantages over the traditional event-processing model. We started with the Streams library and learned about its programming model. We also wrote some programs to familiarize ourselves with the library and its semantics. The Streams library has excellent documentation and you should consult its documentation to learn more about it. After Streams library, we looked at the Streamulus library, which provides a DSEL approach to the manipulation of event Streams. We wrote a couple of programs and also studied some sample programs that come with the Streamulus library. We also mentioned the Raftlib library, an alternative library for the Stream processing . With the coverage of Event Stream programming model, We have now finished dealing with the prerequisites for understanding reactive programming in general and the RxCpp library in particular. In the next chapter, we will start using the RxCpp library to get into the programming model of the reactive system design.

7
Introduction to Data Flow Computation and the RxCpp Library

From this chapter onward, we will get into meat of the reactive programming model. You can consider earlier chapters as a kind of prerequisite for understanding the reactive programming model, more specifically reactive programming using the C++ programming language. If we look back, we covered the necessary prerequisites, which includes the following:

- The event programming models on various GUI platforms
- A whirlwind tour of the Modern C++ language (including functional programming)
- Language-level concurrency in C++ for better concurrent systems
- Lock-free programming models (as a step towards declarative programming)
- Advanced design patterns and the concept of Observables
- Event Stream programming using C++

All of these topics come together in a systematic manner in the case of **functional reactive programming** (**FRP**). The FRP acronym is used here in the loose sense of programming reactive systems using functional programming constructs.

Simply put, reactive programming is nothing but programming with asynchronous data streams. By applying various operations on streams, we can achieve different computational goals. The primary task in a reactive program is to convert data into streams, regardless of the source of the data. The Event Streams are typically called **Observables** and event Stream subscribers are called **Observers**. Between Observables and Observers, there are Stream Operators (filters/transforms).

Since it is implicitly assumed that the data source won't be mutated while data is passed through Operators, we can have multiple Operator paths between Observables and Observers. Immutability gives options for out-of-order execution, and scheduling can be delegated to a special piece of software called a Scheduler. Thus Observables, Observers, Stream Operators, and Schedulers form the backbone of the reactive programming model.

In this chapter, we will cover following topics:

- A short discussion about the data flow computing paradigm
- Introduction to the RxCpp library and its programming model
- Some basic RxCpp programs to get our feet wet
- Rx Stream Operators
- Marble diagrams
- Scheduling
- `flatmap`/`concatmap` oddities
- Additional Rx Operators

The data flow computation paradigm

Traditionally, programmers encode computer programs in terms of control flow. That means we encode programs as a series of small statements (sequence, branching, iteration) or functions (including recursive), with their associated states. We use constructs, such as selection (`if`/`else`), iteration (`while`/`for`), and functions (recursive functions as well), to encode our computation. Handling concurrency and state management for these types of program are really difficult and they lead to subtle bugs while managing state information which are mutable in nature. We need to place locks and other synchronization primitives around shared mutable states. At the compiler level, the language compiler will parse the source code to generate an **abstract syntax tree** (**AST**), do type analysis, and code generation. In fact, AST is an information flow graph where you can perform data-flow analysis (for data/register level optimization) and control-flow analysis to exploit code pipeline optimization at the processor level. Even though programmers encode programs in terms of control flow, the compiler (at least some part of it) tries to see the program in terms of data flow as well. The bottom line here is the fact that there is an implicit data flow graph dormant in every computer program.

The data flow computation organizes computation as an explicit graph, where nodes are computations and edges are paths for data to flow between the nodes. If we place certain restrictions such as preservation of the data state by working on a copy of the input data, (the avoidance of in-place algorithms) on computations at the nodes in a computational graph, we can exploit opportunities for parallelism. The Scheduler will find opportunities for parallelism by doing a topological sort on the graph data structure. We will construct the graph data structure using streams (`Path`) and operations on streams (`Node`). This can be done declaratively, as Operators can be encoded as lambdas, which do some local computations on node. There is a set of primitive standard (functional/stream) Operators, such as `map`, `reduce`, `filter`, `take and so on`, are identified by the functional programming community which works on streams. There is a provision in every data flow computation framework to convert data into streams. The TensorFlow library for machine learning is one library that uses the data flow paradigm. The RxCpp library can also be considered as a data flow computation library, even though graph creation process is not fully explicit, as in the case of TensorFlow library. Since functional programming constructs support lazy evaluation, we are effectively creating a computation flow graph, when we construct a stream pipeline with asynchronous data streams and operations. These graphs are executed by a scheduling sub system.

An introduction to the RxCpp library

We will be using the RxCpp library to write our reactive programs for rest of the book. The RxCpp library is a header-only C++ library that can be downloaded from a GitHub repo: `http://reactive-extensions.github.io/RxCpp/`. The RxCpp library relies on Modern C++ constructs, such as language-level concurrency, lambda functions/expressions, functional composition/transformation, and operator-overloading, to implement reactive programming constructs. The RxCpp library is structured along the lines of libraries such as `Rx.net` and `Rxjava`. Like any other reactive programming framework, there are some key constructs that everyone should understand before they write the first line of code. They are:

- Observables (Observable Streams)
- Observers (who subscribe to the Observables)
- Operators (for example, filters, transformations, and reductions)
- Schedulers

RxCpp is a header-only library and most of the computation is based on the notion of Observables. The library provides lot of primitives to create Observable Streams from various data sources. The data sources can be Arrays, C++ Ranges, STL containers, and so on. We can place Operators between Observables and their consumers (monikered as Observers). Since functional programming support composition of functions, we can place a chain of operators as a single entity between Observables and Observers who subscribe to the Streams. The Scheduler associated with the library will make sure that when data is available in Observable Streams, it will be passed through the series of Operators and a notification will be issued to subscribers. The Observers will get notification through on_next,on_completed or on_error lambdas, whenever something significant happens in the pipeline. Thus, Observers can focus on tasks for which they are primarily responsible, as data will reach them through notification.

The RxCpp library and its programming model

In this section, we will write some programs that will help the reader to understand the programming model of the RxCpp library. The aim of these programs is to elucidate Rx concepts and they are mostly trivial in nature. The code will be sufficient for a programmer to incorporate them into a production implementation with minor tweaks. In this section, Data producers and their Observables will be based on C++ ranges, STL containers, and so on to make the listings simple enough to digest the core concepts outlined here

A simple Observable/Observer interaction

Let's write a simple program that help us understand the programming model of the RxCpp library. In this particular program, we will have an Observable Stream and an Observer that subscribes to the Stream. We will generate a series of numbers from 1 to 12, using a range object. After creating the range of values and an Observable over them, we will attach them together When we execute the program, it will print a series of numbers to the console. Finally, a literal string ("Oncompleted") will also be printed on the console. :

```
//////////
// First.cpp
// g++ -I<PathToRxCpplibfoldersrc> First.cpp
#include "rxcpp/rx.hpp"
#include <ioStream>
int main() {
  //------------- Create an Observable.. a Stream of numbers
  //------------- Range will produce a sequence from 1 to 12
  auto observable = rxcpp::observable<>::range(1, 12);
```

```
//------------ Subscribe (only OnNext and OnCompleted Lambda given
observable.Subscribe(
    [](int v){printf("OnNext: %dn", v);},
    [](){printf("OnCompleted\n");});
}
```

The preceding program will display numbers to the console and the literal string "OnCompleted "will also be displayed on the console. This program demonstrates how we can create an Observable Stream and connect an Observer to the the created Observable Stream using the subscribe method.

Filters and Transformations with Observables

The following program will help us to understand how filter and map Operators work, besides the usual mechanism of connecting an Observer to Observable Streams ,using the subscribe method. The filter method evaluates a predicate on each item of the Stream, and if the evaluation happens to produce a positive assertion, the item will be present in the output Stream. The map operator applies a lambda expression on each element of its input Stream and helps produce an output value every time (which can be propagated through the pipeline):

```
/////////////////////////////////////
// Second.cpp
#include "rxcpp/rx.hpp"
#include <ioStream>
int main() {
  auto values = rxcpp::observable<>::range(1, 12).
      filter([](int v){ return v % 2 ==0 ;}).
      map([](int x) {return x*x;});
  values.subscribe(
          [](int v){printf("OnNext: %dn", v);},
          [](){printf("OnCompleted\n");});
}
```

The preceding program generates a series of numbers (as an Observable) and passes content of the Stream through a filter function. The filter function tries to detect whether the number is even. if the predicate is true , the data will be passed to the map function, which will square its input. Eventually, the contents of the Stream will be displayed on to the console.

Streaming values from C++ containers

The data in STL containers are considered as the data which exists in space.(data which are already captured). Even though Rx streams are meant for processing data varying over time (dynamic), we can convert an STL container into a Rx Stream. We need to use Iterate operator to do the conversion. This can be handy at times and has been helpful in integrating code from code bases that use STL:

```cpp
// STLContainerStream.cpp
#include "rxcpp/rx.hpp"
#include <ioStream>
#include <array>
int main() {
    std::array< int, 3 > a={{1, 2, 3}};
    auto values = rxcpp::observable<>::iterate(a);
    values.subscribe([](int v){printf("OnNext: %dn", v);},
    [](){printf("OnCompleted\n");});
}
```

Creating Observables from the scratch

So far, we have written code that create an Observable Stream from a range object or STL containers. Let's see how we can create an Observable Stream from the scratch. Well, almost:

```cpp
// ObserverFromScratch.cpp
#include "rxcpp/rx.hpp"
#include "rxcpp/rx-test.hpp"
int main() {
    auto ints = rxcpp::observable<>::create<int>(
            [](rxcpp::subscriber<int> s){
                s.on_next(1);
                s.on_next(4);
                s.on_next(9);
                s.on_completed();
            });
    ints.subscribe( [](int v){printf("OnNext: %dn", v);},
                        [](){printf("OnCompletedn");});
}
```

The preceding program calls the `on_ext` method to emit a series of numbers that are perfect squares. Those numbers (1,4,9) will be printed to the console.

Concatenating Observable Streams

We can concatenate two Streams to form a new Stream and this can be handy in some cases. Let's see how this works by writing a simple program:

```
//-------------- Concactatenate.cpp
#include "rxcpp/rx.hpp"
#include "rxcpp/rx-test.hpp"
int main() {
  auto values = rxcpp::observable<>::range(1);
  auto s1 = values.take(3).map([](int prime) { return 2*prime;);});
  auto s2 = values.take(3).map([](int prime) { return prime*prime);});
  s1.concat(s2).subscribe(rxcpp::util::apply_to(
          []( int p) { printf(" %dn", p);}));
}
```

The concat Operator append the contents of constituent Observable Streams one after another by preserving the order. In the preceding code,after creating an Observable (values), we did create two additional Observables (s1 and s2) and did append the content generated by second Observable stream (s2) to produce a combined Observable Stream (s1.concat(s2)). Finally, we subscribed to the Combined Observable.

Unsubscribing from Observable Streams

The following program shows how one can subscribe to an Observable and stop the subscription, if it is warranted. in the case of some programs ,this option is very useful. Please consult the Rxcpp documentation to understand more about the subscription and how one can use them effectively. In the mean time, following program will demonstrate how cone can un-subscribe from a Observable.

```
//--------------- Unsubscribe.cpp
#include "rxcpp/rx.hpp"
#include "rxcpp/rx-test.hpp"
#include <iostream>
int main() {
    auto subs = rxcpp::composite_subscription();
    auto values = rxcpp::observable<>::range(1, 10);
    values.subscribe(
        subs, [&subs](int v){
            printf("OnNext: %dn", v);
            if (v == 6)
                subs.unsubscribe(); //-- Stop recieving events
        },
        [](){printf("OnCompletedn");});
}
```

In the above program, when the value emitted reaches a thresh hold value, we do call unsubscribe (subs.unsubscribe ()) method.

An introduction to marble diagrams for visual representation

It is difficult to visualize Rx Streams, as the data flows asynchronously. The designers of Rx systems have created a set of visualization cues called **marble diagrams**: Let us write a small program and depict logic of the map Operator as a marble diagram.

```
//------------------ Map.cpp
#include "rxcpp/rx.hpp"
#include "rxcpp/rx-test.hpp"
#include <ioStream>
#include <array>
int main() {
    auto ints = rxcpp::observable<>::range(1,10).
                map( [] ( int n  ) {return n*n; });
    ints.subscribe(
            [](int v){printf("OnNext: %dn", v);},
            [](){printf("OnCompletedn");});
}
```

Rather than giving a description of marble diagrams, let's look at a marble diagram that depicts the map operator:

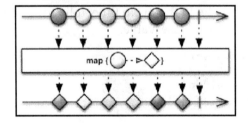

The top part of the marble diagram shows a timeline where a series of values (represented as circles) are displayed. Each of the value will be passing through a map Operator, which takes a lambda as parameter. The lambda will be applied on each element of the Stream to produce the output Stream (shown in the bottom part of the diagram as a diamond).

RxCpp (Stream) Operators

One of the primary advantage of Stream-oriented processing is the fact that we can apply functional programming primitives on them. In RxCpp parlance, the processing is done using Operators. They are nothing but filters, transformations, aggregations, and reductions on Streams. We have already seen how the `map`, `filter`, and `take` operators work in the previous examples. Let us explore them further.

The average Operator

The `average` Operator computes arithmetic mean of values from Observable Streams. The other statistical Operators supported include:

- Min
- Max
- Count
- Sum

The following program just demonstrates the `average` Operator. The schema is the same for other operators in the preceding list:

```cpp
//----------- Average.cpp
#include "rxcpp/rx.hpp"
#include "rxcpp/rx-test.hpp"
#include <ioStream>
int main() {
    auto values = rxcpp::observable<>::range(1, 20).average();
    values.subscribe(
            [](double v){printf("average: %lfn", v);},
            [](){printf("OnCompletedn");});
}
```

The Scan Operator

The `scan` Operator applies a function on each element of a Stream sequentially and accumulates the value into a seed value. The following program produces average of a series of numbers as and when the values are accumulated:

```cpp
//----------- Scan.cpp
#include "rxcpp/rx.hpp"
#include "rxcpp/rx-test.hpp"
#include <ioStream>
```

```
int main() {
    int count = 0;
    auto values = rxcpp::observable<>::range(1, 20).
        scan( 0,[&count](int seed, int v){
                count++;
                return seed + v;
            });
    values.subscribe(
        [&](int v){printf("Average through Scan: %fn", (double)v/count);},
        [](){printf("OnCompletedn");});
}
```

The running average will be printed on to the console. `OnNext  functor` will be called twenty times before `OnCompleted` is called.

Composing Operators through the pipe Operator

The RxCpp library allows devolopers to chain or compose Operators to enable Operator composition. The library allows you to use the `pipe` (|) Operator to compose Operators (instead of the usual fluent interface using the "."), and programmers can pipe the output of one Operator to another as if they are in the command line of a UNIX shell. This assists in comprehension (about what a piece of code does). The following program uses the | Operator to map a range. The RxCpp samples contain many examples using pipe functions:

```
//------------------ Map_With_Pipe.cpp
#include "rxcpp/rx.hpp"
#include "rxcpp/rx-test.hpp"
namespace Rx {
using namespace rxcpp;
using namespace rxcpp::sources;
using namespace rxcpp::operators;
using namespace rxcpp::util;
}
using namespace Rx;
#include <ioStream>
int main() {
    //---------- chain map to the range using the pipe operator
    //---------- avoids the use of . notation.
    auto ints = rxcpp::observable<>::range(1,10) |
                map( [] ( int n  ) {return n*n; });
    ints.subscribe(
            [](int v){printf("OnNext: %dn", v);},
            [](){printf("OnCompletedn");});
}
```

Working with Schedulers

We have already learned about Observables, Operators, and Observers , in the above section. We now know that, between Observables and Observers, we can apply standard Rx Operators to filter and transform streams. In the case of Functional Programming, we write immutable functions (functions without side-effects) and a consequence of immutability is the potential for an out-of-order execution. The order in which we execute a function/functor does not matter, if we can guarantee that the input to an Operator is never modified. Since an Rx program will be manipulating multiple Observables and Observers, we can delegate the task of choosing the execution order to a Scheduler module. By default, Rxcpp is single threaded. The RxCpp will schedule the execution of Operators in the thread which we called the `subscribe` method. It is possible to specify a different thread using the `observe_on` and `subscribe_on` operators. Also, some Observable Operators take a Scheduler as a parameter, where execution can happen in a thread managed by the Scheduler.

The RxCpp library supports the following two Scheduler types:

- `ImmediateScheduler`
- `EventLoopScheduler`

The RxCpp library is single-threaded by default. But you can configure it to run in multiple threads using certain operators:

```
//----------ObserveOn.cpp
#include "rxcpp/rx.hpp"
#include "rxcpp/rx-test.hpp"
#include <ioStream>
#include <thread>
int main(){
 //--------------- Generate a range of values
 //--------------- Apply Square function
 auto values = rxcpp::observable<>::range(1,4).
              map([](int v){ return v*v;});
 //------------ Emit the current thread details
 std::cout  << "Main Thread id => "
            << std::this_thread::get_id()
            << std::endl;
 //---------- observe_on another thread....
 //---------- make it blocking to
 //--------- Consult the Rxcpp documentation on observe_on and schedulers
 values.observe_on(rxcpp::synchronize_new_thread()).as_blocking().
 subscribe( [](int v){
                std::cout << "Observable Thread id => "
                          << std::this_thread::get_id()
```

```
                                << "  " << v << std::endl ;},
                    []()( std::cout << "OnCompleted" << std::endl; });
    //------------------ Print the main thread details
    std::cout << "Main Thread id => "
            << std::this_thread::get_id()
            << std::endl;
    }
```

The preceding program will produce the following output. We will be using the STD C++ thread ID to help us distinguish the items scheduled in the new thread (one of which is different from the main thread):

```
Main Thread id => 1
Observable Thread id => 2    1
Observable Thread id => 2    4
Observable Thread id => 2    9
Observable Thread id => 2    16
OnCompleted
Main Thread id => 1
```

The following program will demonstrate the usage of the subscribe_on method. There are subtle differences between the observe_on and subscribe_on methods in terms of behavior. The purpose of the following listing is to show the options available for declarative scheduling:

```
//----------- SubscribeOn.cpp
#include "rxcpp/rx.hpp"
#include "rxcpp/rx-test.hpp"
#include <ioStream>
#include <thread>
#include <mutex>
//------ A global mutex for output synch.
std::mutex console_mutex;
//------ Print the Current Thread details
void CTDetails() {
    console_mutex.lock();
    std::cout << "Current Thread id => "
            << std::this_thread::get_id()   << std::endl;
    console_mutex.unlock();
}
//---------- a function to Yield control to other threads
void Yield( bool y ) {
    if (y) { std::this_thread::yield(); }

}
int main(){
    auto threads = rxcpp::observe_on_event_loop();
```

```
    auto values = rxcpp::observable<>::range(1);
    //------------- Schedule it in another thread
    auto s1 = values.subscribe_on(threads).
        map([](int prime) {
            CTDetails(); Yield(true); return std::make_tuple("1:",
prime);});
    //-------- Schedule it in Yet another theread
    auto s2 = values. subscribe_on(threads).
        map([](int prime) {
            CTDetails(); Yield(true) ; return std::make_tuple("2:",
prime);});

    s1.merge(s2). take(6).as_blocking().subscribe(rxcpp::util::apply_to(
        [](const char* s, int p) {
            CTDetails();
            console_mutex.lock();
            printf("%s %dn", s, p);
            console_mutex.unlock();
        }));
}
```

A tale of two Operators – flatmap versus concatmap

A source of confusion among developers is often centered around the flatmap and concatmap Operators. Their differences are really important and we will cover them in this section. Let's take a look at the flatmap operator and how it works:

```
//----------- Flatmap.cpp
#include "rxcpp/rx.hpp"
#include "rxcpp/rx-test.hpp"
#include <ioStream>
namespace rxu=rxcpp::util;
#include <array>
int main() {
    std::array< std::string, 4 > a={{"Praseed", "Peter", "Sanjay","Raju"}};
    //---------- Apply Flatmap on the array of names
    //---------- Flatmap returns an Observable<T> ( map returns T )
    //---------- The First lamda creates a new Observable<T>
    //---------- The Second Lambda manipulates primary Observable and
    //---------- Flatmapped Observable
    auto values = rxcpp::observable<>::iterate(a).flat_map(
        [] (std::string v ) {
            std::array<std::string,3> salutation=
                { { "Mr." ,  "Monsieur" , "Sri" }};
```

```
                    return rxcpp::observable<>::iterate(salutation);
            },
            [] ( std::string f , std::string s ) {return s + " " +f;});
    //-------- As usual subscribe
    //-------- Here the value will be interleaved as flat_map merges the
    //-------- Two Streams
    values.subscribe(
            [] (std::string f) { std::cout << f <<  std::endl; } ,
            [] () {std::cout << "Hello World.." << std::endl;} );
    }
```

The previous program produces output sequence which are not predictable. The output of one run of the program is shown as follows. This need not be what we get when we run it again. The reason for this behavior has to do with the post processing of the Stream after the mapping operation: The flatmap uses merge Operator for post processing of Streams.

```
Mr. Praseed
Monsieur Praseed
Mr. Peter
Sri Praseed
Monsieur Peter
Mr. Sanjay
Sri Peter
Monsieur Sanjay
Mr. Raju
Sri Sanjay
Monsieur Raju
Sri Raju
Hello World..
```

The following marble diagram shows schema of the operation. The `flat_map` applies the lambda on the Observable Stream and produces a new Observable Stream. The Streams produced are merged together to provide the output. In the diagram, the red ball gets transformed into a pair of red colored diamonds, whereas the output of the green and blue balls produces interleaved diamonds as output in the newly created Observable:

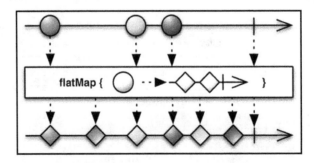

Let us look at the `concat_map` operator by going through the listing given below. The program listing is identical to the earlier program. The only change is the substitution of the `flat_map` with `concat_map`. Even though there is no practical difference in the listing, there is a marked difference in the output behavior. Maybe `concat_map` produces output that suits the synchronized mental model of the programmer:

```cpp
//----------- ConcatMap.cpp
#include "rxcpp/rx.hpp"
#include "rxcpp/rx-test.hpp"
#include <ioStream>
namespace rxu=rxcpp::util;

#include <array>
int main() {

    std::array< std::string,4 > a={{"Praseed", "Peter", "Sanjay","Raju"}};
    //---------- Apply Concat map on the array of names
    //---------- Concat Map returns an Observable<T> ( oncat returns T )
    //---------- The First lamda creates a new Observable<T>
    //---------- The Second Lambda manipulates primary Observable and
    //---------- Concatenated Observable
    auto values = rxcpp::observable<>::iterate(a).flat_map(
            [] (std::string v ) {
                std::array<std::string,3> salutation=
                    { { "Mr." , "Monsieur" , "Sri" }};
                return rxcpp::observable<>::iterate(salutation);
            },
            [] ( std::string f , std::string s ) {return s + " " +f;});

    //-------- As usual subscribe
    //-------- Here the value will be interleaved as concat_map concats
the
    //-------- Two Streams
    values.subscribe(
            [] (std::string f) { std::cout << f <<  std::endl; } ,
            [] () {std::cout << "Hello World.." << std::endl;} );
}
```

Here is how the output will look:

```
Mr. Praseed
Monsieur Praseed
Sri Praseed
Mr. Peter
Monsieur Peter
Sri Peter
Mr. Sanjay
```

```
Monsieur Sanjay
Sri Sanjay
Mr. Raju
Monsieur Raju
Sri Raju
Hello World..
```

The following marble diagram shows `concat_map` in operation. Unlike the Flatmap marble diagram, the output is synchronized (red, green, and blue balls produce the same colored output in the order in which the input is processed):

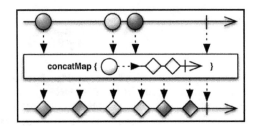

In the case of `flat_map`, we got the output in an interleaved manner. But in the case of `concat_map`, we got the value in the order that we expected the output. What is the real difference here? To make the difference clear, let's take a look at two operators: `concat` and `merge`. Let's look into the way the concatenation of the Streams works. It basically appends the contents of the Stream one after the another, preserving the order:

```
//---------------- Concat.cpp
#include "rxcpp/rx.hpp"
#include "rxcpp/rx-test.hpp"
#include <ioStream>
#include <array>
int main() {
    auto o1 = rxcpp::observable<>::range(1, 3);
    auto o3 = rxcpp::observable<>::from(4, 6);
    auto values = o1.concat(o2);
    values.subscribe(
            [](int v){printf("OnNext: %dn",
v);},[](){printf("OnCompletedn");});
    }
```

The following marble diagram clearly shows what happens when a `concat` Operator is applied on two Streams. We create a new Stream by appending contents of the second Stream to the contents of the first. This preserves the order:

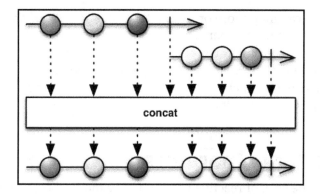

Now, let's see what happens when two Streams are merged. The following code shows how you can merge two Streams:

```cpp
//------------ Merge.cpp
#include "rxcpp/rx.hpp"
#include "rxcpp/rx-test.hpp"
#include <ioStream>
#include <array>
int main() {
    auto o1 = rxcpp::observable<>::range(1, 3);
    auto o2 = rxcpp::observable<>::range(4, 6);
    auto values = o1.merge(o2);
    values.subscribe(
            [](int v){printf("OnNext: %dn", v);},
            [](){printf("OnCompletedn");});
}
```

The following marble diagram clearly shows what happens when we merge two Observable Streams. The contents of the output Stream will be an interleaved combination of two Streams:

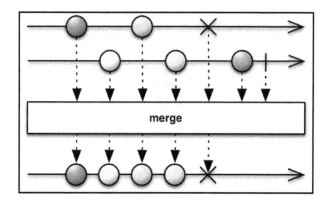

Both flat_map and concat_map more or less do the same operation. The difference lies in the way values are combined together. The `flat_map` uses the `merge` Operator, while the `concact_map` uses the `concact` Operator for post processing of results. In the case of `merge`, the order does not matter. The `concat` operator appends Observables one after the another. That is why you got synchronized output with concat_map and flat_map produced irregularly ordered results.

Other Important Operators

We now understand the crux of reactive programming model, because we covered basic topics such as Observables, Observers, Operators, and Schedulers. There are some more Operators we should know about to write our logic better. In this section, we will cover the `tap`, `defer` and `buffer` Operators. We will first explore the `tap` Operator, which helps peek into the contents of the Stream:

```
//----------- TapExample.cpp
#include "rxcpp/rx.hpp"
#include "rxcpp/rx-test.hpp"
#include <ioStream>
int main() {
    //---- Create a mapped Observable
    auto ints = rxcpp::observable<>::range(1,3).
                map( [] ( int n  ) {return n*n; });
    //---- Apply the tap operator...The Operator
    //---- will act as a filter/debug operator
    auto values = ints.tap(
        [](int v)  {printf("Tap -        OnNext: %dn", v);},
        [](){printf("Tap -        OnCompletedn");
    });
    //------- Do some action
    values.subscribe(
        [](int v){printf("Subscribe - OnNext: %dn", v);},
        [](){printf("Subscribe - OnCompletedn");});
}
```

Now, let's take a look at the `defer` operator. The `defer` operator takes an Observable factory as a parameter to create Observable for each client that subscribes to it. In the following program, we invoke the `observable_factory` lambda when somebody tries to connect to the specified Observable:

```
//----------- DeferExample.cpp
#include "rxcpp/rx.hpp"       '
#include "rxcpp/rx-test.hpp"
#include <ioStream>
```

```
int main() {
    auto observable_factory = [](){
        return rxcpp::observable<>::range(1,3).
            map( [] ( int n ) {return n*n; });
    };
    auto ints = rxcpp::observable<>::defer(observable_factory);
    ints.subscribe([](int v){printf("OnNext: %dn", v);},
        [](){printf("OnCompletedn");});
    ints.subscribe(
        [](int v){printf("2nd OnNext: %dn", v);},
        [](){printf("2nd OnCompletedn");});
}
```

The `buffer` Operator emits an Observable that contains the non-overlapping contents of an Observable, each containing at most the number of items specified by the count parameter. This will help us to process the items in a manner suitable for the content:

```
//----------- BufferExample.cpp
#include "rxcpp/rx.hpp"
#include "rxcpp/rx-test.hpp"
#include <ioStream>
int main() {
    auto values = rxcpp::observable<>::range(1, 10).buffer(2);
    values.subscribe( [](std::vector<int> v){
            printf("OnNext:{");
            std::for_each(v.begin(), v.end(), [](int a){
                printf(" %d", a);
            });
            printf("}n");
        },
        [](){printf("OnCompletedn");});
}
```

The `timer` Operator emits an Observable that takes the interval period as a parameter. There is an option to specify the `Scheduler` object as a parameter. There are various versions of this function in the library; we have shown one in the following code:

```
//----------- TimerExample.cpp
#include "rxcpp/rx.hpp"
#include "rxcpp/rx-test.hpp"
#include <ioStream>
int main() {
    auto Scheduler = rxcpp::observe_on_new_thread();
    auto period = std::chrono::milliseconds(1);
    auto values = rxcpp::observable<>::timer(period, Scheduler).
        finally([](){
            printf("The final actionn");
        });
```

```
values.as_blocking().subscribe(
    [](int v){printf("OnNext: %dn", v);},
    [](){printf("OnCompletedn");});
}
```

A peek into the things we haven't covered yet

The Rx programming model can be considered as confluence of the following:

- Data-flow computation
- Declarative concurrency
- Functional programming
- Stream processing (event)
- Design patterns and idioms

To get a comprehensive view of the whole discipline, you need to work with the programming model extensively. Initially, things won't make much sense. At some point, you'll reach a *click point* where everything will start making sense. So far, we have covered the following topics:

- Observables and Observers
- Basic and intermediate Operators
- Basic and intermediate scheduling

This is just the beginning, and we need to cover many more topics to get familiar with the programming model. They are:

- Hot and cold Observables (Chapter 8, *RxCpp - the Key Elements*)
- A detailed exploration of Rx components (Chapter 8, *RxCpp - the Key Elements*)
- Advanced scheduling (Chapter 8, *RxCpp - the Key Elements)*
- Programming GUI systems (Chapter 9, *Reactive GUI Programming Using Qt/C++*)
- Advanced operators (Chapter 10, Creating Custom Operators in RxCpp)
- Reactive design patterns (Chapter 11, *Design Patterns and Idioms for C++ Rx Programming*)
- Programming for robustness (Chapter 13, *Advanced Streams and Handling Errors*)

Summary

In this chapter, we covered quite a bit of ground in understanding the Rx programming model in general, and the RxCpp library in particular. We started with a conceptual overview of the data flow computing paradigm and moved quickly to writing some basic RxCpp programs. After introducing Rx marble diagrams, we learned about the set of Operators supported by the RxCpp library. We also introduced the important topic of Scheduler, and finally we discussed the difference between the `flatmap` and `concatmap` Operators. In the next chapter, we will cover `hot` and `cold` Observables, Advanced scheduling, and some topics that we have not covered in this chapter.

RxCpp – the Key Elements 8

In the previous chapter, we were introduced to the RxCpp library and its programming model. We wrote some programs to understand workings of the library and also covered the most essential elements of the RxCpp library. In this chapter, we will cover, in some depth, the key elements of reactive programming , which includes the following:

- Observables
- Observers and their variants (Subscribers)
- Subjects
- Schedulers
- Operators

In effect, the key aspects of reactive programming are as follows:

- Observables are Streams to which Observers can subscribe for notifications
- A Subject is a combination of Observable and Observer
- Schedulers execute the Action associated with Operators and help the flow of data from Observables to Observers
- Operators are functions that take an Observable and emit another Observable (well, almost!)

Observables

In the previous chapter, we created Observables from the scratch and subscribed to those Observables. In all of our examples, the Observables created an instance of the (data) `Producer` class. The `Producer` class produces an event Stream. In other words, Observables are functions that connect Subscribers (Observers) to Producers.

Before we proceed, let's dissect an Observable and the core activities related to it:

- An Observable is a function that takes an Observer as a parameter and returns a function
- An Observable connects an Observer to a Producer (Producer is opaque to the Observer)
- A Producer is a source of values for an Observable
- An Observer is an object that has the `on_next`, `on_error`, and `on_completed` methods

What's a Producer?

In a nutshell, A Producer is a source of value for an Observable. Producers can be GUI windows, Timers, WebSockets, DOM trees, Iterators over collections/containers, and so on. They can be anything that can be a source of values that can be passed on to OnNext method of the Observer (In RxCpp, `observer.on_next(value)`.) . Of course, values can passed on to Operators, which in turn will be passed on to the internal Observer of Operators .

Hot versus Cold Observables

In most examples in the previous chapter, we saw that Producers were created in Observable functions. A Producer can also be created outside an Observable function, and a reference to the Producer can be put inside the Observable function. An Observable that refers to a Producer which was created outside its scope is called a hot Observable. Any Observable where we created a Producer instance inside (an Observable) is called a cold Observable. To make matters clear, let's write a program to demonstrate a cold Observable:

```
//---------- ColdObservable.cpp
#include <rxcpp/rx.hpp>
#include <memory>
int main(int argc, char *argv[])
{
  //---------- Get a Coordination
  auto eventloop = rxcpp::observe_on_event_loop();
  //----- Create a Cold Observable
  auto values = rxcpp::observable<>::interval(
             std::chrono::seconds(2)).take(2);
```

In the above code, the interval method created a cold Observable, as the Producer for the event Stream is instantiated int the `interval` function. A cold Observable will emit data when a Subscriber or an Observer is attached to it. Even if there is a delay in subscription between two Observers, the result will be consistent. This means both Observers we will get all the data emitted by the Observable:

```
//----- Subscribe Twice

values.subscribe_on(eventloop).
    subscribe([](int v){printf("[1] onNext: %dn", v);},
        [](){printf("[1] onCompleted\n");});
 values.subscribe_on(eventloop).
    subscribe([](int v){printf("[2] onNext: %dn", v);},
        [](){printf("[2] onCompleted\n");});
  //---- make a blocking subscription to see the results
 values.as_blocking().subscribe();
 //---------- Wait for Two Seconds
 rxcpp::observable<>::timer(std::chrono::milliseconds(2000)).
        subscribe([&](long){ });
}
```

The output emitted by the program is given below. For each run, the order of content in the console may change, as we are scheduling the execution of Observer methods in the same thread. But, there won't be any data loss, due to the delay in subscription:

```
[1] onNext: 1
[2] onNext: 1
[2] onNext: 2
[1] onNext: 2
[2] onCompleted
[1] onCompleted
```

Hot Observables

We can convert a cold Observable into a hot Observable by invoking the Observable's `publish` method. The consequence of converting a cold Observable to a hot Observable will be the fact that data can be missed by later subscriptions. A hot Observable emits data whether there is a subscription or not. The following program demonstrates the behavior:

```
//---------- HotObservable.cpp

#include <rxcpp/rx.hpp>
#include <memory>
int main(int argc, char *argv[]) {
  auto eventloop = rxcpp::observe_on_event_loop();
```

```
//----- Create a Cold Observable
//----- Convert Cold Observable to Hot Observable
//----- using .Publish();
auto values = rxcpp::observable<>::interval(
               std::chrono::seconds(2)).take(2).publish();
//----- Subscribe Twice
values.
   subscribe_on(eventloop).
   subscribe(
       [](int v){printf("[1] onNext: %dn", v);},
       [](){printf("[1] onCompletedn");});
 values.
   subscribe_on(eventloop).
   subscribe(
       [](int v){printf("[2] onNext: %dn", v);},
       [](){printf("[2] onCompletedn");});
//------ Connect to Start Emitting Values
values.connect();
//---- make a blocking subscription to see the results
values.as_blocking().subscribe();
//----------- Wait for Two Seconds
rxcpp::observable<>::timer(
       std::chrono::milliseconds(2000)).
       subscribe([&](long){ });
}
```

In the next example, we will take a look at the `publish_synchronized` mechanism supported by the `RxCpp` library. From a programming interface perspective, this is just a small change. Take a look at the following program:

```
//----------- HotObservable2.cpp
#include <rxcpp/rx.hpp>
#include <memory>

int main(int argc, char *argv[]) {

 auto eventloop = rxcpp::observe_on_event_loop();
 //----- Create a Cold Observable
 //----- Convert Cold Observable to Hot Observable
 //----- using .publish_synchronized();
 auto values = rxcpp::observable<>::interval(
                 std::chrono::seconds(2)).
                 take(5).publish_synchronized(eventloop);
 //----- Subscribe Twice
 values.
    subscribe(
        [](int v){printf("[1] onNext: %dn", v);},
        [](){printf("[1] onCompletedn");});
```

```
values.
    subscribe(
        [](int v){printf("[2] onNext: %dn", v);},
        [](){printf("[2] onCompletedn");});

//------ Start Emitting Values
values.connect();
//---- make a blocking subscription to see the results
values.as_blocking().subscribe();

//----------- Wait for Two Seconds
rxcpp::observable<>::timer(
        std::chrono::milliseconds(2000)).
        subscribe([&](long){ });
}
```

The output of the program is as follows. We can see that the output is well synchronized, that is, the output is displayed in the correct order:

```
[1] onNext: 1
[2] onNext: 1
[1] onNext: 2
[2] onNext: 2
[1] onNext: 3
[2] onNext: 3
[1] onNext: 4
[2] onNext: 4
[1] onNext: 5
[2] onNext: 5
[1] onCompleted
[2] onCompleted
```

Hot Observables and the replay mechanism

A hot Observable emits data, whether there is a Subscriber available or not. This can be an issue in scenarios where we expect, subscribers to receive data consistently. There is a mechanism within reactive programming to cache data so that later subscribers can be notified of the data available with an Observable. We can use the `.replay()` method to create such an Observable. Let's write a program that will demonstrate the replay mechanism, which is useful when writing programs involving hot Observables:

```
//---------- ReplayAll.cpp
#include <rxcpp/rx.hpp>
#include <memory>
int main(int argc, char *argv[]) {
```

```
    auto values = rxcpp::observable<>::interval(
            std::chrono::milliseconds(50),
            rxcpp::observe_on_new_thread()).
            take(5).replay();
    // Subscribe from the beginning
    values.subscribe(
        [](long v){printf("[1] OnNext: %ldn", v);},
        [](){printf("[1] OnCompletedn");});
    // Start emitting
    values.connect();
    // Wait before subscribing
    rxcpp::observable<>::timer(
        std::chrono::milliseconds(125)).subscribe([&](long){
        values.as_blocking().subscribe(
            [](long v){printf("[2] OnNext: %ldn", v);},
            [](){printf("[2] OnCompletedn");});
    });
//----------- Wait for Two Seconds
rxcpp::observable<>::timer(
        std::chrono::milliseconds(2000)).
        subscribe([&](long){ });

}
```

When writing reactive programs, you really need to understand the semantic difference between hot and cold Observables. We have only touched up on some aspects of this topic. Please refer to the RxCpp documentation and ReactiveX documentation to learn more. about hot and cold Observables There are countless articles available on internet about this topic.

Observers and their variants (Subscribers)

An Observer subscribes to an Observable and waits for events to be notified. Observers were already covered in the previous chapter. Hence, we will be focusing on Subscribers, which are a combination of Observers and subscriptions. A Subscriber has the facility to unsubscribe from the Observer,where as with a "vanilla" Observer, you can only subscribe. The following program explain these concepts very well:

```
//---- Subscriber.cpp
#include "rxcpp/rx.hpp"
int main() {
    //----- create a subscription object
    auto subscription = rxcpp::composite_subscription();
    //----- Create a Subscription
    auto subscriber = rxcpp::make_subscriber<int>(
```

```
            subscription,
        [&](int v){
            printf("OnNext: --%dn", v);
            if (v == 3)
                subscription.unsubscribe(); // Demonstrates Un Subscribes
        },
        [](){ printf("OnCompletedn");});

    rxcpp::observable<>::create<int>(
        [](rxcpp::subscriber<int> s){
            for (int i = 0; i < 5; ++i) {
                if (!s.is_subscribed())
                    break;
                s.on_next(i);
            }
            s.on_completed();
    }).subscribe(subscriber);
    return 0;
}
```

For writing nontrivial programs with concurrency and dynamism (asynchronous time varying events), the ability to subscribe and unsubscribe can be very handy. Take a deeper look at the topic by consulting the RxCpp documentation.

Subjects

A Subject is an entity that is both an Observer and an Observable. It helps to relay notifications from one Observable (typically) to a set of Observers. We can implement sophisticated techniques such as the caching and buffering of data using a Subject. We can also use a Subject to transform a hot Observable into a cold Observable. There are four variants of subjects implemented in RxCpp library. They are as follows:

- SimpleSubject
- BehaviorSubject
- ReplaySubject
- SynchronizeSubject

Let's write a simple program that will demonstrate the work of a Subject. The code listing will demonstrate how we can push data to a Subject and retrieve them using the Observer side of the Subject.

```cpp
//-------- SimpleSubject.cpp
#include <rxcpp/rx.hpp>
#include <memory>
int main(int argc, char *argv[]) {
    //----- Create an instance of Subject
    rxcpp::subjects::subject<int> subject;
    //----- Retreive the Observable
    //----- attached to the Subject
    auto observable = subject.get_observable();
    //------ Subscribe Twice
    observable.subscribe( [] ( int v ) { printf("1------%dn",v ); });
    observable.subscribe( [] ( int v ) { printf("2------%dn",v );});
    //--------- Get the Subscriber Interface
    //--------- Attached to the Subject
    auto subscriber = subject.get_subscriber();
    //---------------- Emit Series of Values
    subscriber.on_next(1);
    subscriber.on_next(4);
    subscriber.on_next(9);
    subscriber.on_next(16);
    //---------- Wait for Two Seconds
    rxcpp::observable<>::timer(std::chrono::milliseconds(2000)).
        subscribe([&](long){ });
}
```

The `BehaviorSubject` is a variant of Subject that stores the last emitted (current) value as part of its implementation. Any new Subscriber will get the *current value* immediately. Otherwise, it behaves like a normal Subject. The `BehaviorSubject` is also called a property or a cell in some realm. It is useful in scenarios where we update a particular cell or memory area with a series of data, such as in a transaction context. Let's write a program that demonstrates the workings of `BehaviorSubject`:

```cpp
//--------- BehaviorSubject.cpp
#include <rxcpp/rx.hpp>
#include <memory>

int main(int argc, char *argv[]) {

    rxcpp::subjects::behavior<int> behsubject(0);

    auto observable = behsubject.get_observable();
    observable.subscribe( [] ( int v ) {
        printf("1------%dn",v );
```

```
   });

   observable.subscribe( [] ( int v ) {
      printf("2------%dn",v );
   });

   auto subscriber = behsubject.get_subscriber();
   subscriber.on_next(1);
   subscriber.on_next(2);

   int n = behsubject.get_value();

   printf ("Last Value ....%dn",n);


}
```

The `ReplaySubject` is a variant of Subject that stores data that has already been emitted. We can specify parameters to indicate how many values have to be retained by a Subject. This is very handy when dealing with hot Observables. The function prototypes of various replay overloads are as follows:

```
replay (Coordination cn,[optional] composite_subscription cs)
replay (std::size_t count, Coordination cn,
[optional]composite_subscription cs)
replay (duration period, Coordination cn, [optional] composite_subscription
cs)
replay (std::size_t count, duration period, Coordination cn,[optional]
composite_subscription cs).
```

Let's write a program to understand the semantics of `ReplaySubject`:

```
//------------- ReplaySubject.cpp
#include <rxcpp/rx.hpp>
#include <memory>
int main(int argc, char *argv[]) {
    //----------- instantiate a ReplaySubject
    rxcpp::subjects::replay<int,rxcpp::observe_on_one_worker>
          replay_subject(10,rxcpp::observe_on_new_thread());
    //---------- get the observable interface
    auto observable = replay_subject.get_observable();
    //---------- Subscribe!
    observable.subscribe( [] ( int v ) {printf("1------%dn",v );});
    //-------- get the subscriber interface
    auto subscriber = replay_subject.get_subscriber();
    //---------- Emit data
    subscriber.on_next(1);
    subscriber.on_next(2);
    //-------- Add a new subscriber
```

```
//-------- A normal subject will drop data
//-------- Replay subject will not
observable.subscribe( [] ( int v ) {  printf("2------%dn",v );});
  //----------- Wait for Two Seconds
rxcpp::observable<>::timer(
    std::chrono::milliseconds(2000)).
    subscribe([&](long){ });
}
```

We have covered three variants of a Subject in this section. The primary use case is harnessing events and data from different sources by using the Observable interface and allowing a group of subscribers to consume the harnessed data. A SimpleSubject can act as both an Observable and an Observer to process a stream of values.
The BehaviorSubject is useful for monitoring changes in a property or variable over a period of time and a ReplaySubject will help you to avoid loss of data due to latency in a subscription. Finally, a SynchronizeSubject is a subject that has synchronization logic built into its implementation.

Schedulers

The RxCpp library has got a declarative threading mechanism, thanks to the robust scheduling subsystem packaged with it. From an Observable, data can be streamed through different paths along the change propagation graph. By giving hints to the Stream processing pipeline, we can schedule the execution of Operators and Observer methods in the same thread,different threads, or a background thread. This helps to capture the intent of the programmer much better.

The declarative scheduling model in RxCpp is possible because of the immutability of the Streams in an Operator's implementation. A Stream Operator takes an Observable as a parameter and returns a fresh Observable as the result. The input parameter is not mutated at all (the behavior is implicitly expected from the Operator implementation). This helps in out-of-order execution. The scheduling subsystem of RxCpp contains the following constructs: (specific to Rxcpp v2)

- Scheduler
- Worker
- Coordination
- Coordinator
- Schedulable
- TimeLine

The Version 2 of RxCpp borrows its scheduling architecture from the `RxJava` system. It relies on Scheduler and Worker idioms used by `RxJava`. Here are some important facts about Scheduler:

- The Scheduler has a timeline.
- The Scheduler can create lot of Workers in the timeline.
- The Worker owns a queue of schedulable in the timeline.
- The `schedulable` owns a function (often called `Action`) and has a lifetime.
- A `Coordination` functions as a factory for a coordinator and has a Scheduler.
- Every Coordinator has a Worker and is a factory for the following:
    - Coordinated `schedulable`
    - Coordinated Observables and subscribers

We have been using Rx Schedulers in our programs, without bothering about how they work under the hood. Let's write a toy program, which will help us understand how scheduling works under the hood:

```
//-------------- SchedulerOne.cpp
#include "rxcpp/rx.hpp"
int main(){
    //---------- Get a Coordination
    auto Coordination function= rxcpp::serialize_new_thread();
    //------- Create a Worker instance  through a factory method
    auto worker = coordination.create_coordinator().get_worker();
    //--------- Create a action object
    auto sub_action = rxcpp::schedulers::make_action(
        [] (const rxcpp::schedulers::schedulable&) {
            printf("Action Executed in Thread # : %dn",
            std::this_thread::get_id());
            } );
    //------------- Create a schedulable and schedule the action
    auto scheduled =
rxcpp::schedulers::make_schedulable(worker,sub_action);
    scheduled.schedule();
    return 0;
}
```

In `RxCpp`, all Operators that take multiple streams as input, or deal with tasks that have a bearing on time, take a `Coordination` function as a parameter. Some of the `Coordination` functions using a particular Scheduler are as follows:

- `identity_immediate()`
- `identity_current_thread()`

- identity_same_worker(worker w)
- serialize_event_loop()
- serialize_new_thread()
- serialize_same_worker(worker w)
- observe_on_event_loop()
- observe_on_new_thread()

In the previous program, we manually scheduled an Action (which, in fact, is nothing but a lambda). Let's move on to the declarative aspects of the Scheduler. We will write a program that will schedule tasks using a Coordination function:

```cpp
//----------- SchedulerTwo.cpp
#include "rxcpp/rx.hpp"
int main(){
    //-------- Create a Coordination function
    auto Coordination function= rxcpp::identity_current_thread();
    //-------- Instantiate a coordinator and create a worker
    auto worker = coordination.create_coordinator().get_worker();
    //--------- start and the period
    auto start = coordination.now() + std::chrono::milliseconds(1);
    auto period = std::chrono::milliseconds(1);
    //----------- Create an Observable (Replay )
    auto values = rxcpp::observable<>::interval(start,period).
    take(5).replay(2, coordination);
    //--------------- Subscribe first time using a Worker
    worker.schedule([&](const rxcpp::schedulers::schedulable&){
        values.subscribe( [](long v){ printf("#1 -- %d : %ldn",
                    std::this_thread::get_id(),v);   },
                        [](){ printf("#1 --- OnCompletedn");});
    });
    worker.schedule([&](const rxcpp::schedulers::schedulable&){
        values.subscribe( [](long v){printf("#2 -- %d : %ldn",
                    std::this_thread::get_id(),v); },
                        [](){printf("#2 --- OnCompletedn");});
    });
    //----- Start the emission of values
    worker.schedule([&](const rxcpp::schedulers::schedulable&)
    { values.connect();});
    //------- Add blocking subscription to see results
    values.as_blocking().subscribe(); return 0;
}
```

We created a hot Observable using the replay mechanism to take care of the late subscription by some Observers. We also created a Worker to do the scheduling for subscription and to connect the Observers with the Observable. The previous program demonstrates how the Scheduler works in RxCpp.

ObserveOn versus SubscribeOn

The ObserveOn and SubscribeOn operators behave in a different manner, and this has been a source of confusion for reactive programming newbies. The ObserveOn operator changes the thread of the Operators and Observers below it. In the case of SubscribeOn, it affects Operators and methods that are above and below it as well. The following program demonstrates subtle changes in the runtime behavior of a program, caused by the way the SubscribeOn and ObserveOn operators behave. Let's write a program that uses the ObserveOn operator:

```
//-------- ObservableOnScheduler.cpp
#include "rxcpp/rx.hpp"
int main(){
    //------- Print the main thread id
    printf("Main Thread Id is %dn",
            std::this_thread::get_id());
    //-------- We are using observe_on here
    //-------- The Map will use the main thread
    //-------- Subscribed Lambda will use a new thread
    rxcpp::observable<>::range(0,15).
        map([](int i){
            printf("Map %d : %dn", std::this_thread::get_id(),i);
            return i; }).
        take(5).observe_on(rxcpp::synchronize_new_thread()).
        subscribe([&](int i){
            printf("Subs %d : %dn", std::this_thread::get_id(),i);
        });
    //---------- Wait for Two Seconds
    rxcpp::observable<>::timer(
        std::chrono::milliseconds(2000)).
        subscribe([&](long){ });
    return 0;
}
```

The output of the preceding program is as follows:

```
Main Thread Id is 1
Map 1 : 0
Map 1 : 1
Subs 2 : 0
Map 1 : 2
Subs 2 : 1
Map 1 : 3
Subs 2 : 2
Map 1 : 4
Subs 2 : 3
Subs 2 : 4
```

The output of the preceding program clearly shows that map worked in the primary thread and the subscribe methods got scheduled in a secondary thread. This clearly shows that ObserveOn only worked on Operators and Subscribers below it. Let's write a more or less identical program that uses the SubscribeOn operator instead of the ObserveOn operator. Take a look at this:

```cpp
//-------- SubscribeOnScheduler.cpp
#include "rxcpp/rx.hpp"
int main(){
    //------- Print the main thread id
    printf("Main Thread Id is %dn",
            std::this_thread::get_id());
    //-------- We are using subscribe_on here
    //-------- The Map and subscribed Lambda will
    //--------- use the secondary thread
    rxcpp::observable<>::range(0,15).
        map([](int i){
            printf("Map %d : %dn", std::this_thread::get_id(),i);
            return i;
        }).
        take(5).subscribe_on(rxcpp::synchronize_new_thread()).
        subscribe([&](int i){
            printf("Subs %d : %dn", std::this_thread::get_id(),i);
        });
    //----------- Wait for Two Seconds
    rxcpp::observable<>::timer(
        std::chrono::milliseconds(2000)).
        subscribe([&](long){ });
    return 0;
}
```

The output of the preceding program is as follows:

```
Main Thread Id is 1
Map 2 : 0
Subs 2 : 0
Map 2 : 1
Subs 2 : 1
Map 2 : 2
Subs 2 : 2
Map 2 : 3
Subs 2 : 3
Map 2 : 4
Subs 2 : 4
```

The output of the preceding program shows that both map and subscription methods worked in the secondary thread. This clearly shows that SubscribeOn changes the threading behavior of items before and after it.

The RunLoop Scheduler

The RxCpp library does not have a notion of built-in main thread Scheduler. The closest you can do is to leverage the run_loop class to simulate scheduling in the main thread. In the following program, the Observable executes in a background thread, and the subscription methods run in the main thread. We are using subscribe_on and observe_on to achieve this objective:

```
//------------- RunLoop.cpp
#include "rxcpp/rx.hpp"
int main(){
    //------------ Print the Main Thread Id
    printf("Main Thread Id is %dn",
                std::this_thread::get_id());
    //------- Instantiate a run_loop object
    //------- which will loop in the main thread
    rxcpp::schedulers::run_loop rlp;
    //------ Create a Coordination functionfor run loop
    auto main_thread = rxcpp::observe_on_run_loop(rlp);
    auto worker_thread = rxcpp::synchronize_new_thread();
    rxcpp::composite_subscription scr;
    rxcpp::observable<>::range(0,15).
        map([](int i){
            //----- This will get executed in worker
            printf("Map %d : %dn", std::this_thread::get_id(),i);
            return i;
        }).take(5).subscribe_on(worker_thread).
```

```
        observe_on(main_thread).
        subscribe(scr, [&](int i){
            //--- This will get executed in main thread
            printf("Sub %d : %dn", std::this_thread::get_id(),i); });
    //------------ Execute the Run Loop
    while (scr.is_subscribed() || !rlp.empty()) {
        while (!rlp.empty() && rlp.peek().when < rlp.now())
        { rlp.dispatch(); }
    }
    return 0;
}
```

The output of the preceding program is as follows:

```
Main Thread Id is 1
Map 2 : 0
Map 2 : 1
Sub 1 : 0
Sub 1 : 1
Map 2 : 2
Map 2 : 3
Sub 1 : 2
Map 2 : 4
Sub 1 : 3
Sub 1 : 4
```

We can see that map was scheduled in the worker thread and subscription methods were executed in the main thread. This is enabled because of the judicious placement of the subscribe_on and observe_on Operators, which we covered in the previous section.

Operators

An Operator is a function that applies on an Observable to produce a new Observable. In the process, the original Observable is not mutated and can be considered as a pure function. We have already covered lot of Operators in our sample programs that we have written. In Chapter 10, *Creating Custom Operators in Rxcpp*, we will learn how to create custom Operators which work on Observables. The fact that an Operator does not mutate an (input) Observable is the reason why declarative scheduling works in the Rx programming model. Rx Operators can be categorized as follows:

- Creation Operators
- Transformation Operators
- Filtering Operators
- Combining Operators

- Error-handling Operators
- Utility Operators
- Boolean Operators
- Mathematical Operators

There are some more Operators available that do not fall into any of these categories. We will provde a list of key Operators from preceding categories , as a table for quick reference. As a developer one can pick Operators depending on the context, by consulting the tables given below

Creational Operators

These Operators will help a developer to create various kind of Observables,from the input data. We have already demonstrated the use of create, from, interval, and range Operators in our example code. Consult those examples and the RxCpp documentation to learn more about them. A table containing some of the Operators are given below :

Observables	Description
create	Create an observable by calling the Observer method programmatically
defer	Create a fresh Observable for each Observer/Subscriber
empty	Create an Observable that does not emit anything (emits only on_completed)
from	Create an Observable based on the parameters (Polymorphic)
interval	Create an Observable that emits a sequence of values in a time interval
just	Create an Observable that emits a single value
range	Create an Observable that emits a range of values
never	Create an Observable that never emits anything
repeat	Create an Observable that repeats a stream of values
timer	Create an Observable that emits a value after a delay factor, which can be specified as a parameter
throw	Create an Observable that emits an error

Transformation Operators

These Operators help developers to create a new Observable without modifying the source Observable. They act on individual items in the source Observable by applying a lambda or a functor on them. A table containing some of the most useful transformation Operators are given below.

Observables	Description
`buffer`	Observable that collects values in the past and emits them when signaled
`flat_map`	Observable that emits results of applying a function to a pair of values emitted by the source Observable and the collection Observable
`group_by`	Observable that helps to group values from an Observable
`map`	Observable that emits items from the source Observable, transformed by the specified function
`scan`	Observable that emits results of each call to the accumulator function
`window`	Observable that emits connected, non-overlapping windows of items. Each window will contain a particular number of item, which is given as a parameter. The parameter name is count.

Filtering Operators

The ability to filter Streams is a common activity in Stream processing. It is not unusual that the Rx programming model defines a lot of Operators in the filtering category. Filtering operators are mostly predicate functions or lambdas. The following table contains a list of filtering Operators:

Observables	Description
`debounce`	Observable that emits an item if a particular time span has passed without emitting another item from the source Observable
`distinct`	Observable that emits those items from the source Observable that are distinct
`element_at`	Observable that emits an item located at a specified index location
`filter`	Observable that emits only those items emitted by the source Observable that the filter evaluates as true
`first`	Observable that emits only the very first item emitted by the source Observable
`ignore_eleements`	Observable that emits a termination notification from the source Observable

last	Observable that emits only the very last item emitted by the source Observable
sample	Observable that emits the most recent items emitted by the source Observable within a periodic time interval.
skip	Observable that is identical to the source Observable, except that it does not emit the first t items that the source Observable emits
skip_last	Observable that is identical to the source Observable, except that it does not emit the last t items that the source Observable emits
take	Observable that emits only the first t items emitted by the source Observable, or all of the items from the source Observable if that Observable emits fewer than t items
take_last	Observable that emits only the last t items emitted by the source Observable

Combining Operators

One of the primary goals of the Rx programming model is to decouple the event source from event sinks. Obviously, there is a need for Operators that can combine Streams from various sources. The RxCpp library implements a set of such Operators. The following table outlines a set of commonly used combining Operators:

Observables	Description
combine_latest	When an item is emitted by either of two Observables, combine the latest item emitted by each Observable via a specified function and emit items based on the results of this function
merge	This combines multiple Observables into one by merging their emissions
start_with	This emits a specified sequence of items before beginning to emit the items from the source Observable
switch_on_next	This converts an Observable that emits Observables into a single Observable that emits the items emitted by the most recently emitted of those Observables
zip	This combines the emissions of multiple Observables together via a specified function and emits single items for each combination based on the results of this functions

Error-handling Operators

These are operators that help us to do error recovery when exceptions occur while pipeline execution is going on.

Observables	Description
Catch	Not supported by RxCpp
retry	An observable that mirrors the source Observable, resubscribing to it if it calls on_error up to a specified number of retries

Observable utility Operators

The following is a toolbox of useful utility Operators for working with Observables:. The observe_on and subscribe_on Operators help us to do declarative scheduling. We have already covered them in the previous chapter.

Observables	Description
finally	Observable that emits the same items as the source Observable, then invokes the given action
observe_on	Specify the Scheduler on which an Observer will observe this Observable
subscribe	Operate upon the emissions and notifications from an Observable
subscribe_on	Specify the Scheduler an Observable should use when it is subscribed to
scope	Create a disposable resource that has the same lifespan as the Observable

Conditional and Boolean Operators

The Conditional and Boolean Operators are Operators that evaluate one or more Observables or items emitted by Observables:

Observables	Description
all	Observable that emits true if every item emitted by the source Observable satisfies a specified condition; otherwise, it emits false
amb	Observable that emits same sequence as whichever of source Observables first emitted an item or sent a termination notification
contains	An Observable that emits true if the source Observable emitted a specified item; otherwise it emits false
default_if_empty	An Observable that emits true if the source Observable emitted a specified item; otherwise it emits false

sequence_equal	Observable that emits true only if both sequences terminate normally after emitting the same sequence of items in the same order; otherwise, it will emit false
skip_until	Discard items emitted by an Observable until a second Observable emits an item
skip_while	Discard items emitted by an Observable until a specified condition becomes false
take_until	Discard items emitted by an Observable after a second Observable emits an item or terminates
take_while	Discard items emitted by an Observable after a specified condition becomes false

Mathematical and Aggregate operators

These Mathematical and Aggregate Operators are a category of Operators which operate on an entire sequence of items emitted by an Observable: They basically reduce an Observable<T> to some value of the type T. They do not return an Observable.

Observables	Description
average	Calculate the average of numbers emitted by an Observable and emit this average
concat	Emit the emissions from two or more Observables without interleaving them
count	Count the number of items emitted by the source Observable and emit only this value
max	Determine and emit the maximum-valued item emitted by an Observable
min	Determine and emit the minimum-valued item emitted by an Observable
reduce	Apply a function to each item emitted by an Observable, sequentially, and emit the final value
sum	Calculate the sum of numbers emitted by an Observable and emit this sum

Connectable Observable Operators

The Connectable Observable are special Observables that have more precisely controlled subscription dynamics. The following table lists some key Operators with advanced subscription semantics

Observables	Description
connect	Instruct a Connectable Observable to begin emitting items to its subscribers
publish	Convert an ordinary Observable into a Connectable Observable
ref_count	Make a Connectable Observable behave like an ordinary Observable
replay	Ensure that all Observers see the same sequence of emitted items, even if they subscribe after the Observable has begun emitting items. This Operator is used with hot Observables

Summary

In this chapter, we gained an understanding of how pieces of the Rx programming model fits together. We started with Observables and quickly moved on to the topic of hot and cold Observables. Then, we covered the subscription mechanism and its use. We then moved on to the important topic of Subjects and understood how a number of variants of Scheduler implementation works. Finally, we classified various Operators available with the RxCpp system. In the next chapter, we will learn how we can use the knowledge gained so far, to write GUI programs in a reactive manner, using the Qt framework.

Reactive GUI Programming Using Qt/C++ 9

The Qt (pronounced *cute*) ecosystem is a comprehensive C++ based framework for writing cross-platform and multiplatform GUI applications. If you write your programs using the portable core of the library, you can leverage the *Write Once and Compile Everywhere* paradigm supported by the framework. In some cases, people use the platform-specific features, such as support for the ActiveX programming model for writing Windows-based applications.

We come across situations where Qt is preferred over MFC for writing applications in Windows. A plausible reason for this could be ease of programming, as Qt uses a very tiny subset of C++ language features for its library. The original goal of the framework was, of course, cross-platform development. Qt's single source portability across platforms, feature richness, availability of source code, and well-updated documentation, make it a very programmer-friendly framework. This has helped it thrive for more than two decades, ever since its first release, in 1995.

Qt provides a complete interface environment, with support for developing multiplatform GUI applications, Webkit APIs, media streamers, filesystem browsers, OpenGL APIs, and so on. Covering the full features of this wonderful library would take a book of its own. The purpose of this chapter is to introduce how to write reactive GUI applications, by leveraging Qt and the RxCpp library. We have already covered the core of the Reactive programming model in Chapter 7, *Introduction to Data Flow Computation and the RxCpp Library*, and Chapter 8, *RxCpp – the Key Elements*. Now, it is time to put what we learned in the previous chapters into practice! The Qt framework itself has a robust event processing system, and one needs to learn these library features before he or she can incorporate RxCpp constructs into the mix.

In this chapter, we will explore:

- A quick introduction to Qt GUI programming
- Hello World – Qt program
- The Qt event model, with signals/slots/MOC – an example
- Integrating the RxCpp library with the Qt event model
- Creating Custom Operators in Rxcpp

A quick introduction to Qt GUI programming

Qt is a cross-platform application development framework for writing software that can run on numerous platforms as a native application without changing much code, with native platform capabilities and speed. Aside from GUI applications, we can also write console or command-line applications using the framework—but the primary use cases are graphical user interfaces.

Although applications using Qt are usually written in C++, QML bindings to other languages also exist. Qt simplifies many aspects of C++ development, using comprehensive and powerful APIs and tools. Qt supports many compiler toolchains, such as the GCC C++ compiler and the Visual C++ compiler. Qt also provides Qt Quick (which includes QML, a declarative scripting language based on ECMAScript) to write logic. This helps with rapid application development for mobile platforms, although the logic can be written using native code for the best possible performance. The ECMAScript/C++ combination provides the best of declarative development and native code speed.

Qt is currently being developed and maintained by The Qt Company, and the framework is available with open source and proprietary licenses. When first launched, Qt used its own paint engine and controls by emulating the look and feel of a different platform (thanks to the custom paint engine, one can create a Windows look and feel under GNU Linux). This helped developers easily port across platforms, because of the minimal target platform dependency. As the emulation was imperfect, Qt started to use native-style APIs for the platforms, with its own native widget set. This resolved the issue with emulation of Qt's own paint engine, but at the cost of no more uniform look and feel across the platforms. The Qt library has an excellent binding with the Python programming language, christened as PyQt.

There are some essential things a programmer must understand before he/she leverages the library. In the following sections, we will quickly cover aspects of the Qt object model, signals and slots, the event system, and the meta-object system.

Qt object model

In a GUI framework, both run-time efficiency and high-level flexibility are key factors. The standard C++ object model provides very efficient run-time support, but its static nature is inflexible in certain problematic domains. The Qt framework combines the speed of C++ with the flexibility of the Qt object model.

The Qt object model supports the following features:

- **Signals and slots**, for seamless object communication
- Queryable and designable **object properties**
- Powerful events and event filters
- Powerful internally driven timers, enabling smooth, non-blocking work in many of the tasks in an event-driven GUI
- **Internationalization** with contextual string translation
- Guarded pointers (**QPointers**) that are automatically set to 0 when the referenced object is destroyed
- A **dynamic cast** working across library boundaries

Many of these features are implemented as standard C++ classes, based on inheritance from `QObject`. Others, like signals and slots and the object properties system, require the meta-object system provided by Qt's own **Meta-object compiler** (**MOC**). The meta-object system is an extension of the C++ language, to make it better suited for GUI programming. The MOC acts as an pre-compiler, which generates code based on the hints embedded in the source, and removes those hints for an ANSI C++ compiler to perform its normal compilation tasks.

Let us look at some classes in the Qt object model:

Class Name	Description
QObject	The base class of all Qt objects (http://doc.qt.io/archives/qt-4.8/qobject.html)
QPointer	The template class that provides guarded pointers to QObject (http://doc.qt.io/archives/qt-4.8/qpointer.html)
QSignalMapper	Bundles signals from identifiable senders (http://doc.qt.io/archives/qt-4.8/qsignalmapper.html)
QVariant	Acts like a union for the most common Qt data types (http://doc.qt.io/archives/qt-4.8/qvariant.html)

QMetaClassInfo	Additional information about a class (http://doc.qt.io/archives/qt-4.8/qmetaclassinfo.html)
QMetaEnum	Metadata about an enumerator (http://doc.qt.io/archives/qt-4.8/qmetaenum.html)
QMetaMethod	Metadata about a member function (http://doc.qt.io/archives/qt-4.8/qmetamethod.html)
QMetaObject	Contains meta-information about Qt objects (http://doc.qt.io/archives/qt-4.8/qmetaobject.html)
QMetaProperty	Metadata about a property (http://doc.qt.io/archives/qt-4.8/qmetaproperty.html)
QMetaType	Manages named types in the meta-object system (http://doc.qt.io/archives/qt-4.8/qmetatype.html)
QObjectCleanupHandler	Watches the lifetimes of multiple QObject (http://doc.qt.io/archives/qt-4.8/qobjectcleanuphandler.html)

Qt objects are generally treated as identities, not values. Identities are cloned, not copied or assigned; cloning an identity is a more complex operation than copying or assigning a value. Therefore, QObject and all subclasses of QObject (direct or indirect) have their copy constructors and assignment operators disabled.

Signals and slots

Signals and slots are mechanisms used in Qt to achieve communication between objects. The signals and slots mechanism is a central feature of Qt, as a GUI framework. Widgets get notified about changes in other widgets in Qt through this mechanism. In general, objects of any kind communicate with one another using this mechanism. For example, when a user clicks on a close button, we probably want the window's close() function to be called.

Signals and slots are alternatives to the callback technique in C/C++. A signal gets emitted when a particular event occurs. All of the widgets in the Qt framework have predefined signals, but we can always subclass a widget to add our own signals to it. A slot is a function that gets called in response to a signal. Similar to predefined signals, the Qt widgets have many predefined slots, but we can add custom slots to handle the signals that we are interested in.

The following diagram from Qt's official documentation (`http://doc.qt.io/archives/qt-4.8/signalsandslots.html`), demonstrates how inter-object communication happens through signals and slots:

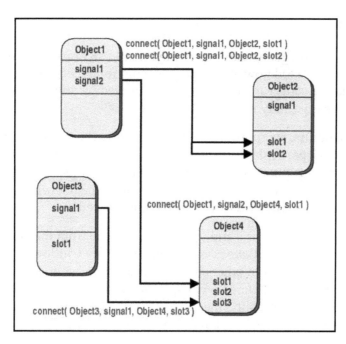

Signals and slots are loosely coupled communication mechanisms; the class that emits a signal doesn't care about the slot which receives the signal. Signals are a perfect example of fire and forget systems. The signals and slots system ensures that if a signal is connected to a slot, the slot will be called with the signal's parameters at the right time. Both signals and slots can take any number of arguments of any type, and they are completely type safe. The signatures of both signals and receiving slots must match; hence, the compilers can help us to detect type mismatches, as a bonus.

All objects inherited from `QObject`, or any of its subclasses (such as `QWidget`), can contain signals and slots. Signals are emitted by an object when it changes its state, which may be interesting to other objects. The object doesn't know (or care) if there are any objects at the receiving end. A signal can be connected to as many slots as needed. Similarly, we can connect as many signals as we want to a single slot. It is even possible to connect a signal to another signal; thus, signal chaining is possible.

Hence, together, signals and systems make an extremely flexible and pluggable component programming mechanism.

Event system

In Qt, events represent things that have happened within an application or a user activity that the application needs to know about. In Qt, events are the objects derived from an abstract QEvent class. Events can be received and handled by any instance of a QObject subclass, but they are especially relevant to widgets.

Whenever an event occurs, an appropriate QEvent subclass instance gets constructed and gives its possession to a particular instance of QObject (or any relevant subclass) by calling its event() function. This function does not handle the event itself; based on the type of event delivered, it calls an event handler for that specific type of event and sends a response based on whether the event was accepted or ignored.

Some events, such as QCloseEvent and QMoveEvent, come from the application itself; some, such as QMouseEvent and QKeyEvent, come from the window system; and some, such as QTimerEvent, come from other sources. Most events have specific subclasses derived from QEvent, and sometimes event-specific functions to meet the specific behavior of the extended events. To exemplify, the QMouseEvent class adds x() and y() functions to enable widgets to discover the positions of the mouse cursor.

Every event has a type associated with it, defined under QEvent::Type, and this is a convenient source of run-time type information that is used to quickly identify what subclass the event has been constructed from.

Event handlers

Generally, events are rendered by calling associated virtual functions. The virtual function is responsible for responding as intended. If custom virtual function implementations do not perform all that is necessary, we may need to call the base class's implementations.

For example, the following example handles the left mouse button clicks on a custom label widget, while passing all other button clicks to the base QLabel class:

```
void my_QLabel::mouseMoveEvent(QMouseEvent *evt)
{
    if (event->button() == Qt::LeftButton) {
        // handle left mouse button here
        qDebug() <<" X: " << evt->x() << "t Y: " << evt->y() << "n";
```

```
    }
    else {
        // pass on other buttons to base class
        QLabel::mouseMoveEvent(event);
    }
}
```

If we want to replace base class functionality, we must implement everything in the virtual function override. If the requirement is to simply extend base class functionality, we can implement what we want, and call the base class function for any other case that we don't want to handle.

Sending events

Many applications that are using the Qt framework want to send their own events, just like the framework-provided events. Suitable custom events can be constructed by using event objects and sending them with `QCoreApplication::sendEvent()` and `QCoreApplication::postEvent()`.

`sendEvent()` is synchronous in execution; therefore, it processes the event immediately. For many event classes, there is a function called `isAccepted()`, which tells us whether the event was accepted or rejected by the last handler that was called.

`postEvent()` is asynchronous in execution; hence, it posts the event in a queue for later dispatch. The next time Qt's main event loop runs, it dispatches all posted events, with some optimization. For example, if there are several resize events, they are compressed into one, as a union of all resize events, which avoids flickering in the user interface.

Meta-object system

The Qt meta-object system realizes the signals and slots mechanism for inter-object communication, the dynamic property system, and run-time type information.

The Qt meta-object system is based on three key aspects:

- `QObject` class: The base class that provides the advantages of the meta-object system to Qt objects
- `Q_OBJECT` macro: The macro to provide in the private section of the class declarations, used to enable meta-object features, such as dynamic properties, signals, and slots

- The MOC: It supplies each `QObject` subclass with the necessary code to implement meta-object features

The MOC executes before the actual compilation of a Qt source file. When the MOC finds class declarations that contain the `Q_OBJECT` macro, it produces another C++ source file, with meta-object code, for each of those classes. This generated source file is either included in the class's source file using `#include` or, more usually, compiled and linked with the class's implementation.

Hello World – Qt program

Now, let's get started with GUI application development using Qt/C++. Before getting into the following sections, download Qt SDK and Qt Creator from Qt's official site (`https://www.qt.io/download`). The codes that we are going to discuss in this chapter are entirely LGPL compatible and will be hand-coded by writing pure C++ code. The Qt framework is designed to be pleasant and intuitive so that you can handcode an entire application without using the Qt Creator IDE.

 Qt Creator is a cross-platform C++, JavaScript, and QML integrated development environment, a part of the SDK for the Qt GUI application development framework. It includes a visual debugger and an integrated GUI layout and forms designer. The editor's features include syntax highlighting and autocompletion. Qt Creator uses the C++ compiler from the GNU Compiler Collection on Linux and FreeBSD. On Windows, it can use MinGW or MSVC, with the default install, and can also use Microsoft Console Debugger, when compiled from source code. Clang is also supported. – *Wikipedia* (`https://en.wikipedia.org/wiki/Qt_Creator`)

Let's begin with a simple *Hello World* program, using a label widget. In this example, we will create and show a label widget, with the text `Hello World, QT!`:

```
#include <QApplication>
#include <QLabel>

int main (int argc, char* argv[])
{
    QApplication app(argc, argv);
    QLabel label("Hello World, QT!");
    Label.show();
    return app.execute();
}
```

In this code, we have included two libraries: `<QApplication>` and `<QLabel>`. The `QApplication` object is defined in the `QApplication` library, which manages the resources in an application, and it is required to run any Qt GUI-based application. This object accepts the command-line arguments from the program, and, when `app.execute()` is called, the Qt event loop gets launched.

An **event loop** is a program structure that permits events to be prioritized, queued, and dispatched to objects. In an event-based application, certain functions are implemented as passive interfaces that get called in response to certain events. The event loop generally continues running until a terminating event occurs (the user clicks on the **QUIT** button, for example).

`QLabel` is the simplest widget among all Qt widgets, defined in `<QLabel>`. In this code, the label is instantiated with the text `Hello World, QT`. When `label.show()` gets called, a label with instantiated text will appear on the screen in its own window frame.

Now, to build and run the application, the first thing we need is a project file. To create a project file and compile the application, we need to follow these steps:

1. Create a directory and save the source code in a CPP file, residing in this directory.
2. Open a shell and verify the version of `qmake` installed by using the `qmake -v` command. If `qmake` can't be found, the installation path needs to be added to the environment variable.
3. Now, change the directory into the Qt file path in the shell, and execute the `qmake -project` command. This will create a project file for the application.
4. Open the project file and add the following line to the `.pro` file after `INCLUDEPATH`:

   ```
   . . .
   INCLUDEPATH += .
   QT += widgets
   . . .
   ```

5. Then, run `qmake` without arguments to create the `make` file that contains the rules to build your application.
6. Run `make` (`nmake` or `gmake`, depending on the platform), which builds the application according to the rules specified in `Makefile`.
7. If you run the application, a small window with a label saying **Hello World, QT!** will appear.

The steps to building any Qt GUI applications are the same, except for the changes that may be required in project files. For all of the future examples that we will discuss in this chapter, *build and run* means to follow these steps.

Before we go on to the next example, let's have some fun. Replace the `QLabel` instantiation with the following code:

```
QLabel label("<h2><i>Hello World</i>, <font color=green>QT!</font></h2>");
```

Now, rebuild and run the application. As this code illustrates, it is easy to customize the Qt's user interface by using some simple HTML-style formatting.

In the next section, we will learn how to handle the Qt events and the use of signals and slots for object communication.

Qt event model with signals/slots/MOC – an example

In this section, we will create an application to handle mouse events in `QLabel`. We will override the mouse events in a custom `QLabel` and handle them in the dialog where the custom label is placed. The approach to this application is as follows:

1. Create a custom `my_QLabel` class, inherited from the framework `QLabel` class, and override the mouse events, such as mouse-move, mouse-pressed, and mouse-leave.

2. Define the signals that correspond to these events in `my_QLabel`, and emit them from the corresponding event handlers.

3. Create a dialog class inherited from the `QDialog` class, and handcode the positions and layouts of all of the widgets, including the custom widget created to handle mouse events.

4. In the dialog class, define the slots to handle the emitted signals from the `my_QLabel` object, and display the appropriate results in the dialog.

5. Instantiate this dialog under the `QApplication` object, and execute.

6. Create the project file to build a widget application and get it up and running.

Creating a custom widget

Let's write the header file `my_qlabel.h` to declare the class `my_QLabel`:

```
#include <QLabel>
#include <QMouseEvent>

class my_QLabel : public QLabel
{
    Q_OBJECT
public:
    explicit my_QLabel(QWidget *parent = nullptr);

    void mouseMoveEvent(QMouseEvent *evt);
    void mousePressEvent(QMouseEvent* evt);
    void leaveEvent(QEvent* evt);

    int x, y;

signals:
    void Mouse_Pressed();
    void Mouse_Position();
    void Mouse_Left();
};
```

`QLabel` and `QMouseEvent` are defined under the included libraries, `<QLabel>` and `<QMouseEvent>`. The class is derived from `QLabel` to inherit its default behavior, and `QObject` is propertied to handle the signaling mechanism.

In the private section of the header file, we have added a `Q_OBJECT` macro to notify the MOC that it must generate meta-object code for this class. The meta-object code is required for the signals and slots mechanism, the run-time type information, and the dynamic property system.

In the class header, along with the constructor declaration, the mouse events such as mouse-move event, mouse-press event, and mouse-leave event are overridden. Also, the public integer variables hold the current X and Y coordinates of the mouse pointer. Finally, the signals emitted from each mouse event are declared under the signals section.

Now, let's define these items in a CPP file, `my_qlabel.cpp`:

```
#include "my_qlabel.h"

my_QLabel::my_QLabel(QWidget *parent) : QLabel(parent), x(0), y(0)  {}

void my_QLabel::mouseMoveEvent(QMouseEvent *evt)
```

```
{
    this->x = evt->x();
    this->y = evt->y();
    emit Mouse_Position();
}
```

In the constructor, the parent is passed on to the `QLabel` base class to inherit the unhandled cases in the overridden class, and the coordinate variables are initialized to zero. In the `mouse-move` event handler, the member variables holding the mouse coordinates get updated, and a signal `Mouse_Position()` is emitted. The dialog using `my_QLabel` can connect this signal to the corresponding `mouse-move` slot in the parent dialog class and update the GUI:

```
void my_QLabel::mousePressEvent(QMouseEvent *evt)
{
    emit Mouse_Pressed();
}

void my_QLabel::leaveEvent(QEvent *evt)
{
    emit Mouse_Left();
}
```

From the `mouse-press` event handlers, the signal `Mouse_Pressed()` is emitted, and from the `mouse-leave` event, the `Mouse_Left()` signal is emitted. These signals get connected to corresponding slots in the parent widget (`Dialog` class) and update the GUI. Hence, we have written a custom label class to handle the mouse events.

Creating the application dialog

As the label class has been implemented, we need to implement the dialog class to place all of the widgets and handle all of the signals emitted from the `my_QLabel` object. Let's start with the `dialog.h` header file:

```
#include <QDialog>

class my_QLabel;
class QLabel;

class Dialog : public QDialog
{
    Q_OBJECT
public:
    explicit Dialog(QWidget *parent = 0);
```

```
    ~Dialog();

private slots:
    void Mouse_CurrentPosition();
    void Mouse_Pressed();
    void Mouse_Left();

private:
    void initializeWidgets();
    my_QLabel *label_MouseArea;
    QLabel *label_Mouse_CurPos;
    QLabel *label_MouseEvents;
};
```

Here, we are creating a `Dialog` class inherited from `QDialog`, defined under the `<QDialog>` library. The classes `QLabel` and `my_QLabel` are forward declared in this class header, as the actual libraries will be included in the class definition file. As we already discussed, the `Q_OBJECT` macro must be included to generate meta-object code for enabling signals and slots mechanisms, the run-time type information, and the dynamic property system.

In addition to the constructor and destructor declarations, private slots are declared to connect to the signals emitted from the `my_QLabel` object. The slots are normal functions, and can be called normally; their only special feature is that signals can be connected to them. The `Mouse_CurrentPosition()` slot will be connected to the signal emitted from the `mouseMoveEvent()` of the `my_QLabel` object. Similarly, `Mouse_Pressed()` will be connected to `mousePressEvent()`, and `MouseLeft()` will be connected to the `leaveEvent()` of the `my_QLabel` object.

Finally, the declaration of all widget pointers and one private function called `initializeWidgets()` is done to instantiate and lay out the widgets in the dialog.

The implementation of the `Dialog` class belongs in `dialog.cpp`:

```cpp
#include "dialog.h"
#include "my_qlabel.h"
#include <QVBoxLayout>
#include <QGroupBox>

Dialog::Dialog(QWidget *parent) : QDialog(parent)
{
    this->setWindowTitle("My Mouse-Event Handling App");
    initializeWidgets();

    connect(label_MouseArea, SIGNAL(Mouse_Position()), this,
SLOT(Mouse_CurrentPosition()));
```

```
    connect(label_MouseArea, SIGNAL(Mouse_Pressed()), this,
SLOT(Mouse_Pressed()));
    connect(label_MouseArea, SIGNAL(Mouse_Left()), this,
SLOT(Mouse_Left()));
}
```

In the constructor, the title of the application dialog is set to `My Mouse-Event Handling App`. Then, the `initializeWidgets()` function gets called—that function will be explained shortly. After creating and setting the layouts calling `initializeWidgets()`, the signals that emit from `my_QLabel` objects are connected to the corresponding slots declared in the `Dialog` class:

```
void Dialog::Mouse_CurrentPosition()
{
    label_Mouse_CurPos->setText(QString("X = %1, Y = %2")
                            .arg(label_MouseArea->x)
                            .arg(label_MouseArea->y));
    label_MouseEvents->setText("Mouse Moving!");
}
```

The `Mouse_CurrentPosition()` function is the slot to the signal emitted from the mouse-move event of the `my_QLabel` object. In this function, the label widget `label_Mouse_CurPos` gets updated with the current mouse coordinates, and `label_MouseEvents` updates its text to `Mouse Moving!`:

```
void Dialog::Mouse_Pressed()
{
    label_MouseEvents->setText("Mouse Pressed!");
}
```

The `Mouse_Pressed()` function is the slot to the signal which has been emitted from the mouse-press event that gets called every time a user clicks inside of the mouse area (the `my_QLabel` object). The function updates the text in the `label_MouseEvents` label as `"Mouse Pressed!"`:

```
void Dialog::Mouse_Left()
{
    label_MouseEvents->setText("Mouse Left!");
}
```

Finally, whenever the mouse leaves the mouse area, the mouse-leave event of the `my_QLabel` object emits a signal connected to the `Mouse_Left()` slot function. Then, it updates the text in the `label_MouseEvents` label to `"Mouse Left!"`.

Use the `initializeWidgets()` function to instantiate and set the layouts in the dialog, as follows:

```
void Dialog::initializeWidgets()
{
    label_MouseArea = new my_QLabel(this);
    label_MouseArea->setText("Mouse Area");
    label_MouseArea->setMouseTracking(true);
    label_MouseArea->setAlignment(Qt::AlignCenter|Qt::AlignHCenter);
    label_MouseArea->setFrameStyle(2);
```

In this code, the `label_MouseArea` object is instantiated with the custom label class, `my_QLabel`. Then, the label properties are modified (such as the label text modified to `"Mouse Area"`), mouse tracking is enabled inside the `label_MouseArea` object, the alignment is set to center and the frame style is set to a thick line.

```
    label_Mouse_CurPos = new QLabel(this);
    label_Mouse_CurPos->setText("X = 0, Y = 0");
    label_Mouse_CurPos->setAlignment(Qt::AlignCenter|Qt::AlignHCenter);
    label_Mouse_CurPos->setFrameStyle(2);
    label_MouseEvents = new QLabel(this);
    label_MouseEvents->setText("Mouse current events!");
    label_MouseEvents->setAlignment(Qt::AlignCenter|Qt::AlignHCenter);
    label_MouseEvents->setFrameStyle(2);
```

The label objects `label_Mouse_CurPos` and `label_MouseEvents` are updating its properties, such as text alignment and frame style, similar to the `label_MouseArea` object. But the text in `label_Mouse_CurPos` is initially set to `"X = 0, Y = 0"`, and the `label_MouseEvents` label to `"Mouse current events!"`:

```
    QGroupBox *groupBox = new QGroupBox(tr("Mouse Events"), this);
    QVBoxLayout *vbox = new QVBoxLayout;
    vbox->addWidget(label_Mouse_CurPos);
    vbox->addWidget(label_MouseEvents);
    vbox->addStretch(0);
    groupBox->setLayout(vbox);

    label_MouseArea->move(40, 40);
    label_MouseArea->resize(280,260);
    groupBox->move(330,40);
    groupBox->resize(200,150);
}
```

Finally, a vertical box layout (QVBoxLayout) is created, and the label_Mouse_CurPos and label_MouseEvents label widgets are added to it. Also, a group box is created with the tag Mouse Events, and the layout of the group box is made into a vertical box layout, created with the widgets. At last, the positions and sizes of the mouse area label and the mouse events group box are set to predefined values. Hence, the widget creation and layout settings are done.

Executing the application

We can now write main.cpp to create the Dialog class and display it:

```
#include "dialog.h"
#include <QApplication>

int main(int argc, char *argv[])
{
    QApplication app(argc, argv);
    Dialog dialog;
    dialog.resize(545, 337);
    dialog.show();
    return app.exec();
}
```

This piece of code is exactly like the Hello World Qt application that we discussed. Instead of a QLabel, we are instantiating the Dialog class we created, resizing the dialog window frame to a predefined value by using the resize() function. Now, the application is ready to build and run. But, before building the application, let us handcode the project file:

```
QT += widgets

SOURCES +=
        main.cpp
        dialog.cpp
    my_qlabel.cpp

HEADERS +=
        dialog.h
    my_qlabel.h
```

Now, build the application and run it. A dialog box will pop up as follows (Windows platform):

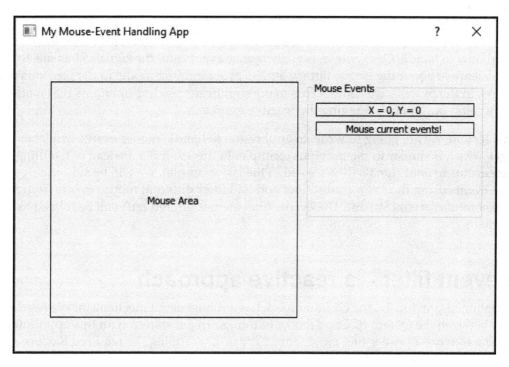

As we hover the mouse pointer through the left side label (**Mouse Area**), the coordinates of the mouse will get updated in the first label on the right side, and the second label on the right side will display the text, **Mouse Moving!** Upon pressing any mouse button in the mouse area, the text in the second label will change to **Mouse Pressed!** When the mouse pointer leaves the mouse area, the text will be updated to **Mouse Left!**

In this section, we learned how to create a dialog window, widgets under a dialog, layouts in the widgets, and so on. We also learned how to enable customizing a widget (the label widget), and how to handle system events. We then learned about the creation and connection of objects using user-defined signals and slots. Finally, we used all of these widgets, including a custom widget, and created an application to handle Qt mouse events in a window.

Now, let's implement a similar application to handle mouse events in a `QLabel` and display mouse coordinates in another label. Here, the event handling is performed by using event subscription and event filtering, with `RxCpp` observables and Qt event filters.

Integrating the RxCpp library with the Qt event model

We already saw the Qt framework from a bird's eye view in the previous sections. We learned how to handle Qt events, especially mouse events and the signals/slots mechanism. We also learned about the RxCpp library and its programming model in the previous two chapters. In the process, we came across many significant reactive operators that matter while writing programs leveraging the reactive approach.

In this section, we are going to write an application to handle mouse events in a label widget, which is similar to the previous example. In this example, instead of handling mouse events to emit signals (like we did in the last example), we will be subscribing to Qt mouse events using the RxCpp subscriber and will filter different mouse events from the resultant mouse events Stream. The events (that are not filtered out) will be related to the subscribers.

Qt event filter – a reactive approach

As mentioned previously, the Qt framework has a robust event mechanism. We need to bridge between the Qt and RxCpp scheme of things. To get started with this application, we are going to write a header file, rx_eventfilter.h, wrapping the required RxCpp headers and the Qt event filter:

```
#include <rxcpp/rx.hpp>
#include <QEvent>
namespace rxevt {
    // Event filter object class
    class EventEater: public QObject  {
    Public:
        EventEater(QObject* parent, QEvent::Type type,
rxcpp::subscriber<QEvent*> s):
        QObject(parent), eventType(type), eventSubscriber(s) {}
        ~EventEater(){ eventSubscriber.on_completed();}
```

The `<rxcpp/rx.hpp>` library is included to get the definitions for `RxxCppsubscriber` and `observable`, which we use in this class, and the `<QEvent>` library for `QEvent` definition. The entire header file is defined under the namespace `rxevt`. Now, the `EventEater` class is a Qt event filter class implanted to `filter-in` the only Qt events the member `eventType` is initialized with. To achieve that, the class has two member variables. The first one is `eventSubscriber`, which is an `rxcpp::subscriber` of the `QEvent` type, and the next one is `eventType`, to hold the `QEvent::Type`.

In the constructor, the parent `QObject` (the widget upon which events need to be filtered) is passed to the base class `QObject`. The member variables `eventType` and `eventSubscriber` get initialized with the `QEvent::Type` that needs to be filtered and the `rxcpp::subscriber` of the corresponding event type:

```
bool eventFilter(QObject* obj, QEvent* event) {
    if(event->type() == eventType)
    { eventSubscriber.on_next(event); }
    return QObject::eventFilter(obj, event);
}
```

We have overridden the `eventFilter()` function to call `on_next()` only if the event type is the same as the initialized type. The `EventEater` is an event filter object that receives all events that are sent to this object. The filter can either stop the event or forward it to this object. The `EventEater` object receives events via its `eventFilter()` function. The `eventFilter()` function (http://doc.qt.io/qt-5/qobject.html#eventFilter) must return true if the event should be filtered (in other words, stopped); otherwise, it must return `false`:

```
private:
    QEvent::Type eventType;
    rxcpp::subscriber<QEvent*> eventSubscriber;
};
```

So, let's write a utility function under the same header file to create and return an `rxcpp::observable` from the event Stream using the `EventEater` object:

```
// Utility function to retrieve the rxcpp::observable of filtered
events
rxcpp::observable<QEvent*> from(QObject* qobject, QEvent::Type type)
{
    if(!qobject) return rxcpp::sources::never<QEvent*>();
     return rxcpp::observable<>::create<QEvent*>(
        [qobject, type](rxcpp::subscriber<QEvent*> s) {
            qobject->installEventFilter(new EventEater(qobject, type,
s));
        }
```

```
        );
    }
} // rxevt
```

In this function, we are returning the observable of `QEvent` from the stream of events that we will filter using the `EventEater` object. A `QObject` instance can be set to monitor the events of another `QObject` instance before the latter object even sees them. This a really powerful feature of Qt's event model. The call of the `installEventFilter()` function makes it possible, and the `EventEater` class has the conditions to perform filtering.

Creating the window – setting layouts and alignments

Now, let's write the application code to create the widget window, which contains two label widgets. One label will be used as the mouse area, similar to the previous example, and the latter will be used to display the filtered mouse event and the mouse coordinates.

Let's look into the code in `main.cpp` as two sections. Initially, we will discuss the code to create and set the layout for the widgets:

```
#include "rx_eventfilter.h"
int main(int argc, char *argv[])
{
    QApplication app(argc, argv);
    // Create the application window
    auto widget = std::unique_ptr<QWidget>(new QWidget());
    widget->resize(280,200);
        // Create and set properties of mouse area label
    auto label_mouseArea    = new QLabel("Mouse Area");
    label_mouseArea->setMouseTracking(true);
    label_mouseArea->setAlignment(Qt::AlignCenter|Qt::AlignHCenter);
    label_mouseArea->setFrameStyle(2);
    // Create and set properties of message display label
    auto label_coordinates = new QLabel("X = 0, Y = 0");
    label_coordinates->setAlignment(Qt::AlignCenter|Qt::AlignHCenter);
    label_coordinates->setFrameStyle(2);
```

We have included the `rx_eventfilter.h` header file to use the event filtering mechanism implemented using the RxCpp library. In this application, instead of creating these widgets inside of a dialog, a `QWidget` object is created, and the two `QLabel` widgets are added into a `QVBoxLayout` layout; this is set as the layout of the application widget. The size of the application window is a predefined value of `200pixels` wide and `280pixels` high. Similar to the previous application, mouse tracing is enabled for the first label:

```
      // Adjusting the size policy of widgets to allow stretching
      // inside the vertical layout
      label_mouseArea->setSizePolicy(QSizePolicy::Expanding,
QSizePolicy::Expanding);
      label_coordinates->setSizePolicy(QSizePolicy::Expanding,
QSizePolicy::Expanding);
      auto layout = new QVBoxLayout;
      layout->addWidget(label_mouseArea);
      layout->addWidget(label_coordinates);
      layout->setStretch(0, 4);
      layout->setStretch(1, 1);
      widget->setLayout(layout);
```

The size policy of both widgets is set to `QSizePolicy::Expanding` to allow for the stretching of widgets inside the vertical layout box. This allows us to make the mouse area label larger than the status display label. The `setStretch()` function sets the stretch factor at the position index to stretch.

Event type specific observables

The code to subscribe to the `rxcpp::observable` of mouse events is as follows:

- Mouse move
- Mouse button press
- Mouse button double-click

The program is as follows:

```
      // Display the mouse move message and the mouse coordinates
      rxevt::from(label_mouseArea, QEvent::MouseMove)
            .subscribe([&label_coordinates](const QEvent* e){
        auto me = static_cast<const QMouseEvent*>(e);
        label_coordinates->setText(QString("Mouse Moving : X = %1, Y = %2")
                                     .arg(me->x())
                                     .arg(me->y()));
      });
```

The `rxevt::from()` function returns the `rxcpp::observable` of the events from `label_mouseArea`, based on the `QEvent::Type` we are passing as the argument. In this code, we are subscribing to an Observable of events in `label_mouseArea`, which are of the `QEvent::MouseMove` type. Here, we are updating the `label_coordinates` text with the current X and Y positions of the mouse pointer:

```
        // Display the mouse signle click message and the mouse coordinates
        rxevt::from(label_mouseArea, QEvent::MouseButtonPress)
                .subscribe([&label_coordinates](const QEvent* e){
            auto me = static_cast<const QMouseEvent*>(e);
            label_coordinates->setText(QString("Mouse Single click at X = %1, Y
    = %2")
                                        .arg(me->x())
                                        .arg(me->y()));
        });
```

Similar to mouse-move filtering, an observable of QEvent is returned by the `rxevt::from()` function, including only events of the type `QEvent::MouseButtonPress`. Then, the text is updated in `label_coordinates`, with the position of the mouse click:

```
        // Display the mouse double click message and the mouse coordinates
        rxevt::from(label_mouseArea, QEvent::MouseButtonDblClick)
                .subscribe([&label_coordinates](const QEvent* e){
            auto me = static_cast<const QMouseEvent*>(e);
            label_coordinates->setText(QString("Mouse Double click at X = %1, Y
    = %2")
                                        .arg(me->x())
                                        .arg(me->y()));
        });
        widget->show();
        return app.exec();
    } // End of main
```

Finally, the event type `QEvent::MouseButtonDblClick` is also handled similar to a single mouse click, and the text in `label_coordinates` is also updated with the double-click position. Then, the `show()` function of the application window widget is called, and the `exec()` function is called to start the event loop.

The project file, `Mouse_EventFilter.pro`, is as follows:

```
QT += core widgets
CONFIG += c++14

TARGET = Mouse_EventFilter
INCLUDEPATH += include

SOURCES +=
    main.cpp
HEADERS +=
    rx_eventfilter.h
```

Since the RxCpp library is a header-only library, a folder named `include` is created inside of the project directory, and the RxCpp library folder is copied there. Updating `INCLUDEPATH` will help the application to fetch any include files present in the directories specified there. Now, let's build and run the application.

An introduction to RxQt

The `RxQt` library is a public domain library written over the `RxCpp` library and makes it easy to program with Qt events and signals in a reactive manner. To understand the library, let us jump into an example so that we can track the mouse events and filter them using the observable supplied by the library. The library can be downloaded from the GitHub repository at `https://github.com/tetsurom/rxqt`:

```cpp
#include <QApplication>
#include <QLabel>
#include <QMouseEvent>
#include "rxqt.hpp"

int main(int argc, char *argv[])
{
    QApplication app(argc, argv);

    auto widget = new QWidget();
    widget->resize(350,300);
    widget->setCursor(Qt::OpenHandCursor);

    auto xDock = new QLabel((QWidget*)widget);
    xDock->setStyleSheet("QLabel { background-color : red}");
    xDock->resize(9,9);
    xDock->setGeometry(0, 0, 9, 9);

    auto yDock = new QLabel((QWidget*)widget);
```

```
yDock->setStyleSheet("QLabel { background-color : blue}");
yDock->resize(9,9);
yDock->setGeometry(0, 0, 9, 9);
```

The preceding code creates QWidget, which acts as the parent of two other QLabels. Two label widgets are created to move inside the parent widget, along the top and left border of the windows. The dockable label along the *X*-axis is colored red, and the one along the *Y*-axis is blue in color:

```
rxqt::from_event(widget, QEvent::MouseButtonPress)
        .filter([](const QEvent* e) {
    auto me = static_cast<const QMouseEvent*>(e);
    return (Qt::LeftButton == me->buttons());
})
        .subscribe([&](const QEvent* e) {
    auto me = static_cast<const QMouseEvent*>(e);
    widget->setCursor(Qt::ClosedHandCursor);
    xDock->move(me->x(), 0);
    yDock->move(0, me->y());
});
```

In the preceding code, the rxqt::from_event() function filters all of the events from the widget class, except for the QEvent::MouseButtonPress event, and returns a rxcpp::observable<QEvent*> instance. The rxcpp::observable here is already filtered with those mouse events if the button is the left mouse button. Then, inside the Lambda function of the subscribe() method, we are changing the cursor into Qt::ClosedHandCursor. We also set the position of xDock to the mouse *x*-position value, along with the top edge of the window, and the yDock position to the mouse *y*-position, along with the left edge of the window:

```
rxqt::from_event(widget, QEvent::MouseMove)
        .filter([](const QEvent* e) {
    auto me = static_cast<const QMouseEvent*>(e);
    return (Qt::LeftButton == me->buttons());
})
        .subscribe([&](const QEvent* e) {
    auto me = static_cast<const QMouseEvent*>(e);
    xDock->move(me->x(), 0);
    yDock->move(0, me->y());
});
```

In this code, we are filtering all the mouse-move events from the widget window using the RxQt library. The observable here is a stream of mouse events with both mouse-move and left mouse button press events are present. Inside the subscribe method, the code updates the position of xDock and yDock along the top and left edges of the window:

```
rxqt::from_event(widget, QEvent::MouseButtonRelease)
        .subscribe([&widget](const QEvent* e) {
    widget->setCursor(Qt::OpenHandCursor);
});

widget->show();
return app.exec();
}
```

Finally, the filtered mouse button release events are filtered, and the mouse cursor is set back to Qt::OpenHandCursor. To add some more fun to this application, let's create one more widget, similar to xDock and yDock; this will be a gravity object. The gravity object will follow the mouse cursor when it is pressed:

```
#ifndef GRAVITY_QLABEL_H
#define GRAVITY_QLABEL_H

#include <QLabel>

class Gravity_QLabel : public QLabel
{
    public:
      explicit Gravity_QLabel(QWidget *parent = nullptr):
          QLabel(parent), prev_x(0), prev_y(0){}

      int prev_x, prev_y;
};

#endif // GRAVITY_QLABEL_H
```

Now, we must create an instance of the gravity widget under the application window (from the newly created Gravity_QLabel class):

```
auto gravityDock = new Gravity_QLabel((QWidget*)widget);
gravityDock->setStyleSheet("QLabel { background-color : green}");
gravityDock->resize(9,9);
gravityDock->setGeometry(0, 0, 9, 9);
```

Similar to the creation and size settings of `xDock` and `yDock`, the new `gravityDock` object has been created. Also, the position of this object must be set in the mouse coordinate values whenever a `press` event is thrown. Therefore, inside of the Lambda function of the subscribe method for `QEvent::MouseButtonPress`, we need to add the following line of code:

```
gravityDock->move(me->x(),me->y());
```

Lastly, the position of `gravityDock` needs to be updated, as per the mouse move. To achieve that, inside of the Lambda function of the `subscribe` method for `QEvent::MouseMove`, we need to add the following code:

```
gravityDock->prev_x = gravityDock->prev_x * .96 + me->x() * .04;
gravityDock->prev_y = gravityDock->prev_y * .96 + me->y() * .04;
gravityDock->move(gravityDock->prev_x, gravityDock->prev_y);
```

Here, the position of `gravityDock` is updated to a new value, which is the sum of 96% of the previous value and 4% of the new position. Hence, we are filtering the Qt events using the `RxQt` and RxCpp libraries to create an *X-Y* mouse position indicator and a gravity object. Now, let's build and run the application.

Summary

In this chapter, we dealt with the topic of reactive GUI programming using Qt. We started with a quick overview of GUI application development using Qt. We learned about concepts in the Qt framework, such as the Qt object hierarchy, the meta-object system, and signals and slots. We wrote a basic *Hello World* application using a simple label widget. Then, we wrote a mouse event handling application using a custom label widget. In that application, we learned more about how the Qt event system works, and how to use the signals and slots mechanism for object communication. Finally, we wrote an application to handle mouse events and filter them by using the `RxCpp` subscription model and Qt event filters. We covered how RxCpp can be used in a GUI framework (such as Qt) to follow a Reactive programming model. We also covered the `RxQt` library, a public domain that integrates RxCpp and the Qt library.

Before proceeding to the next chapter, you need to learn about writing *custom operators for RxCpp observables*. This topic is covered in the online section. You can refer to the following link: `https://www.packtpub.com/sites/default/files/downloads/Creating_Custom_Operators_in_RxCpp.pdf`.

After you have completed reading the preceding mentioned topic, we can proceed to the next chapter, where we will take a look at design patterns and idioms for C++ reactive programming.

10
Creating Custom Operators in RxCpp

In the last three chapters, we learned about the RxCpp library and its programming model. We also applied what we learned, in the context of GUI programming. From a mental model perspective, any developer who wants to write programs in a reactive manner has to understand Observable, Observer, and the operators that work between them. Of course, Schedulers and Subjects are important as well. The bulk of the logic of reactive programs resides in operators. The RxCpp library provides a lot of built-in (stock) operators as part of its implementation. We have already used some of them in our programs. In this chapter, we will learn how we can implement custom operators. To write custom operators, we need to delve deep into some advanced topics related to the RxCpp library. The topics covered in this chapter are the following:

- Philosophy of Rx operators
- Chaining stock operators
- Writing basic RxCpp operators
- Writing different genres of custom operators
- Custom operators using the lift<T> meta operator
- Adding operators to the RxCpp library source code

Philosophy of Rx operators

If you take any reactive program, we see a chain of operators stacked between the Observable and the Observer. The developers use a fluent interface to chain operators. In RxCpp, one can use a dot (.) or pipe (|) to perform the operator chaining. From a software interface point of view, every operator takes an Observable and returns an Observable of the same kind or a different kind.

The general usage of an RxCpp Observable/Observer interaction (given as pseudo-code) is as follows:

```
Observable().       // Source Observable
       Op1().       // First operator
       Op2().       // Second operator
              ..
              ..
       Opn().subscribe( on_datahandler,
                        on_errorhandler,
                        on_completehandler);
```

Even though we are using fluent interfaces when it comes to operator chaining, we are effectively composing functions together. To compose functions together, the return value of a function should be type compatible with the parameter of the function that comes in the composition chain.

An operator takes an Observable as a parameter and returns another Observable. There are some cases where it returns a value other than the Observable. Only those operators that return an Observable can be part of a process called operator chaining.

 To write a new operator that can be part of the operator chaining method, the best way is to add them as a method of the observable<T> type. However, writing a production-quality operator that can run in different contexts is best left to experts in RxCpp internals. Another option is to use the lift<t>(...) operator available in the RxCpp library. We will cover both these strategies in this chapter.

Another very important property that every operator implementation should have is that they should be side effect-free. At least, they should not mutate contents of the input Observable. In other words, the function or functor that acts as an operator should be a pure function.

Chaining stock operators

We have already learned that RxCpp operators operate on Observables (received as input) and return Observables. This allows these operators to be invoked one after the other using operator chaining. Each individual operator in the chain transforms elements in the stream received from the previous operator. The source stream is not mutated in the process. We use the fluent interface syntax when chaining operators.

Developers usually use the fluent interface in the context of the consumption of classes that implement the GOF Builder pattern. Builder pattern implementations are implemented in an order-independent manner. Even though the syntax of operator chaining is similar, the order in which operators are invoked does matter in the reactive world.

Let's write a simple program that will help us understand the significance of the order of execution in Observable operator chaining. In this particular example, we have an Observable stream where we apply the map operator twice: once to find out the square, and then to find two instances of a value. We apply the square function first, followed by the twice function:

```cpp
//----- operatorChaining1.cpp
//----- Square and multiplication by 2 in order
#include "rxcpp/rx.hpp"
int main()
{
    auto values = rxcpp::observable<>::range(1, 3).
        map([](int x) { return x * x; }).
        map([](int x) { return x * 2; });
    values.subscribe(
        [](int v) {printf("OnNext: %dn", v); },
        []() {printf("OnCompletedn"); });
    return 0;
}
```

The preceding program will produce the following output:

```
OnNext: 2
OnNext: 8
OnNext: 18
OnCompleted
```

Now, let's reverse the order of application (scaling by 2, twice, followed by the square of the argument), and then peruse the output to see that we will get a different output (in the first case, square was applied first, then scaling by 2). The following program will explain the order of execution, if we compare the output generated by the program with the previous program:

```cpp
//----- operatorChaining2.cpp
//----- Multiplication by 2 and Square in order
#include "rxcpp/rx.hpp"
int main()
{
    auto values = rxcpp::observable<>::range(1, 3).
        map([](int x) { return x * 2; }).
        map([](int x) { return x * x; });
```

```
    values.subscribe(
        [](int v) {printf("OnNext: %dn", v); },
        []() {printf("OnCompletedn"); });
    return 0;
}
```

The output produced by the program is given here:

```
OnNext: 4
OnNext: 16
OnNext: 36
OnCompleted
```

In C++, we can compose functions together very well because of Lambda functions and the lazy evaluation of Lambda functions. The RxCpp library exploits this fact while implementing operators. If there are three functions (F, G, H) that take observable<T> as the input parameter and return observable<T>, we can compose them symbolically as follows:

```
F(G( H(x))
```

If we are using operator chaining, this can be written as follows:

```
x.H().G().F()
```

We have now learned that operator chaining is effectively doing operator composition. Both produce similar results, but operator chaining is more readable and intuitive. One purpose of this section is to establish the fact that operator composition and operator chaining provide similar functionality. The operators that we implement initially can be composed together (cannot be chained) and we will learn how to create operators that are amenable to operator chaining.

Writing basic RxCpp custom operators

In the previous section, we covered the topic of operator chaining. Operator chaining was possible because, the stock operators are implemented as part of the observable<T> type. The operators that we are going to implement initially cannot be part of the operator chaining strategy. In this section, we will implement some RxCpp operators that can transform an Observable and return another Observable.

Writing an RxCpp operator as a function

To kickstart the discussion, let's write a simple operator that works on observable<string>. The operator just prepends the literal text `Hello` before each item in the stream:

```
//----------- operatorSimple.cpp
#include "rxcpp/rx.hpp"
#include "rxcpp/rx-test.hpp"
#include <iostream>
namespace rxu=rxcpp::util;
#include <array>
using namespace rxcpp;
using namespace rxcpp::operators;
// Write a Simple Reactive operator Takes an Observable<string> and
// Prefix Hello to every item and return another Observable<string>
observable<std::string> helloNames(observable<std::string> src ) {
    return src.map([](std::string s) { return "Hello, " + s + "!"; });
}
```

The custom operator that we have implemented is written to demonstrate how you can write an operator that can work on an Observable. The operator written has to be invoked using the function semantics, and the implementation is not fit for operator chaining. Now that we have implemented an operator, let's write a main function to test how the operator works:

```
int main() {
    std::array< std::string,4 > a={{"Praseed", "Peter", "Sanjay","Raju"}};
    // Apply helloNames operator on the observable<string>
    // This operator cannot be part of the method chaining strategy
    // We need to invoke it as a function
    // If we were implementing this operator as part of the
    //          RxCpp observable<T>
    //    auto values = rxcpp::observable<>:iterate(a).helloNames();
    auto values = helloNames(rxcpp::observable<>::iterate(a));
    //-------- As usual subscribe
    values.subscribe(
            [] (std::string f) { std::cout << f <<  std::endl; } ,
            [] () {std::cout << "Hello World.." << std::endl;} );
}
```

The program will produce the following output:

```
Hello, Praseed!
Hello, Peter!
Hello, Sanjay!
Hello, Raju!
Hello World..
```

Writing an RxCpp operator as a Lambda

We have written our first custom operator as a `unary` function. All operators are `unary` functions that take Observables as a parameter. The function took `observable<string>` as a parameter and returned another `observable<string>`. We can achieve the same effect by writing an operator (inline) as a Lambda. Let's see how it can be done:

```
//----------- operatorInline.cpp
#include "rxcpp/rx.hpp"
#include "rxcpp/rx-test.hpp"
#include <iostream>
namespace rxu=rxcpp::util;
#include <array>
using namespace rxcpp;
using namespace rxcpp::operators;
int main() {
    std::array< std::string,4 > a={{"Praseed", "Peter", "Sanjay","Raju"}};
    auto helloNames = [] (observable<std::string> src ) {
        return src.map([](std::string s) {
          return "Hello, " + s + "!";
          });
    };
    // type of values will be observable<string>
    // Lazy Evaluation
    auto values = helloNames(rxcpp::observable<>::iterate(a));
    //-------- As usual subscribe
    values.subscribe(
          [] (std::string f) { std::cout << f <<  std::endl; } ,
          [] () {std::cout << "Hello World.." << std::endl;} );
}
```

The output of the program is given here:

```
Hello, Praseed!
Hello, Peter!
Hello, Sanjay!
Hello, Raju!
Hello World..
```

The output shows that the program behavior is identical whether one uses an ordinary function or the Lambda function. The advantage of the Lambda function is the call site creation and consumption of functions.

Composing custom RxCpp operators

We have already learned about function-composition in this book (Chapter 2, *A Tour of Modern C++ and Its Key Idioms*). Function composition is possible when the return value of a function is type compatible with the input parameter of another function. In the case of operators, since most of them return Observables and take Observables as a parameter, they are compatible for function composition. In this section, our operators are compatible for composition, but they cannot be chained yet. Let's see how we can compose operators:

```cpp
//----------- operatorCompose.cpp
#include "rxcpp/rx.hpp"
#include "rxcpp/rx-test.hpp"
#include <iostream>
namespace rxu=rxcpp::util;
#include <array>
using namespace rxcpp;
using namespace rxcpp::operators;
int main() {
    std::array< int ,4 > a={{10, 20,30,40}};
    // h-function (idempotent)
    auto h = [] (observable<int> src ) {
      return src.map([](int n ) { return n; });
    };
    // g-function
    auto g = [] (observable<int> src ) {
        return src.map([](int n ) { return n*2; });
    };
    // type of values will be observable<string>
    // Lazy Evaluation ... apply h over observable<string>
    // on the result, apply g
    auto values = g(h(rxcpp::observable<>::iterate(a)));
    //-------- As usual subscribe
    values.subscribe(
            [] (int f) { std::cout << f <<  std::endl; } ,
            [] () {std::cout << "Hello World.." << std::endl;} );
}
```

The output of the program is given here:

```
20
40
60
80
Hello World..
```

Different genres of custom operators

The RxCpp library contains different genres of operators as part of the stock offering. The default collection of RxCpp operators is enough for most applications. The different genres of available operators are as follows:

- Creation operators
- Transformation operators
- Filtering operators
- Combining operators
- Error-handling operators
- Utility operators
- Boolean operators
- Mathematical operators

The classification of operators gives developers a nice framework for choosing the appropriate operator for the context. In this section, we will implement the following:

- Custom creational operators
- Custom transformation operators
- Custom operations that involve Schedulers

Writing a custom creational operator

The majority of RxCpp operator functions accept Observables and return an Observable to achieve composition of operators. We need to do some extra work to make the composition in a chainable fashion (in the next section, we will cover lift<t> and the topic of adding operators to the [observable<T>] Observable in the RxCpp library). The operators we implement in this section will help us create an Observable from the input data. We can create an Observable stream of any type,from individual value of the type, from a range of values, from an iterator to a STL container, from another Observable, and so on. Let's discuss an example program that accepts an STL container and creates an Observable, followed by some transformations:

```
//------ CustomOperator1.cpp
#include "rxcpp/rx.hpp"
namespace rx {
    using namespace rxcpp;
    using namespace rxcpp::operators;
    using namespace rxcpp::sources;
```

```
    using namespace rxcpp::util;
}

template<typename Container>
rx::observable<std::string> helloNames(Container items) {
    auto str = rx::observable<>::iterate(items);
    return str.
    filter([](std::string s){
        return s.length() > 5;
    }).
    map([](std::string s){
        return "Hello, " + s + "!";
    }).
    //------ Translating exception
    on_error_resume_next([](std::exception_ptr){
        return rx::error<std::string>(std::runtime_error("custom
exception"));
    });
}
```

The `helloNames()` function accepts any standard library container and creates an Observable of the type string (`observable<string>`). The Observable is then filtered to get items longer than five characters to prepend the `Hello` string to each item. The exceptions that occur will be translated by the use of the standard RxCpp operator, `on_error_resume_next()`: Now, let's write the main program to see how this operator can be used:

```
int main() {
    //------ Create an observable composing the custom operator
    auto names = {"Praseed", "Peter", "Joseph", "Sanjay"};
    auto value = helloNames(names).take(2);
    auto error_handler = [=](std::exception_ptr e) {
        try { rethrow_exception(e); }
        catch (const std::exception &ex) {
            std::cerr << ex.what() << std::endl;
        }
    };
    value.
    subscribe(
            [](std::string s){printf("OnNext: %sn", s.c_str());},
            error_handler,
            [](){printf("OnCompletedn");});
}
```

The list of names is passed as an argument into the newly defined operator and we get the following output:

```
OnNext: Hello, Praseed!
OnNext: Hello, Joseph!
OnCompleted
```

Writing a custom transformation operator

Let's write a simple program to implement a custom operator by combining other operators, where we filter stream of numbers for odd numbers, transform numbers into its square, and take only first three elements from the stream:

```cpp
//------ CustomOperator1.cpp
#include "rxcpp/rx.hpp"
namespace rx {
    using namespace rxcpp;
    using namespace rxcpp::operators;
    using namespace rxcpp::sources;
    using namespace rxcpp::util;
}
//------ operator to filter odd number, find square & take first three
items
std::function<rx::observable<int>(rx::observable<int>)> getOddNumSquare() {
    return [](rx::observable<int> item) {
        return item.
        filter([](int v){ return v%2; }).
        map([](const int v) { return v*v; }).
        take(3).
        //------ Translating exception
        on_error_resume_next([](std::exception_ptr){
            return rx::error<int>(std::runtime_error("custom exception"));
});
    };
}
int main() {
    //------ Create an observable composing the custom operator
    auto value = rxcpp::observable<>::range(1, 7) |
    getOddNumSquare();
    value.
    subscribe(
            [](int v){printf("OnNext: %dn", v);},
            [](){printf("OnCompletedn");});
}
```

In this example, the custom operator is implemented with a different approach. Instead of returning a simple Observable of the desired type, the operator function returns a function object that takes and returns an Observable of the *int* type. This allows the user to perform the execution of higher-order functions using the pipe (|) operator. The ability to implement custom operators using user-defined transformations and combining them with existing operators comes in very handy when writing nontrivial programs. It is usually better to compose new operators by combining existing ones rather than implementing a new operator from the scratch (do not re-invent the wheel!).

Writing a custom operator that involves Schedulers

The RxCpp library is single-threaded by default, and RxCpp will schedule execution in the thread where we called the subscriber method. There are some operators that take a Scheduler as a parameter, where execution can happen in the thread managed by the Scheduler. Let's write a program to implement a custom operator to work with a Scheduler parameter:

```
//----------- CustomOperatorScheduler.cpp
#include "rxcpp/rx.hpp"
template <typename Duration>
auto generateObservable(Duration durarion) {
    //--------- start and the period
    auto start = rxcpp::identity_current_thread().now();
    auto period = durarion;
    //--------- Observable upto 3 items
    return rxcpp::observable<>::interval(start, period).take(3);
}

int main() {
    //-------- Create a coordination
    auto coordination = rxcpp::observe_on_event_loop();
    //-------- Instantiate a coordinator and create a worker
    auto worker = coordination.create_coordinator().get_worker();
    //----------- Create an Observable (Replay )
    auto values = generateObservable(std::chrono::milliseconds(2)).
        replay(2, coordination);
    //--------------- Subscribe first time
    worker.schedule([&](const rxcpp::schedulers::schedulable&) {
        values.subscribe([](long v) { printf("#1 -- %d : %ldn",
            std::this_thread::get_id(), v); },
                    []() { printf("#1 --- OnCompletedn"); });
    });
```

```
worker.schedule([&](const rxcpp::schedulers::schedulable&) {
    values.subscribe([](long v) { printf("#2 -- %d : %ldn",
        std::this_thread::get_id(), v); },
                    []() { printf("#2 --- OnCompletedn"); }); });
//----- Start the emission of values
worker.schedule([&](const rxcpp::schedulers::schedulable&) {
    values.connect();
});
//------- Add blocking subscription to see results
values.as_blocking().subscribe();
return 0;
}
```

Writing custom operators that can be chained

One of the key benefits of built-in operators provided by the RxCpp library is the possibility to chain operators using fluent interfaces. This significantly improves code readability. The custom operators that we've created so far can be composed together, but cannot be chained together in the way the standard operator can be chained. In this section, we will implement operators that can be chained by using the following methods:

- Using the lift<T> meta operator
- Writing a new operator by adding code to the RxCpp library

Using the lift<t> operator to write a custom operator

The RxCpp library has an operator as part of the observable<T> implementation, called lift (lift<t>). In fact, it can be called a meta-operator as it has the capability to convert a unary function or functor that takes an ordinary variable (int, float, double, struct, and so on) to be compatible for processing observable<T> Streams. The RxCpp implementation of observable<T>::lift expects a Lambda that takes rxcpp::subscriber<T> as a parameter, and within the body of the Lambda, we can apply an action (a Lambda or a function). In this section, one can get an overview of the purpose of the lift<t> operator.

The lift operator takes any function or Lambda that will take a Subscriber for an Observable and produce a new Subscriber. This is intended to allow externally-defined operators that use `make_subscriber` to be connected into the composition chain. The function prototype of the lift is as follows:

```
template<class ResultType , class operator >
auto rxcpp::operators::lift(Operator && op) ->
                    detail::lift_factory<ResultType, operator>
```

The signature and body of the Lambda expected by `lift<t>` is given here:

```
[=](rxcpp::subscriber<T> dest){
        return rxcpp::make_subscriber<T>(
            dest,rxcpp::make_observer_dynamic<T>(
                [=](T n){
                    //---- Apply an action Lambda on each items
                    //---- typically "action_lambda" is declared in
the
                    //---- outside scope (captured)
                    dest.on_next(action_lambda(n));
                },
                [=]( std::exception_ptr e ){dest.on_error(e);},
                [=](){dest.on_completed();}));
};
```

To understand the workings of the `lift<T>` operator, let's write a program that uses it. The advantage of `lift<T>` is that the operator created can be part of the operator chaining infrastructure of the RxCpp library.

```
//----------- operatorLiftFirst.cpp
#include "rxcpp/rx.hpp"
#include "rxcpp/rx-test.hpp"
#include <iostream>
namespace rxu=rxcpp::util;
#include <array>
using namespace rxcpp;
using namespace rxcpp::operators;

int main() {
    std::array< int ,4 > a={{10, 20,30,40}};
    /////////////////////////////////////////////////////////
    // The following Lambda will be lifted
    auto lambda_fn = [] ( int n ) { return n*2; };
    /////////////////////////////////////////////////////////
    // The following Lambda expects a rxcpp::subscriber and returns
    // a subscriber which implements on_next,on_error,on_completed
    // The Lambda lifting happens because, we apply lambda_fn on
```

```
            // each item.
            auto transform = [=](rxcpp::subscriber<int> dest){
                return rxcpp::make_subscriber<int>(
                        dest,rxcpp::make_observer_dynamic<int>(
                            [=](int n){
                                dest.on_next(lambda_fn(n));
                            },
                            [=]( std::exception_ptr e ){dest.on_error(e);},
                            [=](){dest.on_completed();}));
            };
            // type of values will be observable<int>
            // Lazy Evaluation
            auto values = rxcpp::observable<>::iterate(a);
            //-------- As usual subscribe
            values.lift<int>(transform).subscribe(
                    [] (int f) { std::cout << f <<  std::endl; } ,
                    [] () {std::cout << "Hello World.." << std::endl;} );
    }
```

We have now learned how we can use the `lift<t>` operator. The `observable<T>` instance and its lift method take a Lambda with a specific parameter type and produce an `observable<T>`. The advantage of `lift<T>` is that we can use operator chaining.

Converting an arbitrary Lambda to a custom Rx operator

In the previous section, we learned that it is possible to use the `lift<t>` operator to implement custom operators that can be part of the operator chaining infrastructure of the RxCpp library. The workings of `lift<T>` are a bit complicated and we will write an `Adapter` class to convert an arbitrary Lambda that takes a parameter (of the basic types) to a form where the `lift<T>` operator can be applied.

The adapter code will help us to make calls such as this:

```
observable<T>::lift<T>( liftaction( lambda<T> ) )
```

Let's write an `Adapter` class implementation and a generic function wrapper on top of it to be consumed in a program:

```
//----------- operatorLiftSecond.cpp
#include "rxcpp/rx.hpp"
#include "rxcpp/rx-test.hpp"
#include <iostream>
namespace rxu=rxcpp::util;
```

```cpp
#include <array>
using namespace rxcpp;
using namespace rxcpp::operators;
///////////////////////////////////////////////
// The LiftAction class  ( an adapter class) converts an Action ( a Lambda
)
// and wraps it into a form which can help us to connect
// to an observable<T> using the observable<T>::lift<T> method.
template<class Action>
struct LiftAction {
    typedef typename std::decay<Action>::type action_type;
    action_type action;

    LiftAction(action_type t): action(t){}
    ///////////////////////////////////////
    // Create an Internal observer to gather
    // data from observable<T>
    //
    template<class Subscriber>
    struct action_observer : public
            rxcpp::observer_base<typename
            std::decay<Subscriber>::type::value_type>
    {
        ///////////////////////////////////////////
        // typedefs for
        //          * this_type (action_observer)
        //          * base_type (observable_base)
        //          * value_type
        //          * dest_type
        //          * observer_type
        typedef action_observer<Subscriber> this_type;
        typedef rxcpp::observer_base<typename
                std::decay<Subscriber>::type::value_type> base_type;
        typedef typename base_type::value_type value_type;
        typedef typename std::decay<Subscriber>::type dest_type;
        typedef rxcpp::observer<value_type, this_type> observer_type;

        //------ destination subscriber and action
        dest_type dest;
        action_type action;
        action_observer(dest_type d, action_type t)
            : dest(d), action(t){}

        //--------- subscriber/observer methods
        //-------- on_next implementation needs more
        //-------- robustness by supporting exception handling
        void on_next(typename dest_type::value_type v) const
        {dest.on_next(action(v));}
```

```
        void on_error(std::exception_ptr e) const
        { dest.on_error(e);}
        void on_completed() const {
            dest.on_completed();
        }
        //--------- Create a subscriber with requisite parameter
        //--------- types
        static rxcpp::subscriber<value_type, observer_type>
                make(const dest_type& d, const action_type& t) {
            return rxcpp::make_subscriber<value_type>
                (d, observer_type(this_type(d, t)));
        }
    };
```

In RxCpp operator implementations, we will have an internal Observer that intercepts the traffic and applies some logic on items, before passing on the control to the next operator in the chain. The `action_observer` class is structured along those lines. Since we are using Lambdas (lazy evaluation), the execution will happen only when the Scheduler triggers the execution, whenever data is received in the pipeline:

```
    template<class Subscriber>
    auto operator()(const Subscriber& dest) const
        -> decltype(action_observer<Subscriber>::make(dest, action)) {
        return    action_observer<Subscriber>::make(dest, action);
    }
};
/////////////////////////////////////////
// liftaction takes a Universal reference
// and uses perfect forwarding
template<class Action>
auto liftaction(Action&& p) ->  LiftAction<typename
std::decay<Action>::type>
{
    return  LiftAction<typename
            std::decay<Action>::type>(std::forward<Action>(p));
}
```

Now that we have learned how to implement an `Adapter` class to convert a Lambda into a form that `lift<T>` can accept, let's write a program that demonstrates how we can leverage the preceding code:

```
int main() {
    std::array< int ,4 > a={{10, 20,30,40}};
    auto h = [] (observable<int> src ) {
        return src.map([](int n ) { return n; });
    };
    auto g = [] (observable<int> src ) {
```

```
            return src.map([](int n ) { return n*2; });
    };
    // type of values will be observable<int>
    // Lazy Evaluation  ... the Lift operator
    // converts a Lambda to be part of operator chaining
    auto values = g(h(rxcpp::observable<>::iterate(a)))
        .lift<int> (liftaction( [] ( int r ) { return 2*r; }));
    //-------- As usual subscribe
    values.subscribe(
            [] (int f) { std::cout << f <<  std::endl; } ,
            [] () {std::cout << "Hello World.." << std::endl;} );
}
```

The output of the program is given here:

```
40
80
120
160
Hello World..
```

Creating a custom RxCpp operator in the library

Every operator in the RxCpp library is defined under rxcpp::operators namespaces. Within the rxcpp::operators namespace, library designers have created a nested namespace called details, where implementations of the operator logic are typically specified. To demonstrate the implementation of an operator from scratch, we have cloned the implementation of the map operator to create another operator, by the name of eval. The semantics of eval are the same as those of the map operator. The source code listing is available in a folder related to this particular chapter in the GitHub repository associated with this book.

We decided to move the book's code to the GitHub repository because the listing is a bit long and doesn't contribute much to the conceptual understanding of the implementation of an operator in the RxCpp library. The liftaction implementation outlined earlier shows us how to write an internal Observer. There is a standard pattern that every operator implementation follows:

- It subscribes to the source Observable by creating a private Observer
- It transforms elements of the Observable according to the purpose of the operator
- It pushes the transformed value to its own subscribers

The skeleton source listing of the `eval` operator implementation is given here. The implementation of the source file contains the following:

Source file	Key changes

`rx-eval.hpp`	Implementation of the `eval` operator:
	```//rx-eval.hpp```
	```#if !defined(RXCPP_OPERATORS_RX_EVAL_HPP)```
	```#define RXCPP_OPERATORS_RX_EVAL_HPP```
	```//----------- all headers are included here```
	```#include "../rx-includes.hpp"```
	```namespace rxcpp {```
	``` namespace operators {```
	``` namespace detail {```
	``` //------------- operator implementation goes here```
	``` }```
	``` }```
	```}```
	```#endif```

`rx-includes.h`	Modified header files with the inclusion of `Rx-eval.hpp`. `rx-includes.h` will add an additional entry into the file, which goes as follows: ```#include "operators/rx-eval.hpp"```

`rx-operators.h`	Modified header file with the `eval_tag` definition. `rx-operators.h` contains the following tag entry:
	```struct eval_tag {```
	``` template<class Included>```
	``` struct include_header{```
	``` static_assert(Included::value,```
	``` "missing include: please```
	``` #include <rxcpp/operators/rx-eval.hpp>");```
	```};```
	```};```

`rx-observables.h`	Modified header file with the definition of the `eval` operator:
	```template<class... AN>```
	```auto eval(AN&&... an) const->```
	```decltype(observable_member(eval_tag{},```
	``` *(this_type*)nullptr, std::forward<AN>(an)...)){```
	``` return observable_member(eval_tag{},```
	``` *this, std::forward<AN>(an)...);```
	```}```

Let's write a program to use the `eval` operator. The prototype for the `eval` operator (like map) is as follows:

```
observaable<T>::eval<T>( lambda<T>)
```

You can check the source code of the implementation to better understand the `eval` operator. Now, let's write a program that leverages the `eval` operator:

```cpp
//------------ operatorComposeCustom.cpp
#include "rxcpp/rx.hpp"
#include "rxcpp/rx-test.hpp"
#include <iostream>
namespace rxu=rxcpp::util;
#include <array>
using namespace std;
using namespace rxcpp;
using namespace rxcpp::operators;
int main() {
     std::array< string ,4 > a={{"Bjarne","Kirk","Herb","Sean"}};
     auto h = [] (observable<string> src ) {
         return src.eval([](string s ) { return s+"!"; });
     };
     //-------- We will Lift g using eval
     auto g = [](string s) { return "Hello : " + s; };
     // use apply h first and then call eval
     auto values = h(rxcpp::observable<>::iterate(a)).eval(g);
     //-------- As usual subscribe
     values.subscribe(
               [] (string f) { std::cout << f <<  std::endl; } ,
               [] () {std::cout << "Hello World.." << std::endl;} );
}
```

The output of the program is given here:

```
Hello : Bjarne!
Hello : Kirk!
Hello : Herb!
Hello : Sean!
Hello World..
```

To write custom operators that are implemented in a generic manner requires deep expertise in RxCpp internals. You need to understand the implementation of some stock operators before attempting a custom operator. The operator we wrote can be a starting point for you to implement such operators. Once again, writing custom operators from scratch should be a last resort!

Summary

In this chapter, we learned how to write custom operators. We started by writing simple operators that can perform basic tasks. Even though the operators we wrote (initially) were composable, we were not able to chain them together like standard RxCpp operators. After writing different genres of operators, we implemented chainable custom operators using the lift<T> meta operator. Finally, we saw how we can add an operator to observable<T> as well. In the next chapter, we'll delve into the world of design patterns and idioms for Rx programming. We'll start with GOF design patterns and implement different reactive programming patterns.

11
Design Patterns and Idioms for C++ Rx Programming

We have covered quite a bit of ground in using reactive programming model with C++. So far, we have learned about the RxCpp library and its programming model, key elements of the RxCpp library, reactive GUI programming and the topic of writing custom Operators. Now, to take the matter to the next level, we will cover some Design patterns and Idioms which help us in advanced software development tasks.

In this chapter, we will cover following topics:

- An introduction to patterns and the pattern movement
- GOF design patterns and reactive programming
- Some reactive programming patterns and idioms

The OOP and Design patterns movement

The **Object Oriented Programming (OOP)** reached critical mass in early 90s when the C++ programming language began to make inroads into areas where C programming language was the primary programming language. After the advent of Microsoft C++ compiler in the year 1992 , followed by Microsoft Foundation Class (MFC) library, the C++ programming became mainstream under Microsoft Windows. In the POSIX world, C++ GUI toolkits like WxWidgets, and Qt,signaled the arrival of OOP. The early pioneers of the OOP movement wrote articles in various magazines like Dr. Dobb's Journal , C++ Report ,Microsoft Systems Journal and so on., to propagate their ideas.

James Coplien published an influential book titled *Advanced C++ Styles and Idioms*, which dealt with the low-level patterns (idioms) associated with usage of the C++ programming language. Even though it is not widely cited, authors of this book consider it as a notable book for cataloging best practices and techniques of OOP.

Erich Gamma began to work on a pattern catalog as part of his Ph.D. thesis, getting inspiration from Christopher Alexander's *A Pattern of Towns and building* book. While working on the thesis, people with similar thoughts, namely Ralph Johnson, John Vlissides, and Richard Helm, joined hands with Erich Gamma to create a catalog of 23 Design patterns, now known as **Gang of Four** (**GOF**) Design patterns. The Addison Wesley published the book *Design Patterns : Elements of Reusable Object-Oriented Software* in the year 1994, based on their work. This soon became a great reference for programmers, and fueled pattern oriented software development. The GOF catalog was mostly focused on software design and soon pattern catalogs began to appear in areas like architecture,enterprise application integration, enterprise application architecture and so on.

In 1996, a group of engineers from Siemens published the book, *Pattern Oriented Software Architecture (POSA)*, which mainly focused on architectural aspects of building a system. The entire POSA pattern catalog was documented in five books, published by John Wiley and Sons. A flood of activity followed the two preceding initiatives. Other notable pattern catalogs are given below

- *Patterns of Enterprise Application Architecture*, by Martin Fowler, et al.
- *Enterprise Integration Patterns*, by Gregor Hope and Boby Wulf.
- *Core J2EE Patterns*, by Deepak Alur, et al.
- *Domain Driven Design*, by Eric Evans.
- *The Enterprise Patterns and the MDA*, by Jim Arlow and Illa Neustadt.

Even though these books were significant in their own right, they were skewed towards the then-burgeoning area of enterprise software development. For C++ developers, the GOF catalog and POSA catalog are the most important.

Key Pattern catalogs

A pattern is a named solution for a commonly occurring problem in software design. Patterns are most often cataloged in some kind of repository. Some of them are published as books. The most popular and widely used pattern catalog is GOF.

The GOF catalog

The Gang of Four (GOF), named after creators of the catalog, started the pattern movement. The creators were mostly focused on design and architecture of object oriented software. The ideas of Christopher Alexander were borrowed from building architecture and applied to software engineering .Soon, people began pattern initiatives in the area of application architecture, concurrency, security, and so on. The Gang Of Four divided the catalog into structural, creational, and behavioral patterns. The original book used C++ and Smalltalk for explaining the concepts. These patterns have been ported and leveraged in most of the OOP languages that exist today. The table below lists patterns from the GOF catalog.

Sl. No.	Pattern Type	Patterns
1	Creational patterns	Abstract Factory, Builder, Factory Method, Prototype, Singleton
2	Structural patterns	Adapter, Bridge, Composite, Decorator, Facade, Flyweight, Proxy
3	Behavioral patterns	Chain of Responsibility, Command, Interpreter, Iterator, Mediator, Memento, Observer , State, Strategy, Template Method, Visitor

We believe that a good understanding of GOF patterns is necessary for any programmer. These patterns occur everywhere, regardless of the application domain. GOF patterns help us to communicate and reason about software systems in a language agnostic manner. They are widely implemented in the C++, .NET and Java worlds. The Qt framework leverages patterns in the GOF repository extensively, for giving an intuitive programming model in the C++ programming language., primarily for writing GUI applications.

The POSA catalog

Patterns of Software Architecture (five volumes) is an influential book series, which covers most of the applicable patterns for developing mission critical systems. The catalog is good for people who write mission critical sub-systems of large software, especially database engines, distributed systems, middleware systems, and so on. Another advantage of the catalog is that it is well suited for C++ programmers.

The catalog, which spans five published volumes, is worthy of independent study. This catalog is quite handy if we want to write Industrial strength middleware software like web server, protocol servers ,database servers and so on.   The following table contains a list of pattern types and associated patterns

Sl. No.	Pattern Type	Patterns
1	Architectural	Layers, Pipes and Filters, Blackboard, Broker, MVC, Presentation-Abstraction-Control, Microkernel, Reflection
2	Design	Whole-Part, Mater-Slave, Proxy, Command Processor, View Handler, Forwarder-Receiver, Client-Dispatcher-Server, Publisher-Subscriber
3	Service access and configuration patterns	Wrapper Façade, Component Configurator, Interceptor, Extension Interface
4	Event handling patterns	Reactor, Proactor, Asynchronous Completion Token, Acceptor-Connector
5	Synchronization patterns	Scoped Locking, Strategized Locking, Thread-Safe Interface, Double-Checked Locking Optimization
6	Concurrency patterns	Active Object, Monitor Object, Half-Sync/Half-Async, Leader/Followers, Thread-Specific Storage
7	Resource acquisition patterns	Lookup, Lazy Acquisition, Eager Acquisition, Partial Acquisition
8	Resource lifecycle	Caching, Pooling, Coordinator, Resource Lifecycle Manager
9	Resource release patterns	Leasing, Evictor
10	A pattern language for distributive computing	Rather than introducing new patterns , a consolidation of patterns from different catalogs, in being done in the context of distributed programming
11	On patterns and pattern languages	This last volume gives some meta-information about patterns, pattern languages, and usage

The POSA catalog needs to be studied to gain deep insights into the architectural underpinnings of large-scale systems, which are deployed across the world. We believe that, despite its importance, this catalog has not received the attention, it deserves.

The Design pattern redux

The GOF pattern and reactive programming do have a deeper connection than that is obvious from the surface. The GOF pattern is mostly concerned with writing OOP-based software . Reactive programming is a combination of functional programming, stream programming, and concurrent programming. We already learned that reactive programming rectifies some deficiencies in the classic GOF Observer pattern(in the first section of `Chapter 5`, *Introduction to Observables*, we covered this issue).

Writing OOP software is basically about modeling hierarchies, and from the pattern world, the Composite pattern is the way to model Part/Whole hierarchies. Wherever there is a Composite (which models a structure), a collection of Visitor pattern implementations (to model behavior) will follow suit. The primary purpose of Visitor pattern is processing Composites. In other words, the Composite-Visitor duo is the canonical model for writing object oriented systems.

The Visitor implementations should possess some awareness about the structure of Ccmposites. Behavioral processing using the Visitor pattern becomes difficult, as the number of Visitors for a given Composite proliferates. Moreover, adding transformations and filters to the processing layer further complicates the matter.

Enter the Iterator pattern, which is good for the navigation of a sequence,, or list of items. Using object/functional programming constructs, we can filter and transform sequences very easily. Microsoft's LINQ and processing collection classes using lambdas in Java (8 and above) are good examples of the Iterator pattern.

Now, how will we transform hierarchical data into a linear structure? Most hierarchies can be flattened into a list for further processing. Recently, people have started doing the following:

- Modeling their hierarchies using the Composite pattern.
- Flattening the hierarchy into a sequence by using a Visitor meant for the purpose.
- Navigating those sequences using the Iterator pattern.
- Applying a series of transformations and filters to sequences before performing actions on them.

The preceding method is called the `pull` method of programming. Consumers or Clients pull data from the event or data source to process it. This scheme suffers from the following issues:

- The data is unnecessarily pulled into the client.
- The transformations and filters are applied on the event sink (client) side.

- The event sink can block the server.
- The style is not good for asynchronous processing, where data varies over time.

A good solution to the problem is to reverse the gaze, where data is pushed from the server asynchronously as a Stream, and the event sink will react to the Stream. Another advantage of this kind of system is the placement of transformations and filters on the event source side. This leads to a scenario where (only) data that is absolutely essential ,needs to be processed on the sink side.

The scheme is as follows:

- The data is treated as streams, which are called Observables.
- We can apply a series of Operators, or higher order Operators, to them.
- An Operator always takes an Observable and returns another Observable.
- We can subscribe to an Observable for notifications.
- Observers have standard mechanisms to process them.

In this section, we learned how OOP patterns and reactive programming are closely related. Judicious mixing of both paradigms produces high quality, maintainable code. We also discussed how OOP design patterns (Composite/Visitor) can be transformed (flattening the structure) to leverage Iterator pattern. We discussed how the scheme of iteration can be improved with a slight nudge (a fire and forget idiom on the event source side).to arrive at Observables. In the next section, we will demonstrate the whole technique by writing code.

From Design patterns to Reactive programming

Even though the design pattern movement is aligned with OOP, and reactive programming is aligned towards FP, there are close similarities between them. In a previous chapter(Chapter 5, *Introduction to Observables*), we learned the following:

- The OOP model is good for modeling the structural aspects of a system.
- The FP model is good for modeling the behavioral aspects of a system.

To illustrate the connection between OOP and reactive programming, we will write a program that will traverse directories to enumerate files and sub-folders within a given folder.

We will create a composite structure that contains the following:

- A `FileNode` (inherits from the abstract class `EntryNode`) that models file information
- A `DirectoryNode` (inherits from the abstract class `EntryNode`) that models folder information

After defining the preceding Composites, we will define Visitors for the following:

- Printing filenames and folder names
- Converting a composite hierarchy to a list of filenames

Without further ado, let's get into meat of the stuff. Take a look at this code:

```cpp
//---------- DirReact.cpp
#include <rxcpp/rx.hpp>
#include <memory>
#include <map>
#include <algorithm>
#include <string>
#include <vector>
#include <windows.h> // This is omitted in POSIX version
#include <functional>
#include <thread>
#include <future>
using namespace std;
/////////////////////////////////////
//-------------- Forward Declarations
//-------------- Model Folder/File
class FileNode;
class DirectoryNode;
/////////////////////////////////////
//-------------- The Visitor Interface
class IFileFolderVisitor;
```

The preceding forward declarations are undertaken to silence the compiler from issuing errors and warnings while compiling the program. The `FileNode` stores a filename and its size as an instance variable. The `DirectoryNode` stores a folder name and a list of `FileNode`, to indicate files and folders within a directory. The `FileNode/DirectoryNode` hierarchy is processed by the `IFileFolderVisitor` interface. Now, let us the declaration for these data types.

```cpp
/////////////////////////////////////
//------- a Type to store FileInformation
struct FileInformation{
    string name;
```

```
        long size;
        FileInformation( string pname,long psize )
        { name = pname;size = psize; }
};
///////////////////////////////////
//-------------- Base class for File/Folder data structure
class EntryNode{
    protected:
        string  name;
        int isdir;
        long size;
    public:
        virtual bool Isdir() = 0;
        virtual long getSize() = 0;
        virtual void Accept(IFileFolderVisitor& ivis)=0;
        virtual ~EntryNode() {}
};
```

When we create a Composite, we need to create a node class that acts as a base class for all members of the hierarchy. In our case, the `EntryNode` class does that. We store the file or folder name, the size, and so on, in the base class. Other than the three virtual functions, which should be implemented by the derived class, we have a virtual destructor, as well. The presence of a virtual destructor makes sure that destructors are applied properly, to avoid resource leaks. Now, let us see the Visitor base class declaration given below.

```
//--------------The Visitor Interface
class IFileFolderVisitor{
    public:
        virtual void Visit(FileNode& fn )=0;
        virtual void Visit(DirectoryNode& dn )=0;
};
```

Whenever we define a hierarchy using a Composite pattern style implementation, we define a Visitor interface to process nodes in the Composite. For each node in the Composite, there will be a corresponding `visit` method for it in the Visitor interface. Every node in the class hierarchy of the Composite will have an `accept` method, and the Visitor interface, during traversal of the Composite, dispatches call to the respective node's `accept` method. The `accept` method dispatches the call back to the correct `visit` method in the Visitor. This process is called **double dispatch**:

```
// The Node which represents Files
class FileNode : public EntryNode {
    public:
    FileNode(string pname, long psize) {  isdir = 0; name = pname; size =
psize;}
        ~FileNode() {cout << "....Destructor FileNode ...." << name << endl; }
```

```
    virtual bool  Isdir() { return isdir == 1; }
    string getname() { return name; }

    virtual long getSize() {return size; }
    //------------- accept method
    //------------- dispatches call to correct node in
    //------------- the Composite
    virtual void Accept( IFileFolderVisitor& ivis ){ivis.Visit(*this);}
};
```

The `FileNode` class just stores the name and the size of the file. The class also implements all virtual methods declared in the base class (`EntryNode`). The `accept` method redirects the call to the correct Visitor level method, as shown here:

```
// Node which represents Directory
class DirectoryNode : public EntryNode {
  list<unique_ptr<EntryNode>> files;
public:
  DirectoryNode(string pname)
  { files.clear(); isdir = 1; name = pname; }
  ~DirectoryNode() {files.clear();}
  list<unique_ptr<EntryNode>>& GetAllFiles() {return files;}
  bool AddFile( string pname , long size) {
      files.push_back(unique_ptr<EntryNode> (new FileNode(pname,size)));
      return true;
  }
  bool AddDirectory( DirectoryNode *dn ) {
      files.push_back(unique_ptr<EntryNode>(dn));
      return true;
  }
  bool Isdir() { return isdir == 1; }
  string  getname() { return name; }
  void    setname(string pname) { name = pname; }
  long getSize() {return size; }
  //
  //--------------------- accept method
  void Accept( IFileFolderVisitor& ivis ){ivis.Visit(*this); }
};
```

The `DirectoryNode` class models a folder with a list of files and sub-folders. We are using smart pointers to store the entry. As usual, we have also implemented all virtual functions associated with the `EntryNode` class. The methods `AddFile` and `AddDirectory` are meant to populate the list. While traversing the directory using the OS specific functions, we populate contents of a `DirectoryNode` object with the preceding two methods: Let us see prototype of the directory traversal helper function. We have omitted the full listing of the source code (available online)

```
//------Directory Helper Has to be written for Each OS
class DirHelper {
public:
    static  DirectoryNode  *SearchDirectory(
             const std::string& refcstrRootDirectory){
          //-------------- Do some OS specific stuff to retrieve
          //-------------- File/Folder hierarchy from the root folder
          return DirNode;
}};
```

The `DirHelper` logic varies between Windows and GNU Linux/macOS X. We have omitted source code of the implementation, from the book. The associated website contains full source code for the preceding class. Basically, the code recursively traverses directories to populate the data structure. Now, we will move to the topic of traversing the Composite created above. The following code shows how we can traverse the Composite using a Visitor class, which implements the IFileFolderVisitor interface.

```
//////////////////////////////////////
//----- A Visitor Interface that prints
//----- The contents of a Folder
class PrintFolderVisitor : public IFileFolderVisitor
{
  public:
    void Visit(FileNode& fn ) {cout << fn.getname() << endl; }
    void Visit(DirectoryNode& dn ) {
       cout << "In a directory " << dn.getname() << endl;
       list<unique_ptr<EntryNode>>& ls = dn.GetAllFiles();
       for ( auto& itr : ls ) { itr.get()->Accept(*this);}
    }
};
```

The `PrintFolderVisitor` class is a Visitor implementation that displays the file and folder information to the console. The class demonstrates how a basic Visitor can be implemented for a Composite. In our case, the Composite has only two nodes, and it is very easy to write the Visitor implementation.

In certain cases, the number of node types in a hierarchy are numerous, and writing a Visitor implementation is not trivial. Writing filters and transformations for Visitors can be difficult, and the logic is ad hoc. Let's write a program to print the contents of a folder. Here it is:

```
//--------------- has used raw pointers
//--------------- in a production implementation, use smart pointer
void TestVisitor( string directory ){
   // Search files including subdirectories
   DirectoryNode *dirs = DirHelper::SearchDirectory(directory);
   if ( dirs == 0 ) {return;}
   PrintFolderVisitor *fs = new PrintFolderVisitor ();
   dirs->Accept(*fs); delete fs; delete dirs;
}
```

The preceding function recursively traverses a directory and creates a Composite (`DirectoryNode *`). We use `PrintFolderVisitor` to print the contents of the folder, as shown below:

```
int main(int argc, char *argv[]) {  TestVisitor("D:\\Java"); }
```

Flattening the hierarchy to navigate through it

The Visitor implementation has to posses some idea of the structure of the Composite. In some instances of Composite implementation, there will be scores of Visitors needs to be implemented. Moreover, applying transformations and filters on nodes are bit difficult in the case of Visitor interfaces. The GOF pattern catalog has an Iterator pattern that can be used to navigate a sequence of items. The problem is: How can we linearize a hierarchy for processing using the Iterator pattern? Most hierarchies can be flattened to a list, sequence, or stream by writing a Visitor implementation for that purpose. Let us write a flattening Visitor for the said task.

Take a look at the following code:

```
// Flatten the File/Folders into a linear list
class FlattenVisitor : public IFileFolderVisitor{
    list <FileInformation> files;
    string CurrDir;
 public:
    FlattenVisitor() { CurrDir = "";}
    ~FlattenVisitor() { files.clear();}
    list<FileInformation> GetAllFiles() { return files; }
    void Visit(FileNode& fn ) {
        files.push_back( FileInformation{
                CurrDir +"\" + fn.getname(),fn.getSize()));
```

```
        }
      void Visit(DirectoryNode& dn ) {
          CurrDir = dn.getname();
          files.push_back( FileInformation( CurrDir, 0 ));
          list<unique_ptr<EntryNode>>& ls = dn.GetAllFiles();
          for ( auto& itr : ls ) { itr.get()->Accept(*this);}
      }
};
```

The `FlattenVisitor` class collects files and folders in a STL list. For each directory, we iterate through the list of files and issue the `accept` method, using the familiar double dispatch. Let us write a function that returns a list of `FileInformation` for us to iterate through. Here is the code:

```
list<FileInformation> GetAllFiles(string dirname ){
    list<FileInformation> ret_val;
    // Search files including subdirectories
    DirectoryNode *dirs = DirHelper::SearchDirectory(dirname);
    if ( dirs == 0 ) {return ret_val;}
    //--   We have used Raw pointers here...
    //--- In Modern C++, one can use smart pointer here
    //   unique_ptr<FlattenVisitor> fs(new FlattenVisitor());
    //   We can avoid delete fs
    FlattenVisitor *fs = new FlattenVisitor();
    dirs->Accept(*fs);
    ret_val = fs->GetAllFiles();
    //--------- use of Raw pointer
    delete fs; delete dirs;
    return ret_val;
}
int main(int argc, char *argv[]) {
  list<FileInformation> rs = GetAllFiles("D:\JAVA");
  for( auto& as : rs )
    cout << as.name << endl;
}
```

The `FlattenVisitor` class traverses the `DirectoryNode` hierarchy and collects the fully expanded pathname into a STL list container. Once we have linearized the hierarchy into a list, we can iterate over it.

We have learned how to model a hierarchy as a Composite, and eventually flatten it to a form that is suitable for navigation with the Iterator pattern. In the next section, we will learn how Iterators can be transformed into Observables. We will use RxCpp to implement the Observables by using a fire and forget model, pushing values from the event source to the event sink.

From Iterators to Observables

The Iterator pattern is the standard mechanism to pull data from STL containers, generators, and streams. They are well suited for data that has been aggregated in the space. Essentially, this means that we know ahead of time how much data is supposed to be retrieved, or that the data has already been captured. There are scenarios where the data arrives asynchronously and the consumers are not aware of how much data there is or when the data arrives. In such cases, Iterators need to wait, or we need to resort to timeout strategies to handle the scenario. In such a scenario, a push-based approach seems to be a better option. Using the Subject construct of Rx, we can use a fire and forget strategy. Let's write a class that emits the contents of a directory, as shown here:

```cpp
/////////////////////////////////
// A Toy implementation of Active
// Object Pattern... Will be explained as a separate pattern
template <class T>
struct ActiveObject {
    rxcpp::subjects::subject<T> subj;
    // fire-and-forget
    void FireNForget(T & item){subj.get_subscriber().on_next(item);}
    rxcpp::observable<T> GetObservable()
    { return subj.get_observable(); }
    ActiveObject(){}
    ~ActiveObject() {}
};
/////////////////////////////
// The class uses a FireNForget mechanism to
// push data to the Data/Event sink
//
class DirectoryEmitter {
      string rootdir;
      //------------- Active Object ( a Pattern in it's own right )
      ActiveObject<FileInformation> act; // more on this below
  public:
      DirectoryEmitter(string s )    {
         rootdir = s;
         //----- Subscribe
         act.GetObservable().subscribe([] ( FileInformation item ) {
            cout << item.name << ":" << item.size << endl;
         });
      }
      bool Trigger() {
          std::packaged_task<int()> task([&]() {  EmitDirEntry(); return
1; });
          std::future<int> result = task.get_future();
          task();
```

```
                //------------- Comment the below lineto return immediately
                double dresult = result.get();
                return true;
        }
        //----- Iterate over the list of files
        //----- uses ActiveObject Pattern to do FirenForget
        bool EmitDirEntry() {
                list<FileInformation> rs = GetAllFiles(rootdir);
                for( auto& a : rs ) { act.FireNForget(a); }
                return false;
        }
};
int main(int argc, char *argv[]) {
  DirectoryEmitter emitter("D:\\JAVA");
  emitter.Trigger(); return 0;
}
```

The `DirectoryEmitter` class uses modern C++'s `packaged_task` construct to make asynchronous calls in a fire and forget manner. In the preceding listing, we were waiting for the result (using `std::future<T>`). We can comment a line in the above code listing (see the inline comment in the listing) to return immediately.

The Cell pattern

We have already learned that reactive programming is all about processing values that vary over time. The reactive programming model is centered on the notion of Observables. There are two variants of Observables, which are as follows:

- Cells: A cell is an entity (a variable, or a memory location) where values are regularly updated over time. They are also called properties or behaviors, in some contexts.
- Streams: A stream represents a series of events. They are data that is often associated with actions. When people think of Observables, they have got stream variant of Observables in their mind.

We will implement a toy version of a Cell programming pattern. We will only focus on implementing basic functionality. The code needs tidying up for production use.

The following implementation can be optimized, if we are implementing a a controller class called Cell controller. . Then, the Cell controller class (which contains a single Rx Subject for all cells) can receive notifications from all cells (to a central place) and update dependencies by evaluating expressions. Here, we have attached Subjects with every Cell. This implementation shows how the Cell pattern is a viable mechanism for dependent computations:

```cpp
//----------------- CellPattern.cpp
#include <rxcpp/rx.hpp>
#include <memory>
#include <map>
#include <algorithm>
using namespace std;
class Cell
{
  private:
    std::string name;
    std::map<std::string,Cell *> parents;
    rxcpp::subjects::behavior<double> *behsubject;
  public:
    string get_name() { return name; }
    void SetValue(double v )
    { behsubject->get_subscriber().on_next(v); }
    double GetValue()
    { return behsubject->get_value(); }
    rxcpp::observable<double> GetObservable()
    { return behsubject->get_observable(); }
    Cell(std::string pname) {
        name = pname;
        behsubject = new rxcpp::subjects::behavior<double>(0);
    }
    ~Cell() {delete behsubject; parents.clear();}
    bool GetCellNames( string& a , string& b )
    {
        if ( parents.size() !=2 ) { return false; }
        int i = 0;
        for(auto p  : parents ) {
          ( i == 0 )? a = p.first : b = p.first;
          i++;
        }
        return true;
    }
    /////////////////////////////////
    // We will just add two parent cells...
    // in real life, we need to implement an
    // expression evaluator
    bool Recalculate() {
```

```
        string as , bs ;
        if (!GetCellNames(as,bs) ) { return false; }
        auto a = parents[as];
        auto b = parents[bs];
        SetValue( a->GetValue() + b->GetValue() );
        return true;
    }
    bool Attach( Cell& s ) {
        if ( parents.size() >= 2 ) { return false; }
        parents.insert(pair<std::string,Cell *>(s.get_name(),&s));
        s.GetObservable().subscribe( [=] (double a ) { Recalculate() ;});
        return true;
    }
    bool Detach( Cell& s ) { //--- Not Implemented
    } };
```

The Cell class makes an assumption that each cell has two parent dependencies (to make the implementation simple), and whenever there is a change in value of parents, the cell's value will be recalculated. We have only implemented an addition operator (to keep listings small). The `recalculate` method implements the logic, as shown above: Let us write a main program to put everything together.

```
int main(int argc, char *argv[]) {
    Cell a("a");
    Cell b("b");
    Cell c("c");
    Cell d("d");
    Cell e("e");
    //-------- attach a to c
    //-------- attach b to c
    //-------- c is a + b
    c.Attach(a);
    c.Attach(b);
    //---------- attach c to e
    //---------- attach d to e
    //---------- e is c + d or e is a + b + d;
    e.Attach(c);
    e.Attach(d);
    a.SetValue(100);   // should print 100
    cout << "Value is " << c.GetValue() << endl;
    b.SetValue(200);   // should print 300
    cout << "Value is " << c.GetValue() << endl;
    b.SetValue(300);   // should print 400
    cout << "Value is " << c.GetValue() << endl;
    d.SetValue(-400);  // should be Zero
    cout << "Value is " << e.GetValue() << endl;
}
```

The main program demonstrates how we can use the Cell pattern to propagate changes down into the dependencies. By changing values in cless, we force the re-computation of values in the dependent cells.

The Active object pattern

An Active object is a class that decouples method invocations and method executions, and is well suited for fire and forget asynchronous calls. A scheduler attached to the class handles the execution requests. The pattern consists of six elements, which are as follows:

- A proxy, which provides an interface for clients with publicly accessible methods
- An interface that defines the method request on an Active object
- A list of pending requests from clients
- A Scheduler, which decides which request to execute next
- The implementation of the Active object method
- A callback or variable, for the client to receive the result

We will dissect an implementation of the Active object pattern. This program is written for elucidation; for production use, we need to use a bit more sophistication. Attempting a production quality implementation would make the code considerably longer. Let's take a look at the code:

```cpp
#include <rxcpp/rx.hpp>
#include <memory>
#include <map>
#include <algorithm>
#include <string>
#include <vector>
#include <windows.h>
#include <functional>
#include <thread>
#include <future>
using namespace std;
//------- Active Object Pattern Implementation
template <class T>
class ActiveObject {
    //----------- Dispatcher Object
    rxcpp::subjects::subject<T> subj;
    protected:
    ActiveObject(){
        subj.get_observable().subscribe([=] (T s )
        { Execute(s); });
    }
```

```
        virtual void Execute(T s) {}
        public:
        // fire-and-forget
        void FireNForget(T item){ subj.get_subscriber().on_next(item);}
        rxcpp::observable<T> GetObservable() { return subj.get_observable(); }
        virtual ~ActiveObject() {}
    };
```

The preceding implementation declares an instance of the `subject<T>` class, to act as a notification mechanism. The `FireNForget` method places the value into the subject by invoking the `get_subscriber` method. The method immediately returns, and the subscription method will retrieve the value and call the `Execute` method. The class is supposed to be overridden by a concrete implementation. Let's take a look at the code:

```
    class ConcreteObject : public ActiveObject<double> {
        public:
          ConcreteObject() {}
          virtual void Execute(double a )
          { cout << "Hello World....." << a << endl;}
    };
    int main(int argc, char *argv[]) {
      ConcreteObject temp;
      for( int i=0; i<=10; ++i )
          temp.FireNForget(i*i);
      return 0;
    }
```

The previous code snippet calls the `FireNForget` method, with a double value. On the console, we can see the value being displayed. The overridden `Execute` method is automatically invoked.

The Resource Loan pattern

The Loan pattern, as the name suggest, loans a resource to a function In the example given below, a file handle is loaned to consumers of the class. It performs following steps:

1. It creates a resource that you can use (a file handle)
2. It loans the resource (file handle) to functions (lambdas) that will use it
3. This function is passed by the caller and executed by the resource holder
4. The resource (file handle) is closed or destroyed by the resource holder

The following code implements the Resource Loan pattern for resource management. The pattern helps to avoid resource leakage when writing code:

```cpp
//----------- ResourceLoan.cpp
#include <rxcpp/rx.hpp>
using namespace std;
/////////////////////////////
// implementation of Resource Loan  Pattern. The Implementation opens a
file
// and does not pass the file handle to user  defined Lambda. The Ownership
remains with
// the class
class ResourceLoan {
   FILE *file;  // This is the resource which is being loaned
   string filename;
  public:
     ResourceLoan(string pfile) {
         filename = pfile;
         //---------- Create the resource
         file = fopen(filename.c_str(),"rb");
     }
     /////////////////////////////
     // Read upto 1024 bytes to a buffer
     // return the buffer contents and number of bytes
     int ReadBuffer( std::function<int(char pbuffer[],int val )> func )
     {
          if (file == nullptr ) { return -1; }
          char buffer[1024];
          int result = fread (buffer,1,1024,file);
          return func(buffer,result);
     }
     //---------- close the resource
     ~ResourceLoan() { fclose(file); }
};
/////////////////////////////////
// A Sample Program to invoke the preceding
// class
//
int main(int argc, char *argv[]) {
  ResourceLoan res("a.bin");
  int nread ;
  //-------------- The conents of the buffer
  //-------------- and size of buffer is stored in val
  auto rlambda =  [] (char buffer[] , int val ) {
       cout <<  "Size " << val << endl;
       return val;
  };
  //------- The File Handle is not available to the
```

```
//------- User defined Lambda It has been loaned to the
//-------- consumer of the class
while ((nread = res.ReadBuffer(rlambda)) > 0) {}
//---- When the ResourceLoan object goes out of scope
//---- File Handle is closed
return 0;
}
```

The Resource Loan pattern is suitable for avoiding resource leakage. The holder of the resource never hands over handle or pointer of the resource to its consumers. The main program demonstrates how we can consume the implementation. The ResourceLoan class never allows its consumer to access the file handle directly.

The Event bus pattern

The Event bus acts as a intermediary between event sources and event sinks. An event source, or producer, emits the events to a bus, and classes that have subscribed to events (consumers) will get notified. The pattern could be an instance of the Mediator design pattern. In an Event bus implementation, we have the following archetypes

- **Producers**: Classes which produce events
- **Consumers**: Classes which consume events
- **Controllers**: Classes which act as producers and consumers

In the implementation that follows, we have omitted the implementation of Controllers. The following code implements a toy version of an Event bus:

```
//----------- EventBus.cpp
#include <rxcpp/rx.hpp>
#include <memory>
#include <map>
#include <algorithm>
using namespace std;
//---------- Event Information
struct EVENT_INFO{
    int id;
    int err_code;
    string description;
    EVENT_INFO() { id = err_code = 0 ; description ="default";}
    EVENT_INFO(int pid,int perr_code,string pdescription )
    { id = pid; err_code = perr_code; description = pdescription; }
    void Print() {
        cout << "id & Error Code" << id << ":" << err_code << ":";
        cout << description << endl;
```

```
    }
};
```

The `EVENT_INFO` struct models an event, and it has the following content:

- `Id`: Event ID
- `err_code`: Error code
- `description`: Description of the events

The rest of the code is fairly obvious; here it is:

```
//------------ The following method
//------------ will be invoked by
//------------ Consumers
template <class T>
void DoSomeThingWithEvent( T ev )
{ev.Print();}

//---------- Forward Declarations
template <class T>
class EventBus;
//------------- Event Producer
//------------- Just Inserts event to a Bus
template <class T>
class Producer {
  string name;
 public:
   Producer(string pname ) { name = pname; }
   bool Fire(T ev, EventBus<T> *bev ) {
        bev->FireEvent(ev);
        return false;
   }
};
```

Implementation of the Producer class is fairly simple. The skeleton implementation is rather trivial. The `Fire` method takes a compatible `EventBus<T>` as a parameter and calls the `FireEvent` method of the `EventBus<T>` class. A production implementation requires some bells and whistles. Let's take a look at the code for the Consumer class.

```
//------------- Event Consumer
//------------- Subscribes to a Subject
//------------- to Retrieve Events
template <class T>
class Consumer {
  string name;
  //--------- The subscription member helps us to
  //--------- Unsubscribe to an Observable
```

```cpp
    rxcpp::composite_subscription subscription;
public:
  Consumer(string pname) { name = pname;}
  //--------- Connect a Consumer to a Event Bus
  bool Connect( EventBus<T> *bus ) {
      //------ If already subscribed, Unsubscribe!
      if ( subscription.is_subscribed() )
            subscription.unsubscribe();
      //------- Create a new Subscription
      //------- We will call DoSomeThingWithEvent method
      //------- from Lambda function
      subscription = rxcpp::composite_subscription();
      auto subscriber = rxcpp::make_subscriber<T>(
        subscription,[=](T value){
            DoSomeThingWithEvent<T>(value);
        },[](){ printf("OnCompletedn"); });
      //----------- Subscribe!
      bus->GetObservable().subscribe(subscriber);
      return true;
  }
  //-------- DTOR ....Unsubscribe
  ~Consumer() { Disconnect(); }
  bool Disconnect() {
      if (subscription.is_subscribed() )
        subscription.unsubscribe();
  }
};
```

The functionality of `Consumer<T>` is pretty obvious. The `Connect` method does the work of subscribing to the Observable side of the Subject in the `EventBus<T>` class. Each time a new connection request comes in, the existing subscription is unsubscribed, as shown here:

```cpp
//--- The implementation of the EventBus class
//--- We have not taken care of Concurrency issues
//--- as our purpose is to demonstrate the pattern
template <class T>
class EventBus
{
  private:
    std::string name;
    //----- Reference to the Subject...
    //----- Consumers get notification by
    //----- Subscribing to the Observable side of the subject
    rxcpp::subjects::behavior<T> *replaysubject;
  public:
    EventBus<T>() {replaysubject = new rxcpp::subjects::behavior<T>(T());}
    ~EventBus() {delete replaysubject;}
    //------ Add a Consumer to the Bus...
```

```
    bool AddConsumer( Consumer<T>& b ) {b.Connect(this);}
    //------ Fire the Event...
    bool FireEvent ( T& event ) {
        replaysubject->get_subscriber().on_next(event);
        return true;
    }
    string get_name() { return name;}
    rxcpp::observable<T> GetObservable()
    { return replaysubject->get_observable(); }
};
```

The EventBus<T> class acts as a conduit between the Producers and Consumers. We are using a replaysubject under the hood, to notify the Consumers. Now that, we have finished writing Producer and Consumer class, let us see how we can utilize the code written above.

```
/////////////////////
//The EntryPoint
//
//
int main(int argc, char *argv[]) {
    //---- Create an instance of the EventBus
    EventBus<EVENT_INFO> program_bus;
    //---- Create a Producer and Two Consumers
    //---- Add Consumers to the EventBus
    Producer<EVENT_INFO> producer_one("first");
    Consumer<EVENT_INFO> consumer_one("one");
    Consumer<EVENT_INFO> consumer_two("two");
    program_bus.AddConsumer(consumer_one);
    program_bus.AddConsumer(consumer_two);
    //---- Fire an Event...
    EVENT_INFO ev;
    ev.id = 100;
    ev.err_code = 0;
    ev.description = "Hello World..";
    producer_one.Fire(ev,&program_bus);
    //---- fire another by creating a second
    //---- Producer
    ev.id = 100;
    ev.err_code = 10;
    ev.description = "Error Happened..";
    Producer<EVENT_INFO> producer_two("second");
    producer_two.Fire(ev,&program_bus);
}
```

In the main function, we are performing the following tasks:

1. Creating an instance of the `EventBus<T>`
2. Creating an instance of Producers
3. Creating an instance of Consumers
4. Dispatching events to the bus

We have only covered a subset of the design patterns that are suitable for writing reactive programs. Primarily, our focus has been on bridging from GOF design patterns to the reactive programming world. In fact, authors of this book believe that the reactive programming model is an enhanced implementation of classic GOF design patterns. The enhancement is possible due to the functional programming constructs added to modern programming languages. In fact, object/functional programming is a good approach for writing modern C++ code. This chapter was largely based on the very idea.

Summary

In this chapter, we delved into the wonderful world of design patterns/idioms associated with C++ programming and reactive programming. Starting with GOF design patterns, we moved on to reactive programming patterns and gradual transition from OOP to reactive programming is a highlight of this chapter. Later,we covered reactive programming patterns such as Cell, Active object, Resource loan, and Event bus. Bridging from GOF patterns to reactive programming helps you to look at reactive programming in a broader sense.In the next chapter, we will learn about micro-service development using C++.

Reactive Microservices Using C++

12

So far, we have covered essential aspects of reactive programming using C++. Some of the key topics covered include:

- The reactive programming model and its cognitive prerequisites
- The RxCpp library and its programming model
- Reactive GUI programming using Qt/RxCpp
- Writing Custom Operators
- Design patterns and the reactive programming model

If you take a closer look, all examples so far in this book are related to what happens inside a process. Or, we were essentially focusing on shared memory parallel and concurrent techniques. The Rx.net, RxJava and most Rx implementations are   basically concerned with shared memory concurrent and parallel programming. A system such as Akka applies reactive programming model to the distributed world. In Akka, we can write reactive logic that spans processes and machines. The reactive programming model is also good for exposing REST-based web services and consuming them. The RxJs library is mostly used for consuming REST-based services from a browser page. The RxCpp library can be used for writing web clients for aggregating the contents from various service endpoints. We can leverage the RxCpp library from console and GUI applications. Another use case is aggregating data from multiple fine-grained services and delivering it to web clients.

In this chapter, we will write a basic web application, using C++, that will leverage the Microsoft C++ REST SDK to write the server part and use the (C++ REST SDK) client library to consume those services. In the process, we will explain what micro-services are and how to consume them. We will also explain how the RxCpp library can be used to access REST endpoints and HTML pages ,by writing a wrapper on top of the `libcurl` library. We are planning to leverage Kirk Shoop's RxCurl library (written as part of his Twitter analysis application) to demonstrate this technique.

The C++ language and web programming

Nowadays, most web-centric applications are developed using Python, Java, C#, PHP, and other high-level languages. But, for these applications, people place reverse proxies, such as NGINX, Apache Web server, or IIS redirector, to manage the traffic . All of these reverse proxies are written in C++. Likewise, most of the web browsers and HTTP client libraries, such as `libwww`, `libcurl`, and `WinInet`, are written using C++.

One reason why Java, (statically-typed) C#, and other dynamic languages (such as Python, Ruby, and PHP) became popular is the fact that these languages support reflective capabilities (in the case of static languages, such as C#/Java) and duck typing (supported by dynamic languages). These features help web application servers to load web page handlers dynamically. Read about them by searching for keywords such as *Reflection API* and *Duck Typing*.

The REST programming model

The REST, which stands for **REpresentational State Transfer**, is an architectural style spearheaded by Roy Fielding as part of his PhD thesis. Nowadays, it is one of the most popular technique for exposing and consuming web services. REST follows a resource-centric approach and nicely maps to the CRUD pattern, which are popular among programmers who are well versed in writing enterprise business applications. We use **JavaScript Object Notation** (also known as **JSON**) as payload while writing REST services, instead of the XML format (which is in vogue for SOAP services). The REST programming model relies on HTTP verbs (GET,POST,PUT,DELETE and so on)to indicate the kind of operations to be executed while receiving a REST API call. The most popular methods supported are:

- `POST`: Creates a new resource
- `GET`: Retrieves a resource
- `PUT`: Updates an existing resource (if it's a new resource, behaves like `POST`)
- `DELETE`: Deletes a resource

The C++ REST SDK

The C++ REST SDK is a Microsoft project for cloud-based client-server communication in native code using a modern asynchronous C++ API design. This toolkit aims to help C++ developers connect to and interact with HTTP based services. The SDK has the following features that help you to write robust services:

- HTTP client/server
- JSON support
- Asynchronous streams
- WebSocket's client
- oAuth support

The C++ REST SDK relies on the parallel patterns library's task API. The PPL tasks is a powerful model for composing asynchronous operations based on modern C++ features. The C++ REST SDK supports Windows desktop, Windows Store (UWP), Linux, macOS, Unix, iOS, and Android.

HTTP client programming using the C++ REST SDK

The C++ REST SDK programming model is inherently asynchronous in nature, and we can invoke the API calls in a synchronous manner as well. The following program will demonstrate how we can invoke HTTP client API calls asynchronously. The program demonstrates workings of the client side of the HTTP protocol supported by the C++ REST SDK. We use a technique called **task continuation** (a technique of chaining blocks of code) here to retrieve data from a web page and store it in a local disk file. The C++ REST SDK follows an asynchronous I/O model and we chain operations together. Finally, we invoke the composition using the `wait()` method:

```cpp
#include <cpprest/http_client.h>
#include <cpprest/filestream.h>
//----- Some standard C++ headers emitted for brevity
#include "cpprest/json.h"
#include "cpprest/http_listener.h"
#include "cpprest/uri.h"
#include "cpprest/asyncrt_utils.h"
/////////////////////////////////////////////////
// A Simple HTTP Client to Demonstrate
// REST SDK Client programming model
// The Toy sample shows how one can read
// contents of a web page
//
using namespace utility;  // Common utilities like string conversions
using namespace web;      // Common features like URIs.
using namespace web::http;// Common HTTP functionality
using namespace web::http::client;// HTTP client features
using namespace concurrency::streams;// Asynchronous streams
```

```cpp
int main(int argc, char* argv[])
{
    auto fileStream = std::make_shared<ostream>();
    // Open stream to output file.
    pplx::task<void> requestTask =
                fstream::open_ostream(U("google_home.html")).
        then([=](ostream outFile)
    {
        *fileStream = outFile;
        // Create http_client to send the request.
        http_client client(U("http://www.google.com"));
        // Build request URI and start the request.
        uri_builder builder(U("/"));
        return client.request(methods::GET, builder.to_string());

    }).then([=](http_response response)
    {
        printf("Received response status code:%un",
                            response.status_code());
        return response.body().
                    read_to_end(fileStream->streambuf());
    }).then([=](size_t){
        return fileStream->close();
    });

    // We have not started execution, just composed
    // set of tasks in a Continuation Style
    // Wait for all the outstanding I/O to complete
    // and handle any exceptions, If any
    try {
        //-- All Taskss will get triggered here
        requestTask.wait();
    }
    catch (const std::exception &e) {
        printf("Error exception:%sn", e.what());
    }
    //--------------- pause for a key
    getchar();
    return 0;
}
```

The above program demonstrate workings of the task continuation style of programming. The bulk of the code is about composing lambdas, and the actual execution starts when the wait() method is called. The lazy evaluation strategy of lambda functions helps us to compose code in the manner given above.We can invoke the logic in a synchronous manner as well. Consult the Microsoft C++ REST SDK documentation to learn more.

HTTP server programming using the C++ REST SDK

We have already learned about HTTP client programming model supported by the C++ REST SDK. We worked with the asynchronous task-continuation-based API to retrieve contents of a web page and persist it into a disk file. Now, it is time to start concentrating on the REST SDK HTTP server programming. The C++ REST SDK has a listener interface that will handle HTTP requests, and we can place handlers for each type of the HTTP verbs, such as GET, PUT, POST and so on

```
//////////////////////////////////
//  A Simple Web Application with C++ REST SDK
//  We can use Postman Or Curl to test the Server
using namespace std;
using namespace web;
using namespace utility;
using namespace http;
using namespace web::http::experimental::listener;
/////////////////////////////////
// SimpleServer is a Wrapper over
// http_listener class available with C++ REST SDK
class SimpleServer
{
public:

    SimpleServer(utility::string_t url);
    ~SimpleServer() {}
    pplx::task<void> Open() { return m_listener.open(); }
    pplx::task<void> Close() { return m_listener.close(); }

private:
    //--- Handlers for HTTP verbs
    void HandleGet(http_request message);
    void HandlePut(http_request message);
    void HandlePost(http_request message);
    void HandleDelete(http_request message);
    //--------------- The  HTTP listener class
    http_listener m_listener;
};
```

The `SimpleServer` C++ class is basically a wrapper on top of the `http_listener` class supported by the C++ REST SDK. The class listens for the incoming HTTP request, and it is possible to set request handlers for each request type (`GET`, `POST`, `PUT`, and so on). When a request arrives, `http_listener` will dispatch request information to associated handlers, depending upon the HTTP verb.

```
//////////////////////////////////
// The Constructor Binds HTTP verbs to instance methods
// Based on the naming convention, we can infer what is happening
SimpleServer::SimpleServer(utility::string_t url) : m_listener(url)
{
    m_listener.support(methods::GET, std::bind(&SimpleServer::HandleGet,
            this, std::placeholders::_1));
    m_listener.support(methods::PUT, std::bind(&SimpleServer::HandlePut,
            this, std::placeholders::_1));
    m_listener.support(methods::POST, std::bind(&SimpleServer::HandlePost,
            this, std::placeholders::_1));
    m_listener.support(methods::DEL, std::bind(&SimpleServer::HandleDelete,
            this, std::placeholders::_1));

}
```

The previous code snippets bind request handlers to the `http_request` object. We are only focusing on the `GET`, `PUT`, `POST`, and `DELETE` verbs. These verbs are the most popular commands supported by all REST implementations:

```
//////////////////////////////////
// For this implementation, what we do is
// spit the HTTP request details on the Server Console
// and return 200 OK and a String which indicates  Success of Operations
void SimpleServer::HandleGet(http_request message){
    ucout << message.to_string() << endl;
    message.reply(status_codes::OK,L"GET Operation Succeeded");
}
void SimpleServer::HandlePost(http_request message){
    ucout << message.to_string() << endl;
    message.reply(status_codes::OK, L"POST Operation Succeeded");
};

void SimpleServer::HandleDelete(http_request message){
    ucout << message.to_string() << endl;
    message.reply(status_codes::OK, L"DELETE Operation Succeeded");
}
void SimpleServer::HandlePut(http_request message){
    ucout << message.to_string() << endl;
    message.reply(status_codes::OK, L"PUT Operation Succeeded");
};
```

The above code block follows a pattern that can be easily deciphered by any developer. All the handler does is print the request parameters to the console of the server and return a string to the client to indicate that the request was successfully completed. (HTTP status code - 200) We will show how we can access these services through the POSTMAN and CURL utilities in the next section.

```
/////////////////////////////////
// A Smart Pointer for Server Instance...
//
std::unique_ptr<SimpleServer> g_http;
/////////////////////////////////////////////////
// STart the Server with the Given URL
//
void StartServer(const string_t& address)
{
    // Build our listener's URI from the address given
    // We just append DBDEMO/ to the base URL
    uri_builder uri(address);
    uri.append_path(U("DBDEMO/"));
    auto addr = uri.to_uri().to_string();
    /////////////////////////////////////
    // Create an Instance of the Server and Invoke Wait to
    // start the Server...
    g_http = std::unique_ptr<SimpleServer>(new SimpleServer(addr));
    g_http->Open().wait();
    //----- Indicate the start and spit URI to the Console
    ucout << utility::string_t(U("Listening for requests at: ")) <<
                addr << std::endl;

    return;
}


/////////////////////////////////////////
// Simply Closes the Connection... Close returns
// pplx::task<void> ...we need to Call wait to invoke the
// operation...
void ShutDown(){
    g_http->Close().wait();
    return;
}
/////////////////////////////////////
// EntryPoint function
int wmain(int argc, wchar_t *argv[])
{
    utility::string_t port = U("34567");
    if (argc == 2){ port = argv[1]; }
    //--- Create the Server URI base address
```

```
        utility::string_t address = U("http://localhost:");
        address.append(port);
        StartServer(address);
        std::cout << "Press ENTER to exit." << std::endl;
        //--- Wait Indefenintely, Untill some one has
        // pressed a key....and Shut the Server down
        std::string line;
        std::getline(std::cin, line);
        ShutDown();
        return 0;
   }
```

The main function instantiates an instance of the `SimpleListener` class through the `StartServer` function. Then, the `main` function waits for a key to be pressed before the `ShutDown` function is called. Once we have kick-started the application, we can use the `CURL` tool or `POSTMAN` to test whether program works or not.

Testing the HTTP server using CURL and POSTMAN

`CURL` is a command-line tool that is portable across Windows, GNU Linux, MacOS, and other POSIX compliant systems. The tool helps to transfer data using various TCP/IP-based application protocols. Some of the common protocols supported include HTTP, HTTPS, FTP, FTPS, SCP, SFTP, TFTP, DICT, TELNET, and LDAP,to name a few.

We will be using the `CURL` tool to test the HTTP server we wrote. The command-line utility can be invoked by giving the requisite command-line parameters to place HTTP requests with associated verbs. We give the command-line parameters for invoking the `GET` and the `PUT` request to the server we wrote:

```
    curl -X PUT http://localhost:34567/DBDEMO/
          -H "Content-Type: application/json" -d
'{"SimpleContent":"Value"}'
    curl -X GET
          -H "Content-Type: application/json"
  http://localhost:34567/DBDEMO/
```

Embed the previous command in a batch file or shell script, depending upon your platform. The output on the console should be as follows:

```
PUT Operation Succeeded
GET Operation Succeeded
```

Similarly, by consulting the CURL documentation, we can test the other HTTP verbs as well.

POSTMAN is a powerful HTTP client for testing HTTP based services. It started as a side project by an Indian developer by the name Abhinav Asthana. It was a Chrome plugin that went viral. Today, it is an independent platform and there exists a company formed around this application, where Mr. Asthana is the CEO. You can download POSTMAN tool to test these services. Since download URLs can change, please consult your favorite search engine to find the download URL in vogue. (search for "POSTMAN HTTP Client")

The libcurl and the HTTP client programming

We have already come across the CURL utility, which is, in fact a wrapper on top of the libcurl library. We will use the libcurl library to access REST services we wrote, in this chapter. To get you familiar with the libcurl library and its programming model, we will write a basic HTTP client using the library: The program will ping the http://example.com.

```c
/////////////////////////////////////
// A Simple Program to demonstrate
// the usage of libcurl library
//
#include <stdio.h>
#include <curl/curl.h>
/////////////////////////////
// Entrypoint for the program
//
int main(void)
{
  CURL *curl;
  CURLcode res;
  /////////////////////////////
  // Initialize the library
  //
  curl = curl_easy_init();
  if(curl) {
    //----------- Set the URL
    curl_easy_setopt(curl, CURLOPT_URL,
                     "http://example.com");
    /////////////////////////////////////////////
    // To support URL re-direction, we need to configure
    // the lib curl library with CURLOPT_FOLLOWLOCATION
    //
    curl_easy_setopt(curl,
            CURLOPT_FOLLOWLOCATION, 1L);
    /////////////////////////////////////////////
    // Now that, we have setup the options necessary,
```

```
   // invoke the operation to pull data
   //
   res = curl_easy_perform(curl);
   if(res != CURLE_OK) {
     //----- if error, print the error on console
      cout << "curl_easy_perform() failed: "
             << curl_easy_strerror(res) << endl;
   }
   curl_easy_cleanup(curl);
 }
 return 0;
}
```

The previous code pings the http://example.com URL to retrieve its contents and displays them on the console. The programming model is very simple, and the documentation of the library is really good. It is one of the most popular libraries for accessing the TCP/IP application services. In the next section, we will leverage a reactive wrapper on to top of the libcurl library.

Kirk Shoop's libCURL Wrapper library

The primary implementer of the RxCpp library is Kirk Shoop, who is currently associated with the Microsoft. He wrote a Twitter analysis sample app (https://github.com/kirkshoop/twitter) to demonstrate various facets of reactive programming. One of the things he did as part of the initiative was to write a reactive wrapper over libcurl to implement HTTP GET and POST methods. The authors of this book have extended his code to support the PUT and DELETE methods.

Take a look at the RxCurl library bundled with the source code of this book: (The listing is too big to be included here)

```
/////////////////////////////////////
// A Simple program to pull HTTP content
// using a Rx wrapper on top of the Libcurl
//
//
#include <iostream>
#include <stdio.h>
#include <stdlib.h>
#include <map>
#include <chrono>
using namespace std;
using namespace std::chrono;
/////////////////////////
```

```
// include Curl Library and
// Rxcpp library
//
#include <curl/curl.h>
#include <rxcpp/rx.hpp>
using namespace rxcpp;
using namespace rxcpp::rxo;
using namespace rxcpp::rxs;
/////////////////////////
// include the modified rxcurl library from
// Kirk Shoop's Twitter Analysis app
//
#include "rxcurl.h"
using namespace rxcurl;
int main() {
        ////////////////////////////////////////
        //
        // Create a factory object to create
        // HTTP request.  The http_request structure
        // is defined in rxcurl.h
        string url = "http://example.com";
        auto factory = create_rxcurl();
        auto request  = factory.create(http_request{url, "GET",{}, {}}) |
                rxo::map([](http_response r){
                    return r.body.complete;
                });
```

We created an `observable` by using the `factory` class for creating the HTTP `request` object. The `map` function just retrieves body of the response object. The most important structure in the whole code is the `http_request` struct, whose definition is as follows:

```
struct http_request{
    string url;
    string method;
    std::map<string, string> headers;
    string body;
};
```

The purpose of the http_request structure is pretty much obvious from the above declaration. The members are

- url - the target URL
- method - The HTTP verb
- headers - HTTP headers
- body - body of the request

```
        ////////////////////////////////////////////
```

```
        // make a blocking call to the url..
        observable<string>    response_message;
        request.as_blocking().subscribe([&] (observable<string> s) {
                response_message = s.sum();
        } ,[] () {});
```

The `request` Observable can be subscribed for `on_next` using a lambda function that takes `observable<string>` ,as the `map` function returns `observable<string>`. In the body of the `on_next` function, we aggregate the content to produce a string using the `observable<string>::sum()` reducer:

```
        /////////////////////////////////
        // retrieve the html content form the site
        string html;
        response_message.as_blocking().subscribe( [&html] ( string temp ) {
                html = temp;
        }, [&html] () { } );
        //------------ Print to the Console...
        cout << html << endl;
}
```

The `response_message` Observable is subscribed with a lambda, which takes a string as the parameter. In the body of the `on_next` function, we simply assign the string containing the HTML to the `html` variable. Finally, we display the contents on to the console. Please take a look at the `rxcurl.h` header file to see how the library works.

The JSON and HTTP protocol

The payload format for invoking web services were once monopolized by the XML format. The SOAP-based services mostly support the XML format. With the advent of REST-based services, developers use **JavaScript Object Notation (JSON)** as the payload format.

The following table shows a comparison between XML and corresponding JSON object:

XML	JSON
```<person> <firstName>John</firstName> <lastName>Smith</lastName> <age>25</age> <address> <streetAddress>21 2nd Street</streetAddress> <city>New York</city> <state>NY</state> <postalCode>10021</postalCode> </address> <phoneNumber> <type>home</type> <number>212 555-1234</number> </phoneNumber> <phoneNumber> <type>fax</type> <number>646 555-4567</number> </phoneNumber> <gender> <type>male</type> </gender> </person>```	```{ "firstName": "John", "lastName": "Smith", "age": 25, "address": { "streetAddress": "21 2nd Street", "city": "New York", "state": "NY", "postalCode": "10021" }, "phoneNumber": [{ "type": "home", "number": "212 555-1234" }, { "type": "fax", "number": "646 555-4567" }], "gender": { "type": "male" } }```

The JSON format contains following data types:

- String
- Number
- Object (JSON object)
- Array
- Boolean

Let us inspect a JSON object, to see how preceding data types are represented in the real world.

```
{
{ "name":"John" },
{ "age":35 },
{
  "spouse":{ "name":"Joanna",
             "age":30,
             "city":"New York" }
},
{
```

```
        "siblings":["Bob", "Bill", "Peter" ]
    },
    { "employed":true }
}
```

The mappings are:

- name: The value is string type ("john")
- age: The value is number (35)
- spouse: This is a JSON object
- siblings: This is an array
- employed: This is a Boolean (true)

Now that we have a better understanding of JSON and its core aspects, we will write a simple program that demonstrates usage of the JSON API, available as part of the C++ REST SDK:

```cpp
///////////////////////////////////
// A Console Application to demonstrate JSON API
// available as part of the C++ SDK
using namespace std;
using namespace web;
using namespace utility;
using namespace http;
using namespace web::http::experimental::listener;
/////////////////////////////////////////
// Define a Simple struct to demonstrate the
// Working of JSON API
struct EMPLOYEE_INFO{
    utility::string_t name;
    int age;
    double salary;
    ///////////////////////////////////
    // Convert a JSON Object to a C++ Struct
    //
    static EMPLOYEE_INFO JSonToObject(const web::json::object & object){
        EMPLOYEE_INFO result;
        result.name = object.at(U("name")).as_string();
        result.age = object.at(U("age")).as_integer();
        result.salary = object.at(U("salary")).as_double();
        return result;
    }
```

The `JSonToObject` static method converts a JSON object to the `EMPLOYEE_INFO` structure. `json::at` returns a reference to `json::value` based on the string that we used to index it. The resultant `json::value` reference is used to invoke the type-specific conversion methods, such as `as_string`, `as_integer`, and `as_double`:

```cpp
//////////////////////////////////////////////
// Convert a C++ struct to a Json Value
//
web::json::value ObjectToJson() const{
        web::json::value result = web::json::value::object();
        result[U("name")] = web::json::value::string(name);
        result[U("age")] = web::json::value::number(age);
        result[U("salary")] = web::json::value::number(salary);
        return result;
    }
};
```

`ObjectToJson` is an instance method of `EMPLOYEE_STRUCT`, which helps to produce JSON output from the instance data. Here, we use conversion methods to transfer instance data to `json::value`. Next, we will focus on how we can create `json::object` from scratch:

```cpp
//////////////////////////////////////////////
// Create a Json Object group and Embed and
// Array in it...
void MakeAndShowJSONObject(){
    // Create a JSON object (the group)
    json::value group;
    group[L"Title"] = json::value::string(U("Native Developers"));
    group[L"Subtitle"] =
                json::value::string(U("C++ devekioers on Windws/GNU LINUX"));
    group[L"Description"] =
                json::value::string(U("A Short Description here "));
    // Create a JSON object (the item)
    json::value item;
    item[L"Name"] = json::value::string(U("Praseed Pai"));
    item[L"Skill"] = json::value::string(U("C++ / java "));
    // Create a JSON object (the item)
    json::value item2;
    item2[L"Name"] = json::value::string(U("Peter Abraham"));
    item2[L"Skill"] = json::value::string(U("C++ / C# "));
    // Create the items array
    json::value items;
    items[0] = item;
    items[1] = item2;
    // Assign the items array as the value for the Resources key
    group[L"Resources"] = items;
    // Write the current JSON value to wide char string stream
```

```
    utility::stringstream_t stream;
    group.serialize(stream);
    // Display the string stream
    std::wcout << stream.str();
}

int wmain(int argc, wchar_t *argv[])
{
    EMPLOYEE_INFO dm;
    dm.name = L"Sabhir Bhatia";
    dm.age = 50;
    dm.salary = 10000;
    wcout << dm.ObjectToJson().serialize() << endl;
```

We create an `EMPLOYEE_INFO` struct and assign some values into the fields. We then invoke `EMPLOYEE_INFO::ObjectToJSon()` to create a `json::value` object. We call the `serialize()` method to generate the JSON textual output:

```
    utility::string_t port =
        U("{"Name": "Alex Stepanov","Age": 55,"salary":20000}");;
    web::json::value json_par;
    json::value obj = json::value::parse(port);
    wcout << obj.serialize() << endl;
```

The previous code snippets demonstrate the use to parse textual strings to produce `json::value` objects. We invoked the `serialize` method to print the JSON string to the console:

```
    MakeAndShowJSONObject();
    getchar();
    return 0;
}
```

The C++ REST SDK-based REST server

In this section, we have leveraged code from Marius Bancila's excellent article about the C++ REST SDK. In fact, the key/value database code is borrowed from his implementation. The authors are thankful to him for the excellent article, available at `https://mariusbancila.ro/blog/2017/11/19/revisited-full-fledged-client-server-example-with-c-rest-sdk-2-10/`.

Let's write a micro-service application that puts everything together we have learned so far in the context of Microsoft C++ REST SDK. We will consume REST services by leveraging the RxCurl library written by Kirk Shoop, as part of his Twitter analysis application. We have added support to the DELETE and PUT verbs, as the original implementation contained only support for GET and POST verbs. The REST service implemented here supports the following verbs:

- GET: Lists all the key/value pairs in the storage. The response will be in the {key:value,key:value} format.
- POST: Retrieves values corresponding to an array of keys. The request should be in the [key1,...,keyn] format. The response will be in the {key:value,key:value....} format.
- PUT: Inserts a collection of key/value pairs into the storage. The request should be in the {key:value,key:value} format.
- DELETE: Deletes an array of keys and their corresponding values from the storage. The request should be in the [key,key] format.

Let's have a look at the code:

```
// MicroServiceController.cpp : Defines the entry point for the console
application.
#include <cpprest/http_client.h>
#include <cpprest/filestream.h>
//------------- Omitted some standard C++ headers for terse code listing
#include "cpprest/json.h"
#include "cpprest/http_listener.h"
#include "cpprest/uri.h"
#include "cpprest/asyncrt_utils.h"

#ifdef _WIN32
#ifndef NOMINMAX
#define NOMINMAX
#endif
#include <Windows.h>
#else
# include <sys/time.h>
#endif


using namespace std;
using namespace web;
using namespace utility;
using namespace http;
using namespace web::http::experimental::listener;
```

```
/////////////////////////////
//
// The following code dumps a json to the Console...
void  DisplayJSON(json::value const & jvalue){
   wcout << jvalue.serialize() << endl;
}


/////////////////////////////////////////////////
// A Workhorse routine to perform an action on the request data type
// takes a lambda as parameter along with request type
// The Lambda should contain the action logic...whether it is
// GET, PUT,POST or DELETE
//
void RequeatWorker( http_request& request,
function<void(json::value const &, json::value &)> handler) {
   auto result = json::value::object();
   request.extract_json().then([&result,
       &handler](pplx::task<json::value> task)     {
       try{
           auto const & jvalue = task.get();
           if (!jvalue.is_null())
               handler(jvalue, result); // invoke the lambda
        }
        catch (http_exception const & e) {
            //----------- do exception processsing
            wcout << L"Exception ->" << e.what() << endl;
        }
   }).wait();
    request.reply(status_codes::OK, result);
}
```

The `RequestWorker` is a global function, that takes `http_request` as a parameter along, with a lambda with specific signature. The lambda takes two parameters:

- An input JSON object of the `json::value` type (a constant parameter)
- An output JSON object that contains result from the lambda call

The JSON payload is extracted and passed to the `then` continuation. Once the data is retrieved, the handler lambda is invoked. Since the result is passed by reference, we can use the resultant JSON for generating the HTTP response. Now, we will create a simple key/value data store to simulate an industrial-strength key/value database:

```
/////////////////////////////////////////
// A Mock data base Engine which Simulates a key/value DB
// In Real life, one should use an Industrial strength DB
//
class HttpKeyValueDBEngine {
```

```
/////////////////////////////////
//---------- Map , which we save,retrieve,  update and
//---------- delete data
map<utility::string_t, utility::string_t> storage;
public:
    HttpKeyValueDBEngine() {
        storage[L"Praseed"]= L"45";
        storage[L"Peter"] = L"28";
        storage[L"Andrei"] = L"50";
    }
```

The key/value pairs are stored in an STL map for the sake of the ease of implementation. In the constructor, we initialize STL map with some records. We can use PUT and POST to add additional records, and DELETE for deleting records: Let us dissect the source code of the function which handles GET requests.

```
///////////////////////////////////////////////////////////
// GET - ?Just Iterates through the Map and Stores
// the data in a JSon Object. IT is emitted to the
// Response Stream
void GET_HANDLER(http_request& request) {
    auto resp_obj = json::value::object();
    for (auto const & p : storage)
        resp_obj[p.first] = json::value::string(p.second);
    request.reply(status_codes::OK, resp_obj);
}
```

The GET_HANLDER method will be invoked by the HTTP listener, when it encounters an HTTP GET verb as part of the request payload. After creating json::value::object, we stuff contents of the storage map into it. The resulting JSON object is returned to the HTTP client: Let us take a look at source code of the POST handler.

```
////////////////////////////////////////////////////
// POST - Retrieves a Set of Values from the DB
// The PAyload should be in ["Key1" , "Key2"...,"Keyn"]
// format
void POST_HANDLER(http_request& request) {
    RequeatWorker(request, [&](json::value const & jvalue,
                                    json::value & result){
        //---------- Write to the Console for Diagnostics
        DisplayJSON(jvalue);
            for (auto const & e : jvalue.as_array()){
                if (e.is_string()){
                    auto key = e.as_string();
                    auto pos = storage.find(key);
                    if (pos == storage.end()){
                        //--- Indicate to the Client that Key is not found
```

```
                            result[key] = json::value::string(L"notfound");
                    }
                    else {
                    //------------ store the key value pair in the result
                    //------------ json. The result will be send back to
                    //------------ the client
                    result[pos->first] = json::value::string(pos->second);
                    }
                }
            }
        });
}
```

The POST_HANDLER expects an array of JSON values in the body of request, and cycles through each element to retrieve the data corresponding to keys provided. The resultant object stores the returned value. If some keys are not present in the key/value DB, a literal string ("notond") is returned to indicate that the value is not found:

```
/////////////////////////////////////////////////////
// PUT - Updates Data, If new KEy is found
//         Otherwise, Inserts it
// REST Payload should be in
//         { Key1..Value1,...,Keyn,Valuen}  format
//
//
void PUT_HANDLER(http_request& request) {
        RequeatWorker( request,
            [&](json::value const & jvalue, json::value & result){
            DisplayJSON(jvalue);
            for (auto const & e : jvalue.as_object()){
                if (e.second.is_string()){
                    auto key = e.first;
                    auto value = e.second.as_string();
                    if (storage.find(key) == storage.end())
                    {
                            //--- Indicate to the client that we have
                            //--- created a new record
                            result[key] =
                                json::value::string(L"<put>");
                    }
                    else {
                            //--- Indicate to the client that we have
                            //--- updated a new record
                            result[key] =
                                json::value::string(L"<updated>");
                    }
                    storage[key] = value;
                }
```

```
            }
      });
   }
```

The `PUT_HANDLER` expects a list of key/value pairs in the JSON format. The collection of keys is iterated to do the lookup into the storage. If the key already exists in the storage, the value is updated, otherwise the key/value is inserted into the storage. A JSON object (result) is returned to indicate the action performed on each key (whether it was an insert or an update):

```
/////////////////////////////////////////////////
// DEL - Deletes a Set of Records
// REST PayLoad should be in
//       [ Key1,....,Keyn] format
//
void DEL_HANDLER(http_request& request)
{
    RequeatWorker( request,
        [&](json::value const & jvalue, json::value & result)
        {
                //--------------- We aggregate all keys into this set
                //--------------- and delete in one go
                set<utility::string_t> keys;
                for (auto const & e : jvalue.as_array()){
                    if (e.is_string()){
                        auto key = e.as_string();
                        auto pos = storage.find(key);
                        if (pos == storage.end()){
                            result[key] =
                                json::value::string(L"<failed>");
                        }
                        else {
                            result[key] =
                                json::value::string(L"<deleted>");
                            //---------- Insert in to the delete list
                            keys.insert(key);
                        }
                    }
                }
                //---------------Erase all
                for (auto const & key : keys)
                    storage.erase(key);
        });
    }
};
```

The `DEL_HANDLER` expects an array of keys as the input, and it cycles through the array to retrieve the data. If the key is already present in the storage, keys are added to a delete list (- an STL set). A JSON object (result) is populated with the kind of action taken on each key. The resultant object will be returned to the client:

```
///////////////////////////////////////////////
//
// Instantiates the Global instance of key/value DB
HttpKeyValueDBEngine g_dbengine;
```

Now that we have a functional simulated key/value database `engine`, we will use the functionality of the database to the outside world as a REST service endpoint with `GET`, `POST`, `PUT`, and `DELETE` commands. The HTTP handlers will just delegate the call to the `HttpValueDBEngine` instance. The code is very similar to the code that we wrote for the `SimpleServer` class:

```cpp
class RestDbServiceServer{
public:
    RestDbServiceServer(utility::string_t url);
    pplx::task<void> Open() { return m_listener.open(); }
    pplx::task<void> Close() { return m_listener.close(); }
private:
    void HandleGet(http_request message);
    void HandlePut(http_request message);
    void HandlePost(http_request message);
    void HandleDelete(http_request message);
    http_listener m_listener;
};
RestDbServiceServer::RestDbServiceServer(utility::string_t url) :
m_listener(url)
{
    m_listener.support(methods::GET,
        std::bind(&RestDbServiceServer::HandleGet, this,
std::placeholders::_1));
    m_listener.support(methods::PUT,
        std::bind(&RestDbServiceServer::HandlePut, this,
std::placeholders::_1));
    m_listener.support(methods::POST,
        std::bind(&RestDbServiceServer::HandlePost, this,
std::placeholders::_1));
    m_listener.support(methods::DEL,
        std::bind(&RestDbServiceServer::HandleDelete,
        this,std::placeholders::_1));
}
```

The above code binds HTTP verbs to the corresponding handlers. The bodies of the handlers are similar in character, as the handlers are just delegating the HTTPcall to the key/value engine:

```
void RestDbServiceServer::HandleGet(http_request message)
{g_dbengine.GET_HANDLER(message);};
void RestDbServiceServer::HandlePost(http_request message)
{g_dbengine.POST_HANDLER(message);};
void RestDbServiceServer::HandleDelete(http_request message)
{g_dbengine.DEL_HANDLER(message);}
void RestDbServiceServer::HandlePut(http_request message)
{g_dbengine.PUT_HANDLER(message);};
//--------------- Create an instance of the Server
std::unique_ptr<RestDbServiceServer> g_http;
void StartServer(const string_t& address)
{
    uri_builder uri(address);
    uri.append_path(U("DBDEMO/"));
    auto addr = uri.to_uri().to_string();
    g_http = std::unique_ptr<RestDbServiceServer>(new
RestDbServiceServer(addr));
    g_http->Open().wait();
    ucout << utility::string_t(U("Listening for requests at: ")) <<
                addr << std::endl;
    return;
}
void ShutDown(){
        g_http->Close().wait();
        return;
}
////////////////////////////////
// The EntryPoint function
int wmain(int argc, wchar_t *argv[]){
    utility::string_t port = U("34567");
    if (argc == 2){port = argv[1];}
    utility::string_t address = U("http://localhost:");
    address.append(port);
    StartServer(address);
    std::cout << "Press ENTER to exit." << std::endl;
    std::string line;
    std::getline(std::cin, line);
    ShutDown();
    return 0;
}
```

The code for the HTTP controller is not different from `SimpleServer`, which we wrote earlier in the chapter. We provided the listing here for the sake of completeness. With this, we have learned how to expose a REST service endpoint to the outside world, using the C++ REST SDK.

We have already discussed how we can expose a REST endpoint and how to write handlers for the various HTTP verbs. In a micro-services architecture style, we will have lot of REST endpoints deployed independently. The process of breaking a coarse-grained service into a micro-service is an art that is highly dependent upon context. The micro-services are exposed to outside world, sometimes through aggregation services. An aggregation service will make request to multiple end points and the results from different endpoints will be aggregated, before responding to Its client. The aggregation services are a candidate for writing reactive client logic for accessing the REST micro-services. Since network calls are asynchronous, the reactive programming model is natural here.

Invoking REST services using the RxCurl library

The `RxCurl` library, written by Kirk Shoop, originally supported `GET` and `POST` verbs. The Twitter analysis app only warrants that. The authors of the book have added support for the `PUT` and `DELETE` verbs. You can refer to the source of `rxcurl.h`, to see necessary changes made to support these additional verbs, in the Github repository: Let us see how we can use the modified library to make calls to the REST server, we wrote above.

```cpp
#include <iostream>
#include <stdio.h>
#include <iostream>
#include <stdio.h>
#include <stdlib.h>
#include <map>
#include <chrono>
using namespace std;
using namespace std::chrono;
/////////////////////////
// include Curl Library and
// Rxcpp library
//
#include <curl/curl.h>
#include <rxcpp/rx.hpp>
using namespace rxcpp;
using namespace rxcpp::rxo;
using namespace rxcpp::rxs;
```

```
/////////////////////////
// include the modified rxcurl library from
// Kirk Shoop's Twitter Analysis app
//
#include "rxcurl.h"
using namespace rxcurl;
rxcurl::rxcurl factory;
```

Using the `factory` object, we can create request object by calling the `create` method. The `create` method expects:

- The URL endpoint
- The HTTP method
- HTTP headers
- The body of HTTP request:

```
string HttpCall( string url ,
                 string method,
                 std::map<string,string> headers,
                 string  body  ) {
    auto request   = factory.create(http_request{url,method,
                         headers,body}) |
                         rxo::map([](http_response r){
                             return r.body.complete;
                         });
```

The above code creates a `request` object by composing creation of the HTTP request and a function to map from `http_response` to the HTTP body. There is an option to return chunks of data. We are not using it here, as we expect only small amount of data as response.

```
/////////////////////////////////////////
// make a blocking call to the url..
observable<string>   response_message;
request.as_blocking().subscribe([&] (observable<string> s) {
        response_message = s.sum();
} ,[] () {printf("");});
```

The above code makes a blocking call to the `observable` we created earlier. The body of the `subscribe` method's `on_next` function concatenates the content to form another Observable. In real life, we can make this call in an asynchronous manner as well. That involves a little more programming effort. Moreover, the code listing won't fit in the available page budget:

```
/////////////////////////////
//
// retrieve the html content form the site
string html;
response_message.as_blocking().subscribe( [&html] ( string temp ) {
            html = temp;
}, [] () { printf(""); } );
return html;
}
////////////////////////////
// The EntryPoint...
//
int main() {

    /////////////////////////////////////
    // set the url and create the rxcurl object
    string url = "http://localhost:34567/DBDEMO/";
    factory = create_rxcurl();
    ////////////////////////////////
    // default header values
    std::map<string,string> headers;
    headers["Content-Type"] = "application/json";
    headers["Cache-Control"] = "no-cache";

    //------- invoke GET to retrieve the contents
    string html = HttpCall( url,"GET",headers, "" );
    cout << html << endl;

    //------- Retrieve values for the following
    string body = string("["Praseed"]rn");
    html = HttpCall( url,"POST", headers,body);
    cout << html << endl;
    //--------- Add new Values using PUT
    body = string("rn{"Praveen": "29","Rajesh" :"41"}rn");
    html = HttpCall( url,"PUT", headers,body);
    cout << html << endl;
    //-------- See whether values has been added
    html = HttpCall( url,"GET",headers, "" );
    cout << "------------------------current database state" << endl;
    cout << html << endl;
    //--------------- DELETE a particular record
```

```
        body = string("["Praseed"]rn");
        html = HttpCall( url,"DELETE", headers,body);
        cout << "Delleted..." << html << endl;
        html = HttpCall( url,"GET",headers, "" );
        cout << "------------------------current database state" << endl;
        cout << html << endl;
    }
```

The `main` method demonstrates how we can invoke the `HttpCall` function created by us. The code has been provided to show how you can leverage the RxCurl library. We can use the library to issue multiple requests asynchronously and wait for their completion as well. The reader can tweak the code to support such a feature.

A word about the Reactive micro-services architecture

We have learned how to write a microservices controller using the C++ REST SDK. Maybe we can say that the server we just implemented can be a microservice instance. In a real-life microservices architecture scenario, there will be multiple services hosted in different boxes (Docker containers or Virtual machines), and microservices controller will access these independently deployed services to cater to the client. The microservice controller will aggregate output from different services to send as a response to the client. A basic architecture for a microservice application is shown in the following diagram:

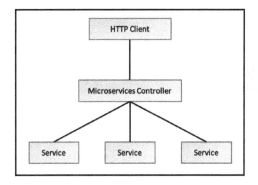

In the previous diagram, the REST (HTTP) client makes an HTTP call to the microservices controller, which wraps `http_listener` object. The controller invokes three microservices to retrieve data, and the resultant data will be assembled or merged to provide a response to the REST client. The endpoints can be deployed in a container or in different containers, using technologies such as Docker.

According to Martin Fowler:

"The term "Microservice Architecture" has sprung up over the last few years to describe a particular way of designing software applications as suites of independently deployable services. While there is no precise definition of this architectural style, there are certain common characteristics around organization around business capability, automated deployment, intelligence in the endpoints, and decentralized control of languages and data."

The topic of microservices architecture is a subject in its own right, and the topic warrants a book of its own. What we have covered here is how we can leverage the C++ programming language to write web applications in this style. The description given here is meant to point readers to the right information. The reactive programming model is suitable for aggregating information from different service endpoints and presenting it uniformly to the client. The aggregation of services is the key concern, which ought to be further researched by the readers.

When we talk about microservices architecture, we need to understand following topics:

- Fine-grained services
- Polyglot persistence
- Independent deployment
- Service orchestration and Service choreography
- Reactive web service calls

We will discuss them in detail in following sections.

Fine-grained services

Traditional SOA- and REST-based services are mostly coarse-grained services and are written with a mindset in which reduction of network roundtrip is the core concern. To reduce the network roundtrip, developers often created payload formats that were composite (multiple data elements packed together) in nature. So, an endpoint or a URI was used to handle more than one concern, and violated the principle of Separation Of Concerns. The microservices architecture expects services to perform a single responsibility, and payload formats are tailored for that. In this way, the service becomes granular.

Polyglot persistence

Polyglot persistence is a term used to denote the use of multiple storage technologies while persisting data. The term come from the term **polyglot programming**, where the choice of programming language is determined by the context. In the case of polyglot programming, we mix different programming languages. The authors of this book have come across systems that use Java for the application server code, Scala for stream processing, C++ for storage-related concerns, C# for writing the web layer, and, of course, TypeScript/JavaScript for the client-side programming. In the case of polyglot persistence, we have the choice of using RDBMS, key/value stores, document databases, graph databases, columnar databases, and even time series databases.

An e-commerce portal is a classic example of a system where polyglot persistence can be really handy. Such a platform will deal with many types of data (for example, shopping cart, inventory, and completed orders). Instead of trying to store all of this data in one database, we might use RDBMS (to record transactions), key/value DBs (caching and lookup), a document database for storing logs, and so on. *Choose the right persistence model for your concern and context* is the main motto here.

Independent deployment

The biggest difference between microservices architecture and traditional SOA is in the area of deployment. With the evolution of container technologies, we can deploy services independently and in isolation, very easily. The DevOps movement helped a lot in popularizing the independent deployment model of services and applications. We can now automate the process of provisioning a VM and associated containers with CPU, memory, storage, additional disks, virtual networks, firewalls, load balancing, auto scaling and so on, in deployment policies attached to a cloud service, such as AWS,Azure or Google Cloud. Policies help you deploy microservices in an automatic manner, using automation scripts.

While developing applications using the microservices architectural style, the notion of container technology will pop up again and again. An associated movement, called DevOps, is brought into the realm of discussion. Covering DevOps and containerization (and cluster management) in the context of independent deployment is beyond the scope of this book. You can search for Docker, Kubernetes, and "Infrastructure as code", to gain more insight into these technologies.

Service orchestration and choreography

Let's start with service orchestration. You put together several services by a fixed logic. This logic is described in a single place. But we might deploy multiple instances of same services, for availability. An aggregator service will call these services independently and aggregate the data for the downstream systems. On the other hand, in service choreography, the decision logic is distributed with no centralized point. A call to service will trigger multiple calls between services, before data reaches the downstream system. Service choreography requires more effort than implementing orchestration. You can read more about service orchestration and choreography by searching the web using your favorite search engine.

Reactive web service call

The processing of web requests is nicely mapped to the reactive programming model. In the case of applications with responsive UI, we typically make a call to the server once. An aggregator service running on the server will spawn a series of requests asynchronously. The resulting responses are aggregated to give a response to the UI layer. The modified `RxCurl` can be used as a mechanism to invoke multiple services in projects which use C++ programming language.

Summary

In this chapter, we covered how the Rx programming model can be used to write reactive microservices using C++. As part of the process, we introduced you to the Microsoft C++ REST SDK and its programming model. The C++ REST SDK follows an asynchronous programming model based on a technique called task continuation style, while writing client-side code. To write REST clients, we leveraged Kirk Shoop's `RxCurl` library, with some modifications to support the `PUT` and `DELETE` verbs. Finally, we wrote a REST server and consumed it in a reactive manner.In the next chapter, we will learn how to handle errors and exceptions using constructs available in the RxCpp library.

13
Advanced Streams and Handling Errors

In this book, we have covered quite a bit of ground in explaining modern C++ techniques and the RxCpp library. We started with a set of prerequisites for undertaking reactive programming using C++. The first six chapters were mostly about prerequisites and getting acclimatized with the features that are embodied in functional reactive programming in general, and in the RxCpp library in particular. We have used the term functional reactive programming in a loose sense—we are leveraging functional programming techniques to write reactive programs. Some purists differ from us on this. They do not consider the Rx family of libraries to be a complete implementation of functional reactive programming. The biggest shift a programmer has to undergo is the mindset change to adopt a declarative programming paradigm.

Traditionally, we design elaborate data structures, and write algorithms upon those data structures, to write our programs. This is appropriate for programs that manipulate data that exists in space. When time comes into the picture, asynchrony is a natural consequence. In reactive programming, we reduce complicated data structures into Streams of data and place Operators in the Streams, before getting notified to perform some action, based on the notification. We have seen how this can simplify programming in the case of GUI programs, web programs, and console applications, using the C++ programming language.

In our examples, we have omitted exception handling (and error handling) logic in reactive programs. This was on purpose, so as to focus on the core reactive elements and their interactions. Now that we have covered all of the essentials, and beyond, we will focus on exception handling in a reactive program. Before getting into error and exception handling, we will cover the characteristics of reactive systems.

In this chapter, we will cover the following topics:

- A short recap of the characteristics of a reactive system
- RxCpp—error handling Operators
- Scheduling and error handling
- Event-based Stream handling—some examples

A short recap of the characteristics of a reactive system

We now live in a world that warrants increased scalability and rapid response. The concept of reactive programming is a need that has arisen to meet the demands of high availability, scalability, and quick response. As per the reactive manifesto (https://www. reactivemanifesto.org/), reactive systems are:

- **Responsive**: The ability (of a system) to complete assigned tasks within a timeframe. Responsiveness also means that the problems are detected quickly, and dealt with effectively. The key point is the consistent behavior of a system. Consistency helps the users to build confidence in the system.
- **Resilient**: In the context of changes in behavior, the ability of a system to defend itself from failure is resilience. It is correlated to the responsiveness, as the consistency guarantees error handling as well. Resilience is achieved by the isolation and containment of components subject to error situation and protecting the system from failures.
- **Elastic**: Elasticity is the ability of a system to adapt to workload changes by reallocating the resources required in an automated manner. In turn, at each instance of time, the resources in use match the demand as closely as possible. reactive systems achieve elasticity by providing relevant live performance measures.
- **Message-driven**: Reactive systems achieve isolation and the loose coupling of systems through the ability to communicate through the asynchronous message-passing mechanism. With the use of a message queue, the interdependent processing of different modules and commands is made possible in reactive systems. Non-blocking communication through message-driven architecture allows the recipients to consume resources only when active:

The following diagram from the Reactive Manifesto demonstrates how all the pillars of a reactive system are inter-related:

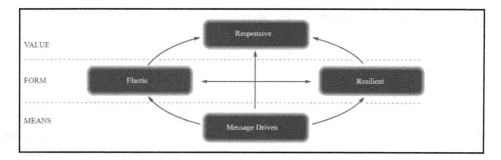

The reactive systems are made composable by applying these principles at all levels of their construction.

The focus of this chapter will be the resilient properties of the reactive systems, through explaining advanced Streams and error handling.

RxCpp error and exception handling Operators

In a real-world scenario, no system is perfect. As we discussed in the previous section, resilience is one of the qualities of a reactive system. How a system handles errors and exceptions decides the future of that system. Early detection and the seamless handling of errors makes a system consistent and responsive. Compared to imperative programming approaches, the reactive programming model helps the user to handle errors separately, as and when the system detects an error or throws an exception.

In this section, we will take a look at how to handle exceptions and errors by using the RxCpp library. There are a variety of RxCpp Operators that can be used to react to on_error notifications from Observables. For instance, we might:

- Handle the error by exiting from the sequence gracefully
- Ignore the error and switch over to a backup Observable to continue the sequence
- Ignore the error and emit a default value
- Ignore the error and immediately try to restart the failed Observable
- Ignore the error and try to restart the failed Observable, after some back-off interval

The exception handling is possible because the `observer<>` contains three methods:

- `on_next`
- `on_completed`
- `on_error`

The `on_error` method is meant to handle exceptions when they occur, or when they are thrown by `observable<>` or any Operators in the composition chain. The examples so far have ignored the error handling aspects of the system. The prototypes for the observer methods are as follows:

- `void observer::on_next(T);`
- `void observer::on_error(std::exception_ptr);`
- `void observer::on_completed();`

Executing an action on an error

When an error occurs, we need to handle it in a graceful manner. So far, in the RxCpp programs discussed in this book, the programs were written to only handle the `on_next` and `on_completed` scenarios in the `subscribe` method. The `subscribe` function has one more method, where it can accept a Lambda function for `on_error` scenarios as well. Let's look at a simple example to understand how to use the error handler inside the `subscribe` function:

```
//------ OnError1
#include "rxcpp/rx.hpp"

int main()
{
    //------ Creating Observable with an error appended
    //------ A canned example to demonstrate error
    auto values = rxcpp::observable<>::range(1, 3).
               concat(rxcpp::observable<>::
               error<int>(std::runtime_error("Error from producer!")));

    values.
        subscribe(
            //-------------- on_next
            [](int v) { printf("OnNext: %dn", v); },
            //--------------- on_error
            [](std::exception_ptr ep) {
                printf("OnError: %sn", rxcpp::util::what(ep).c_str());
            },
```

```
//--------------- on_completed
[]() { printf("OnCompletedn"); });
}
```

With the second Lambda, the function passed into the `subscribe` function invokes the action that is needed when there is an error. The output of the code will look like this:

OnNext: 1
OnNext: 2
OnNext: 3
OnError: Error from producer!

In the previous code, the error is appended to the Observable Stream to kick-start the discussion on exception/error handling at the subscriber end. Let's see how an exception can be propagated to the subscriber level, through the Observable Streams:

```
//------- OnError2.cpp
#include "rxcpp/rx.hpp"

int main() {
    //-------- Create a subject instance
    //------    and retrieve subscriber abd Observable handle
    rxcpp::rxsub::subject<int> sub;
    auto subscriber = sub.get_subscriber();
    auto observable = sub.get_observable();
    //------------------------- Subscribe!
    observable.subscribe(
        [](int v) { printf("OnNext: %dn", v); },
        [](std::exception_ptr ep) {
            printf("OnError: %sn", rxcpp::util::what(ep).c_str());
        },
        []() { printf("OnCompletedn"); }
    );
```

The previous code creates an instance of a `subject<T>` class, which we covered in chapter-10, Creating Custom Operators in RxCpp. We subscribe to the Observable part of the `subject<T>`. We also retrieve the subscriber handle to emit the value or exception into the Stream:

```
for (int i = 1; i <= 10; ++i) {
    if (i > 5) {
        try {
            std::string().at(1);
        }
        catch (std::out_of_range& ex) {
            //------------ Emit exception.
            subscriber.on_error(std::make_exception_ptr(ex));
```

```
            break;
        }
    }
    subscriber.on_next(i * 10);
    }
    subscriber.on_completed();
    }
}
```

The `on_next()` function emits a new value to the subscriber, and the function will be called multiple times. The `on_next()` function won't be called once `on_completed()` or `on_error()` is being invoked on the Stream. The `on_completed()` function notifies the subscriber that the Observable has finished sending **push-based notifications**. The Observable will not call this function if it has already invoked the `on_error()` function. Finally, the `on_error()` function notifies the subscriber that the Observable has experienced an error condition, and if the Observable calls this function, it will not call `on_next()` or `on_completed()` thereafter.

Resuming when an error occurs

An error occurrence breaks the sequence flow of a standard reactive Stream. The RxCpp library provides mechanisms to invoke actions on an error occurrence, also. Sometimes, however, users want to resume the sequence with a default option; that's what `on_error_resume_next()` does:

```cpp
//------- OnError3.cpp
#include "rxcpp/rx.hpp"

int main()
{
    //------- Create an Observable with appended error
    auto values = rxcpp::observable<>::range(1, 3).
        concat(rxcpp::observable<>::
        error<int>(std::runtime_error("Error from producer!   "))).
        //------- Resuming with another Stream
        on_error_resume_next([](std::exception_ptr ep) {
            printf("Resuming after: %sn", rxcpp::util::what(ep).c_str());
            return rxcpp::observable<>::range(4,6);
        });

    values.
        subscribe(
            [](int v) {printf("OnNext: %dn", v); },
            [](std::exception_ptr ep) {
                printf("OnError: %sn", rxcpp::util::what(ep).c_str()); },
```

```
[]() {printf("OnCompletedn"); });
}
```

The Observable Operator `on_error_resume_next()` gets executed if there is an error in the Stream. In this code, a new Stream is returned from the Lambda given as a parameter, to resume the sequence with this new Stream. This way, the error propagation can be prevented, by continuing with a meaningful sequence. The output of the previous program will look like this:

```
OnNext: 1
OnNext: 2
OnNext: 3
Resuming after: Error from producer!
OnNext: 4
OnNext: 5
OnNext: 6
OnCompleted
```

As well as resuming with another sequence, the sequence can be resumed with a default single item. In the previous example, replace the invocation of the Operator `on_error_resume_next()` with the following lines:

```
//-------- Resuming with a default single value
on_error_resume_next([](std::exception_ptr ep) {
    printf("Resuming after: %sn", rxcpp::util::what(ep).c_str());
    return rxcpp::observable<>::just(-1);
});
```

The output, after replacing the code, will look like this:

```
OnNext: 1
OnNext: 2
OnNext: 3
Resuming after: Error from source
OnNext: -1
OnCompleted
```

Let's look at the marble diagram that depicts the `on_error_resume_next()` Operator:

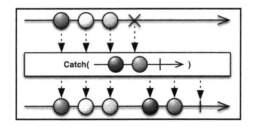

In short, the `on_error_resume_next()` function returns an Observable instance when it encounters an error from a particular Observable. The Stream switches to the new Observable and resumes the execution.

The `on_error_resume_next()` Operator comes in handy in many places, where the user needs to continue the propagation of an error. For instance, between the creation and subscription of the Streams, there is a chance that the Streams may undergo different transformations and reductions. Also, as explained in Chapter 9, *Reactive GUI Programming Using Qt/C++*, the user-defined Operators can be constructed by composing existing RxCpp Operators. In such cases, it is intended to use the `on_error_resume_next()` Operator at every single stage of aggregation and transformations to translate the exceptions/errors till the subscription phase. Similar to the default value or a sequence emitted from this Operator, the error itself can be retransmitted, to resume the flow of the error until the `subscribe()` Operator's error handler:

```
auto processed_strm = Source_observable.
map([](const string& s) {
return do_string_operation(s);
        }).
// Translating exception from the source
on_error_resume_next([](std::exception_ptr){
return
rxcpp::sources::error<string>(runtime_error(rxcpp::util::what(ep).c_str()))
;
        });
```

The previous fragment of code explains how the `on_error_resume_next()` Operator can be used to translate the error.

Retry when an error occurs

In many situations, the normal sequence may be broken by a temporary failure on the producer end. In such scenarios, it is worthwhile to have an option to wait until the anomalies are fixed at the producer end, to continue the normal execution flow. RxCpp gives the users a very similar option to retry when an error occurs. The retry option is best suited to when you are expecting the sequence to encounter predictable issues.

The retry Operator responds to an `on_error` notification from the source Observable by resubscribing to the source Observable, instead of passing that call through to its Observers. This gives the source another opportunity to complete its sequence without an error. The retry always passes `on_next` notifications through to its Observers, even from sequences that terminate with an error; this can cause duplicate emissions. The following marble diagram will explain this further:

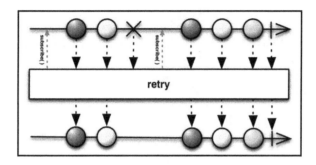

Here is an example that uses the `retry()` Operator:

```
//-------- Retry1.cpp
#include "rxcpp/rx.hpp"

int main()
{
    auto values = rxcpp::observable<>::range(1, 3).
        concat(rxcpp::observable<>::
        error<int>(std::runtime_error("Error from producer!"))).
        retry().
        take(5);

    //----- Subscription
    values.
        subscribe(
            [](int v) {printf("OnNext: %dn", v); },
            []() {printf("OnCompletedn"); });
}
```

In this example, as the error is appended to the Stream using the `concat()` Operator, we are using the `take()` Operator to avoid the infinite wait. Because of the infinite wait on the retry Operator in error scenarios, the subscriber can omit error handler used in the subscription.

The output of this code will be:

```
OnNext: 1
OnNext: 2
OnNext: 3
OnNext: 1
OnNext: 2
OnCompleted
```

Most of the time, it is better to use a fixed number of retries for error situations. This can be achieved by another overload of `retry()`, which accepts the number of retries:

```cpp
//------- Retry2.cpp
#include "rxcpp/rx.hpp"

int main()
{
    auto source = rxcpp::observable<>::range(1, 3).
        concat(rxcpp::observable<>::
        error<int>(std::runtime_error("Error from producer!"))).
        retry(2);

    source.
        subscribe(
            [](int v) {printf("OnNext: %dn", v); },
            [](std::exception_ptr ep) {
                printf("OnError: %sn", rxcpp::util::what(ep).c_str()); },
            []() {printf("OnCompletedn"); });
}
```

The output for the code will look like this:

```
OnNext: 1
OnNext: 2
OnNext: 3
OnNext: 1
OnNext: 2
OnNext: 3
OnError: Error from producer!
```

Cleanup with the finally() Operator

So far, in this chapter, we have seen that the source sequence in RxCpp can terminate gracefully after throwing exceptions. The `finally()` Operator is useful when we are using external resources, or when there's a need to free up some resources allocated in some other parts of the program. As we know, there are millions of lines of code that are already written for building various systems in C++, and it is highly likely that we need to handle resource management when using legacy external dependencies. This is a place where `finally()` comes in handy in RxCpp:

```
//------- Finally.cpp
#include "rxcpp/rx.hpp"

int main()
{
    auto values = rxcpp::observable<>::range(1, 3).
        concat(rxcpp::observable<>::
        error<int>(std::runtime_error("Error from producer!"))).
        //----- Final action
        finally([]() { printf("The final actionn");
    });

    values.
        subscribe(
            [](int v) {printf("OnNext: %dn", v); },
            [](std::exception_ptr ep) {
                printf("OnError: %sn", rxcpp::util::what(ep).c_str()); },
            []() {printf("OnCompletedn"); });
}
```

The `finally()` Operator adds a new action at the end of the newly created Observables. The output of the previous program is as shown:

```
OnNext: 1
OnNext: 2
OnNext: 3
OnError: Error from producer!
The final action
```

It can be seen, in the previous output, that if the source generates an error, the final action is still called.

If we remove the error concatenated to the source Observable, the output of the program will look as follows:

```
OnNext: 1
OnNext: 2
OnNext: 3
OnCompleted
The final action
```

Schedulers and error handling

We already covered the topic of scheduling in Chapter 8, *RxCpp – the Key Elements*. The schedulers in RxCpp queue up the values and deliver the queued up value using the supplied coordination. The coordination could be the current execution thread, the RxCpp run loop, the RxCpp event loop, or a new thread. The execution of scheduler operations can be achieved by using the RxCpp Operators, such as observe_on() or subscribe_on(). These Operators accept the chosen coordination as an argument. By default, the RxCpp library is single-threaded, so it does the scheduler operations. The user has to explicitly choose the thread in which execution happens:

```cpp
//----------OnError_ObserveOn1.cpp
#include "rxcpp/rx.hpp"
#include <iostream>
#include <thread>

int main() {
    //--------------- Generate a range of values
    //--------------- Apply Square function
    auto values = rxcpp::observable<>::range(1, 4).
        transform([](int v) { return v * v; }).
        concat(rxcpp::observable<>::
        error<int>(std::runtime_error("Error from producer!")));

    //------------- Emit the current thread details
    std::cout << "Main Thread id => "
        << std::this_thread::get_id()
        << std::endl;
```

We have created an Observable Stream using the range Operator, and have concatenated an error, to demonstrate how basic error handling works with schedulers in RxCpp:

```cpp
    //---------- observe_on another thread....
    //---------- make it blocking too
    values.observe_on(rxcpp::synchronize_new_thread()).as_blocking().
```

```
        subscribe([](int v) {
            std::cout << "Observable Thread id => "
            << std::this_thread::get_id()
            << " " << v << std::endl; },
            [](std::exception_ptr ep) {
            printf("OnError: %sn", rxcpp::util::what(ep).c_str()); },
            []() { std::cout << "OnCompleted" << std::endl; });

    //------------------- Print the main thread details
    std::cout << "Main Thread id => "
        << std::this_thread::get_id()
        << std::endl;
}
```

Using `observe_on()` Operator, the Observable stream is subscribed into a new thread as its coordination. Similar to the previous examples that we discussed in this chapter, the error handler is provided with the `subscribe()` function. The output of the code may look like this:

```
Main Thread id => 5776
Observable Thread id => 12184 1
Observable Thread id => 12184 4
Observable Thread id => 12184 9
Observable Thread id => 12184 16
OnError: Error from producer!
Main Thread id => 5776
```

Now, let's take a look at another example, with two subscribers from the same source. The subscribers are supposed to be notified in two different threads:

```
//------- OnError_ObserveOn2.cpp
#include "rxcpp/rx.hpp"
#include <mutex>

std::mutex printMutex;

int main() {

    rxcpp::rxsub::subject<int> sub;
    auto subscriber = sub.get_subscriber();
    auto observable1 = sub.get_observable();
    auto observable2 = sub.get_observable();
```

A `subject` instance is created to add data to the source Stream; from the subject instance, one subscriber and two Observables are created, to be scheduled in two distinct threads:

```
auto onNext = [](int v) {
    std::lock_guard<std::mutex> lock(printMutex);
    std::cout << "Observable Thread id => "
        << std::this_thread::get_id()
        << "t OnNext: " << v << std::endl;
};

auto onError = [](std::exception_ptr ep) {
    std::lock_guard<std::mutex> lock(printMutex);
    std::cout << "Observable Thread id => "
        << std::this_thread::get_id()
        << "t OnError: "
        << rxcpp::util::what(ep).c_str() << std::endl;
};
```

Two Lambda functions are declared for use with the `subscribe` method, with mutex synchronization applied on the usage of the `std::ostream` Operator to get an organized output. Placing a mutex around `std::ostream` will avoid interleaved output if the thread switch happens during a write to the Stream:

```
//------------- Schedule it in another thread
observable1.
    observe_on(rxcpp::synchronize_new_thread()).
    subscribe(onNext, onError,
        []() {printf("OnCompletedn"); });

//------------- Schedule it in yet another thread
observable2.
    observe_on(rxcpp::synchronize_event_loop()).
    subscribe(onNext, onError,
        []() {printf("OnCompletedn"); });
```

Two Observables are retrieved from the source Stream, and they are scheduled to observe from separate threads. For the `observable1` function object, a separate C++ thread is specified as the coordinator by passing `rxcpp::synchronize_new_thread()` as the argument in the `observe_on()` Operator. For the `observable2` object, an event loop is specified as the coordinator by passing `rxcpp::observe_on_event_loop()` into `observe_on()`:

```
//------------- Adding new values into the source Stream
//------------- Adding error into Stream when exception occurs
for (int i = 1; i <= 10; ++i) {
    if (i > 5) {
```

```
            try {
                std::string().at(1);
            }
            catch (...) {
                std::exception_ptr eptr = std::current_exception();
                subscriber.on_error(eptr);
                break;
            }
        }
        subscriber.on_next(i * 10);
    }
    subscriber.on_completed();

    //----------- Wait for Two Seconds
    rxcpp::observable<>::timer(std::chrono::milliseconds(2000)).
        subscribe([&](long) {});
}
```

Finally, the values are added to the Observable Stream by using a subject instance, and an exception is passed into the Stream explicitly, to understand the behavior of the schedulers and error handlers together. The output of this code will be as follows:

```
Observable Thread id => 2644    OnNext:  10
Observable Thread id => 2304    OnNext:  10
Observable Thread id => 2644    OnNext:  20
Observable Thread id => 2304    OnNext:  20
Observable Thread id => 2644    OnNext:  30
Observable Thread id => 2304    OnNext:  30
Observable Thread id => 2644    OnNext:  40
Observable Thread id => 2304    OnNext:  40
Observable Thread id => 2304    OnNext:  50
Observable Thread id => 2304    OnError: invalid string position
Observable Thread id => 2644    OnNext:  50
Observable Thread id => 2644    OnError: invalid string position
```

This example demonstrates how the propagation of data happens through two separate Observables that are subscribed to a common source. The error generated in the source is received and handled by both of the Observables at the corresponding `subscribe` functions. Now, let's look at an example that demonstrates how error handling can be done in scheduling by using the `subscribe_on()` Operator:

```
//----------- SubscribeOn.cpp
#include "rxcpp/rx.hpp"
#include <thread>
#include <mutex>

//------- A global mutex for output sync.
```

```
std::mutex printMutex;

int main() {
    //-------- Creating Observable Streams
    auto values1 = rxcpp::observable<>::range(1, 4).
        transform([](int v) { return v * v; });

    auto values2 = rxcpp::observable<>::range(5, 9).
                        transform([](int v) { return v * v; }).
                        concat(rxcpp::observable<>:
:error<int>(std::runtime_error("Error from source")));
```

Two random Observable Streams on integers are created using the `rxcpp::observable<>::range()` Operator and one Stream is concatenated with an error, to explain error handling in scheduled sequences:

```
    //-------- Schedule it in another thread
    auto s1 = values1.subscribe_on(rxcpp::observe_on_event_loop());

    //-------- Schedule it in Yet another thread
    auto s2 = values2.subscribe_on(rxcpp::synchronize_new_thread());
```

The Observable Streams are queued up in different threads using the `subscribe_on()` Operator. The first Stream is scheduled with an event loop as its coordination thread, and the second Stream is scheduled on another C++ thread:

```
    auto onNext = [](int v) {
        std::lock_guard<std::mutex> lock(printMutex);
        std::cout << "Observable Thread id => "
                  << std::this_thread::get_id()
                  << "tOnNext: " << v << std::endl;
    };

    auto onError = [](std::exception_ptr ep) {
        std::lock_guard<std::mutex> lock(printMutex);
        std::cout << "Observable Thread id => "
                  << std::this_thread::get_id()
                  << "tOnError: "
                  << rxcpp::util::what(ep).c_str() << std::endl;
    };
```

The preceding Lambda functions are defined to be passed as parameters in place of the `on_next` and `on_error` functions of the `subscribe` method. These Lambda functions are protected with mutex, to synchronize the calls to the `std::ostream` Operator:

```
    //-------- Subscribing the merged sequence
    s1.merge(s2).as_blocking().subscribe(
```

```
        onNext, onError,
        []() { std::cout << "OnCompleted" << std::endl; });

    //-------- Print the main thread details
    std::cout << "Main Thread id => "
        << std::this_thread::get_id()
        << std::endl;
}
```

The output of the code will look like this:

```
Observable Thread id => 12380    OnNext: 1
Observable Thread id => 9076     OnNext: 25
Observable Thread id => 12380    OnNext: 4
Observable Thread id => 9076     OnNext: 36
Observable Thread id => 12380    OnNext: 9
Observable Thread id => 12380    OnNext: 16
Observable Thread id => 9076     OnNext: 49
Observable Thread id => 9076     OnNext: 64
Observable Thread id => 9076     OnNext: 81
Observable Thread id => 9076     OnError: Error from producer!
Main Thread id => 10692
```

Event-based Stream handling – some examples

Before we conclude this chapter, let's discuss a few examples, to work with an event-based system using the RxCpp library. In this section, we'll discuss two examples to understand how effective the RxCpp library can be in meeting real-world scenarios. We will discuss an example that demonstrates the aggregation of data in a Stream and application event handling, using the RxCpp library.

Aggregation based on Stream data

In this section, the Stream item is a user-defined type to represent an employee, and the code is intended to group the input Stream based on the roles and salaries of employees:

```
#include "rxcpp/rx.hpp"

namespace Rx {
    using namespace rxcpp;
    using namespace rxcpp::sources;
```

```
            using namespace rxcpp::subjects;
            using namespace rxcpp::util;
    }

using namespace std;

struct Employee {
    string name;
    string role;
    int salary;
};
```

The libraries and namespaces required in the code are included, and the data structure to represent an `Employee` is declared. The `Employee` type is a simple structure, with data items such as `name`, `role`, and `salary`. We have treated the salary field as an integer:

```
int main()
{
    Rx::subject<Employee> employees;

    // Group Salaries by Role
    auto role_sal = employees.
    get_observable().
        group_by(
            [](Employee& e) { return e.role; },
            [](Employee& e) { return e.salary; });
```

In the `main()` function, a subject is created with the `Employee` type, to create a **hot Observable**. The grouping based on the role is performed and salary attribute is extracted out of it to form the resultant Grouped Observable. The RxCpp Operator, `group_by()`, returns an Observable that emits `grouped_observables`, each of which corresponds to a unique key/value pair from the source Observable:

```
    // Combine min max and average reductions based on salary.
    auto result = role_sal.
        map([](Rx::grouped_observable<string, int> group) {
            return group.
                count().
                zip([=](int count, int min, int max, double average) {
                return make_tuple(group.get_key(), count, min, max,
average);
            },
            group.min(),
            group.max(),
            group.map([](int salary) -> double { return salary; }).average());
        }).
        merge();
```

Here, the resultant Observable combines the Observable based on the role, and the reduction, based on the salary, is performed by appending the minimum salary, maximum salary, and average salary per role. The Lambda inside of the `zip()` will be called when all of the arguments have a value. In this case, when a particular group completes, all of the values inside of the Streams corresponding to the group are reduced to single tuples. Therefore, the Lambda is called only once per role, with the final value of each iteration. Here, the map applied on the `group` returns an Observable of the type `observable<tuple<string, int, int, int, double>>`, and the `merge()` Operator returns an Observable of the type `tuple<string, int, int, int, double>`. The merge is applied to prevent the data loss, as the grouped Observable is hot, and the data will be lost if it is not subscribed to immediately:

```
    // Display the aggregated result
    result.
        subscribe(Rx::apply_to(
        [](string role, int count, int min, int max, double avg) {
          std::cout << role.c_str() << ":tCount = " << count <<
          ", Salary Range = [" << min
              << "-" << max << "], Average Salary = " << avg << endl;
        }));

    // Supplying input data
    Rx::observable<>::from(
        Employee{ "Jon", "Engineer", 60000 },
        Employee{ "Tyrion", "Manager", 120000 },
        Employee{ "Arya", "Engineer", 92000 },
        Employee{ "Sansa", "Manager", 150000 },
        Employee{ "Cersei", "Accountant", 76000 },
        Employee{ "Jaime", "Engineer", 52000 }).
        subscribe(employees.get_subscriber());

    return 0;
}
```

The resultant Observable is then subscribed, in order to display the aggregated result of input data. The data items are supplied to the subscriber from the `employees` subject, created with the `Employees` type. In the previous code, the source can be anything, such as data retrieved from the network or from another thread. Since the Observable created here is a hot Observable, aggregation is performed based on the latest data supplied.

The output of this code is as follows:

```
Accountant:     Count = 1, Salary Range = [76000-76000], Average Salary =
76000
Engineer:       Count = 3, Salary Range = [52000-92000], Average Salary =
68000
Manager:        Count = 2, Salary Range = [120000-150000], Average Salary =
135000
```

Application event handling example

The following example is a command-line program, with events to represent the primitive operations of a user interface application. We will be handling the flow of these events by using RxCpp in this program. This has been done for brevity in the code listing:

```cpp
//--------- UI_EventsApp.cpp
#include <rxcpp/rx.hpp>
#include <cassert>
#include <cctype>
#include <clocale>

namespace Rx {
    using namespace rxcpp;
    using namespace rxcpp::sources;
    using namespace rxcpp::operators;
    using namespace rxcpp::util;
    using namespace rxcpp::subjects;
}

using namespace Rx;
using namespace std::chrono;

// Application events
enum class AppEvent {
    Active,
    Inactive,
    Data,
    Close,
    Finish,
    Other
};
```

The libraries and namespaces that we will be using in the programs are included (declared) here. Also, an enum AppEvent is declared, to represent some of the basic event states that can be emitted from a generic system:

```
int main()
{
    //--------------------
    // A or a - Active
    // I or i - Inactive
    // D or d - Data
    // C or c - Close
    // F or f - Finish
    // default - Other
    auto events = Rx::observable<>::create<AppEvent>(
        [](Rx::subscriber<AppEvent> dest) {
        std::cout << "Enter Application Events:\n";
        for (;;) {
            int key = std::cin.get();
            AppEvent current_event = AppEvent::Other;

            switch (std::tolower(key)) {
            case 'a': current_event = AppEvent::Active; break;
            case 'i': current_event = AppEvent::Inactive; break;
            case 'd': current_event = AppEvent::Data; break;
            case 'c': current_event = AppEvent::Close; break;
            case 'f': current_event = AppEvent::Finish; break;
            default:  current_event = AppEvent::Other;
            }

            if (current_event == AppEvent::Finish) {
                dest.on_completed();
                break;
            }
            else {
                dest.on_next(current_event);
            }
        }
    }).
    on_error_resume_next([](std::exception_ptr ep) {
        return rxcpp::observable<>::just(AppEvent::Finish);
    }).
    publish();
```

In the previous code, we created an Observable Stream of the `AppEvent` type by mapping some of the keyboard entries to defined event types. The infinite loop inside the Lambda of the `create` function represents the `event_loop/message_loop` in GUI applications. To convert the cold Observable into a hot Observable and to get the connections to the source independent of following subscriptions, the `publish()` Operator is used. It also helps to send the most recent value in the Stream to new subscribers:

```cpp
// Observable containing application active events
auto appActive = events.
    filter([](AppEvent const& event) {
    return event == AppEvent::Active;
});

// Observable containing application inactive events
auto appInactive = events.
    filter([](AppEvent const& event) {
    return event == AppEvent::Inactive;
});

// Observable containing application data events
auto appData = events.
    filter([](AppEvent const& event) {
    return event == AppEvent::Data;
});

// Observable containing application close events
auto appClose = events.
    filter([](AppEvent const& event) {
    return event == AppEvent::Close;
});
```

Some filtered Observables are defined, to handle the use cases of the reactive system. The `appActive` is an Observable contains `AppEvent::Active` event filtered from source Observable whenever it is available in the source stream. Similarly, `appInactive` Observable contains `AppEvent::Inactive` events, `appData` Observable contains `AppEvent::Data` events, and `appClose` Observable extracts `AppEvent::Close` events out of the source Observable:

```cpp
auto dataFromApp = appActive.
    map([=](AppEvent const& event) {
    std::cout << "**Application Active**n" << std::flush;
    return appData. // Return all the data events
        take_until(appInactive). // Stop recieving data when the
application goes inactive
        finally([]() {
```

```
            std::cout << "**Application Inactive**n";
        });
    }).
        switch_on_next(). // only listen to most recent data
        take_until(appClose). // stop everything when Finish/Close event
recieved
        finally([]() {
        std::cout << "**Application Close/Finish**n";
    });

    dataFromApp.
        subscribe([](AppEvent const& event) {
        std::cout << "**Application Data**n" << std::flush;
    });

    events.connect();

    return 0;
}
```

The program will start accepting the data Streams from the events Observable only if the AppEvent::Active event is received. Then, the application will accept the data until AppEvent::Inactive is received. The event flow will resume only when the next AppEvent::Active is emitted. When AppEvent::Close or AppEvent::Finish is emitted, the application will exit gracefully, similar to a **Close** or **Apply** event/message in a GUI application.

Summary

In this chapter, we discussed error handling in RxCpp, along with some of the advanced constructs and Operators to handle Streams in the RxCpp library. We visited the basic principles of a reactive system, and gave more emphasis to one of the key pillars of a reactive system, resilience, when we discussed error handling mechanisms. We discussed features such as error handlers (on_error), which need to be used with subscription. Also, we discussed RxCpp Operators, such as on_error_resume_next(), retry(), and finally(), to discuss how to continue Streams when an error comes, how to wait for the producer of the Stream to correct the error and continue the sequence, and how to perform common operations that are applicable to both success and error paths. Finally, we discussed two sample programs, to understand more about Stream processing. These programs illustrated how the RxCpp library can be used to process a Stream of UX events (simulated using a console program) and aggregate data Streams.

Other Books You May Enjoy

If you enjoyed this book, you may be interested in these other books by Packt:

C++ Data Structures and Algorithms
Wisnu Anggoro

ISBN: 978-1-78883-521-3

- Know how to use arrays and lists to get better results in complex scenarios
- Build enhanced applications by using hashtables, dictionaries, and sets
- Implement searching algorithms such as linear search, binary search, jump search, exponential search, and more
- Have a positive impact on the efficiency of applications with tree traversal
- Explore the design used in sorting algorithms like Heap sort, Quick sort, Merge sort and Radix sort
- Implement various common algorithms in string data types
- Find out how to design an algorithm for a specific task using the common algorithm paradigms

C++ High Performance
Viktor Sehr

ISBN: 978-1-78712-095-2

- Benefits of modern C++ constructs and techniques
- Identify hardware bottlenecks, such as CPU cache misses, to boost performance
- Write specialized data structures for performance-critical code
- Use modern metaprogramming techniques to reduce runtime calculations
- Achieve efficient memory management using custom memory allocators
- Reduce boilerplate code using reflection techniques
- Reap the benefits of lock-free concurrent programming
- Perform under-the-hood optimizations with preserved readability using proxy objects
- Gain insights into subtle optimizations used by STL algorithms
- Utilize the Range V3 library for expressive C++ code
- Parallelize your code over CPU and GPU, without compromising readability

Leave a review - let other readers know what you think

Please share your thoughts on this book with others by leaving a review on the site that you bought it from. If you purchased the book from Amazon, please leave us an honest review on this book's Amazon page. This is vital so that other potential readers can see and use your unbiased opinion to make purchasing decisions, we can understand what our customers think about our products, and our authors can see your feedback on the title that they have worked with Packt to create. It will only take a few minutes of your time, but is valuable to other potential customers, our authors, and Packt. Thank you!

Index

A

Abstract Syntax Tree (AST) 124
acquire-release ordering 110
Active object pattern 265
ActiveX Template Library (ATL) 13
aggregate operator 199
Applicative-order evaluation (AO) 142
applied stream programming
  Streams library, using 141
arbitrary Lambda
  converting, to custom Rx operator 242, 244
atomic operations
  about 98
  load operations 101
  read-modify-write operations 101
  store operations 101
atomic types
  about 98, 99
  atomic 103
  atomic_flag 101
  pointer arithmetic 106
  primary class template 107
  standard atomic integral types 105

C

C++ containers
  values, streaming from 162
C++ language
  web programming 274
C++ programming language
  composition 48
  concerns 30
  currying 48
  enhancements, for writing better code 34
  expressivity 30, 33
  function wrappers 50
  functors 45
  inference 34
  lambda functions 44
  lambdas 45
  partial function application 48
  pointers 42
  RValue references 39
  semantics 40
  substitutability 33
  type deduction 34
  variables, uniform initialization 36
  variadic templates 37
  zero cost abstraction 30
C++ REST SDK-based REST Server 289, 294
C++ REST SDK
  about 274
  used, for HTTP client programming 275
  used, for HTTP Server programming 277
cell pattern 262
compare-and-swap (CAS) 104
Composite pattern
  used, for expression processing 125
concept 119
concurrency
  about 62
  and memory access 97
  Hello World example 63
condition variables 82
Connectable Observable operators 200
creational operators 195
CURL
  used, for testing HTTP server 280
custom operators
  custom creational operator, writing 236
  custom transformation operator, writing 238
  genres 236
  implementing, for chaining together 240

with schedulers, writing 239
writing, lift operator used 240, 242
custom Rx operator
    arbitrary Lambda, converting 242, 244
custom RxCpp operator
    creating, in library 245, 247

D

data flow computation paradigm 159
deadlock
    avoiding 77
design pattern redux 253
design patterns
    hierarchy, flattening 259
    migrating, to reactive programming 254
Domain Specific Embedded Language (DSEL) 27,
    146
double dispatch 256

E

error handling 314
Event bus pattern
    about 271
    consumers 268
    controllers 268
    producers 268
event filter
    URL 219
Event Stream programming
    about 145
    advantages 145
    RaftLib 153
    Rx programming 154
    spreadsheet Library 151
    Streamulus library 146, 149, 150
event-based Stream handling
    about 319
    aggregation, based on Stream data 319
    application event handling, example 322
event-driven programming model
    about 8
    alternatives 14
    limitations 14
    MFC 13
    on Microsoft Windows 10

on X Windows 8
with Qt 12
exception handling operators
    about 305
    action, executing on error 306
    cleaning up, with finally() operator 313
    resuming, on error occurrence 308
    retry option 310

F

features, C++ 17
    about 53
    fold expressions 53
    variant type 54
filter operation
    applying, on list 132
functional reactive programming (FRP) 15, 157
functions
    composing, with pipe operator 51
future 90

G

Gang of Four (GoF) 117, 251
GoF Observer pattern
    about 118, 120, 122
    limitations 121

H

hierarchy
    about 124
hot Observables
    about 320
    replay mechanism 183
    versus cold Observables 180
HTTP protocol 284
HTTP server
    CURL Wrapper library, Kirk Shoop 282
    HTTP client programming 281
    LibCurl 281
    testing, with CURL 280
    testing, with POSTMAN 280

I

IObservable

events, converting 22, 25
iterative processing
  composite, flattening 129, 131
iterator pattern
  migrating, to observables 261

J

JavaScript Object Notation (JSON) 274, 284

L

Lambda function
  ownership management 71
  using 70
lazy evaluation
  about 142
  STL 144
  Stream program 142
  Streams library 144
  values, aggregating with stream paradigm 143
linearizability
  URL 97
lock-free data structure 113

M

map operation
  applying, on list 132
marble diagrams 164
  using, for representation 164
mathematical operator 199
memory access 97
memory model 96
memory ordering
  about 108
  acquire-release ordering 110
  categories 108
  relaxed ordering 112
  sequential consistency 108
Meta Object Compiler (MOC) 12, 203
modification contract 98
modification order consistency 112
mutexes 75

N

Normal-order evaluation (NO) 142

O

Object Oriented Programming (OOP) 124, 249
Observable Utility Operators 198
Observables
  about 179
  creating, from scratch 162
  hot observables 181
  hot Observables, replay mechanism 183
  hot Observables, versus cold Observables 180
  producer 180
  reversing 133, 137
  Streams, concatenation 163
  Streams, unsubscribing 163
  transformation, using with 161
  transformations 161
Observers 158
operators
  about 194
  aggregate operators 199
  boolean operators 198
  combining 197
  conditional operators 198
  Connectable Observable operators 200
  creational operators 195
  error-handling operators 198
  filtering 196
  mathematical operators 199
  Observable Utility Operators 198

P

pattern catalogs
  GOF patterns 251
  POSA catalog 251
Patterns of Software Architecture (POSA) 251
pipe operator
  functions, composing 51
pointer arithmetic 106
Polyglot programming 301
POSTMAN
  used, for testing HTTP server 280
primary class template 107
producers 180
promise 90, 91
pull method 253

push-based reactive program
  IEnumerable/IObservable duality 18
  versus pull-based reactive program 18

Q

Qt event model
  application dialog, creating 212, 216
  application, executing 216
  custom widget, creating 211
  event filter 218, 220
  event type specific observables 221
  RxCpp library, integrating 218
  RxQt library 223
  window, creating 220
  with MOC 210
  with signals 210
Qt GUI programming
  about 202
  event handlers 206
  event system 206
  meta-object system 207
  Qt object model 203
  signals and slots 204
Qt object model
  features 203
Qt program 208, 210
Qt
  URL 208

R

race condition 74
RaftLib
  about 153
  URL 153
range-based
  implementing, for loops 55
  implementing, for observables 55
reactive manifesto
  URL 304
Reactive Microservices Architecture
  about 299
  fine-grained services 300
  independent deployment 301
  Polyglot persistence 301
  service orchestration 302

  web service call 302
reactive program
  interfaces 16
reactive programming model 15
reactive system
  elastic 304
  message-driven 304
  resilient 304
  responsive 304
relaxed ordering 112
Resource Acquisition Is Initialization (RAII)
  about 76
  URL 77
Resource Loan pattern 266
REST programming model 274
Reverse Polish Notation (RPN) form 128
Rx operators
  philosophy 229, 230
RxCpp (Stream) operators
  about 165
  average Operator 165
  composing, through pipe operator 166
  flat map, versus concat map 169, 172
  other operators 174
  Scan Operator 165
  Schedulers, working with 167
RxCpp custom operators
  composing 235
  writing 232
  writing, as function 233
  writing, as Lambda 234
RxCpp error 305
RxCpp library
  about 159
  filters, with Observables 161
  integrating, with Qt event model 218
  Observable/Observer interaction 160
  programming model 160
  transformations, with Observables 161
  URL 159
RxCurl library
  used, for invoking REST services 296
RxQt library 223

S

schedulers
    about 188, 314
    ObserveOn, versus SubscribeOn 191
    RunLoop scheduler 193

sequential consistency 108

signals and slots
    about 204
    URL 205

spurious failure 104

standard template library (STL) 141

stock operators
    chaining 230, 231

stream programming model
    about 140
    advantages 140

subjects 188

subscribers 184

T

task continuation 275

task-based parallelism
    about 90
    async, using 94
    future 90

packaged_task 93
    promise 90

thread-safe stack data structure 84, 86

threads
    arguments, passing 67
    condition variables 82
    data, sharing between 73
    deadlock, avoiding 77
    join() 66
    launching 65
    managing 64
    mutexes 75
    unique_lock, used for locking 80

transformation operators 196

U

user-defined type (UDT) 107

V

visitor pattern
    used, for expression processing 125

W

web programming
    REST programming model 274